AN INTRODUCTION TO CATHOLIC ETHICS

Lucien F. Longtin, SJ
Andrew J. Peach

National Catholic Educational Association

Nihil Obstat:
Monsignor James Mulligan

Imprimatur:
+Most Reverend Harry J. Flynn, D.D.
Archdiocese of Saint Paul and Minneapolis
February 24, 2003

The nihil obstat and imprimatur are a declaration
that a book is considered to be free from doctrinal or moral error.
It is not implied that those who have granted the nihil obstat and imprimatur agree
with the contents, opinions, or statements expressed.

DEDICATION

This book is dedicated to Rev. Jim DiGiacomo, SJ, long-time teacher at New York's Regis High School and Fordham University, in grateful appreciation for his inspiring leadership and generous service to the Catholic apostolate of religious education. You have been both a wonderful friend and a great mentor to many of your colleagues; and for thousands of adolescent students, you have been a venerated and respected teacher. We, who are your fellow "teachers of religion," cannot thank you enough for your leadership, for your encouragement, and for the wisdom you have given us over four decades.

Further, the Mother's Club of Gonzaga College High School and the Society of Jesus also supported this project with generous grants. But most importantly, the authors would like to thank the students of Gonzaga College High School who were the guinea pigs for this book. Their general enthusiasm for learning, as well as their questions, comments, and forthright criticisms have made the writing of this book an enjoyable and fruitful experience.

CONTENTS

ACKNOWLEDGEMENTS

In addition, the authors would like to thank the many people who have contributed to this book. Jim DiGiacomo, SJ, Vince Genovesi, SJ, Kathryn Mahon Peach, Jim Boettcher, Dan Dwyer, Paul McNellis, SJ, Ronald K. Tacelli, SJ, Michael Mahon, and Molly Dunn have read sections of this text and offered helpful suggestions as to how to improve it. Carol Corrigan, Jamie Kelly, SJ, Seton Cuneen, SND, and Mark McManmon have taught earlier versions of this work at Gonzaga College High School, and their advice and suggestions have been invaluable.

Cover concept by Kathryn Mahon Peach
Book design by Sheila Harrington, Studio Five, Washington, DC

CHAPTER ONE:
INTRODUCTION, TEST CASES, AND RELATIVISM

PART ONE:
INTRODUCTION

A. WHAT IS "CATHOLIC ETHICS"?

Is it permissible for a cancer patient, one who has been given no chance of recovery by his doctors, to breathe in carbon monoxide and slowly "go to sleep" forever? Must a woman who has taken every precaution against getting pregnant, short of abstinence, be required to carry her baby to term if she nonetheless conceives? Does "the end justify the means" or are there some things that are so abominable that no outcome, no matter how great, could justify them? Are there situations in which it would be permissible to lie? To cheat on one's spouse? To steal?

These questions and ones similar to them are the questions that are dealt with in the discipline known as "ethics." The word "ethics" is derived from the Greek word *ethos*, which is usually translated as "character." Not surprisingly, then, the discipline of ethics is the discipline that deals with a person's character; it deals with the kinds of decisions that a person makes and the kind of person that he becomes because of those decisions.

Catholic ethics, the subject-matter of this textbook, deals with these same issues, but it deals with them in light of Christianity, specifically the Catholic religion. As would be the case with any ethics textbook, this one aims at helping students develop a sound approach to making ethical decisions, in the hope of living a virtuous and happy life. But Christians believe that the end or goal of human life is not simply virtue and happiness *in this life*; they believe they are called to eternal life—to eternal friendship—with God. And this belief does make (or should make) a significant difference in how the Christian person lives.

B. WHAT ISSUES WILL BE COVERED IN THIS TEXTBOOK?

Whenever anyone thinks about ethics, that person usually thinks of the kinds of questions with which this introduction began: Is euthanasia, abortion, adultery, etc. acceptable? Unquestionably, these questions are fascinating and of particular interest to our society at this time in human history. But all great disciplines, like all great books or lives, must have their less-than-exciting parts. In ethics, in general, and Christian ethics, in particular, it is necessary *to begin with* the less-than-exciting parts. To immediately address the morality of such issues as abortion or adultery without a discussion of human nature, sin, or the role of the Church in the ethical decision-making process would lead to an entirely piecemeal approach to Christian ethics.

The purpose of this textbook is to provide the student with a coherent and living approach to *any* ethical issue. Armed with an understanding of the basic tenets of Catholic ethical *theory*, the student will be well-equipped to deal with most of the issues or problems that he or she will confront *in practice*. This textbook does not directly deal with any of "the big issues" in modern ethical debate; ideally, in a full-year Christian ethics course, the study of abortion, euthanasia, adultery, etc. will be reserved for the second half of the year. This text is intended as the first part, the beginning, of a full-year ethics course. But as Aristotle observed, "The beginning is more than half of the whole," and it is with this insight in mind that this text begins with ethical *theory*.

After presenting a number of preliminary test cases to arouse interest and make a methodological point, the text will wrestle with the rather predominant philosophy of "relativism" and the challenges it poses. The second chapter will present a number of classical ethical philosophies that have enjoyed great success and popularity through history *even though they did not rely, in any significant way, on religion*. Following the lead of chapter two, the third chapter will address the questions, "What difference does Christianity make to ethics? If people such as John Locke, Immanuel Kant, or John Stuart Mill didn't believe Christianity added anything significant to ethical theory, why should we?" The third chapter will illustrate this Christian difference by presenting aspects of the lives and philosophies of Ignatius Loyola, Pedro Arrupe, Dorothy Day, Thomas More, and Martin Luther King, Jr. Your teacher may wish to add several other names of Christians he or she admires. The fourth chapter will deal with the conceptual tools necessary for the formation of a healthy, informed, and active conscience. It will address the notions of freedom and sin, and the parts of moral actions—object, intention, and circumstances. The fifth chapter will address the proper way to use Scripture in the ethical decision-making process, the role of the Church in this process, and the meaning of natural law and its role. Finally, the sixth chapter will put forward some guidelines for dealing with difficult situations, and discuss the role of prayer and discernment in the moral realm.

C.   A METHODOLOGICAL NOTE

In his *Nicomachean Ethics*, Aristotle makes an observation that is particularly relevant to people who are beginning a study of ethics. Aristotle observes, "It is the mark of an educated man to look for precision in each class of things just so far as the nature of the subject admits."[1] Math, for example, gives very *exact and precise* answers; a student of mathematics would certainly not be very pleased with a teacher who declared that 5 + 4 was "probably" or "usually" 9. But not all disciplines can give a mathematical degree of certainty, and thus, it is unreasonable to demand of all disciplines a mathematical degree of precision. Historians, for example, cannot say in a decisive, precise, and final way what *exactly* the causes of World War I were; the *exact* causes of a war usually do not exist. Historians speak of "trends," "movements," and "eras" that bleed into one another and form one complex whole on which they try to draw lines. The historian must be content with general answers because general answers are the only ones that can be given. Likewise, the student of ethics must be content with *general guidelines* and observations about human nature that are, *for the most part*, true. This is not to say that there are not moral absolutes, i.e., moral rules that hold *in every instance*. But the observations that will be presented about human nature, sin, Scripture, and the workings of natural law cannot be as precise as some students would like. This is not a problem with the discipline; it is simply the nature of ethics.

D.   AN INTRODUCTORY EXERCISE

This is a homework assignment to be done on the evening after the first class in this course. It will help your instructor to understand how best to help you learn.

I.   For the next class, write a description of your learning style.

    a.   Specifically, tell what learning experiences have been most rewarding for you up to now.

    b.   Tell whether you feel you are especially gifted in one or another area of learning or in some skill.

    c.   Tell what educational techniques you would deem helpful or unhelpful and why.

II.   Explain where you stand in terms of Christianity, in general, and Catholicism, in particular. What aspects, if any, do you find to be true or most appealing about Christianity/Catholicism? What aspects, if any, do you find troublesome?

PART TWO:
TEST RUN ON SOME ETHICAL CASES

Whenever students enter an advanced astronomy class, they can be fairly sure that they are going to be introduced to relatively new concepts; most people do not know much, if anything, about black holes, curved space, or supernovas. But ethics is not a specialized science like astronomy; most people believe that they already have some level of knowledge of ethical concepts. And they do. Philosophers and theologians who study ethics are not dealing with a subject that only they can understand; they are dealing with human experiences that *everyone* has. Only, they attempt to make sense of this experience in a systematic or orderly fashion.

Everyone, except perhaps a psychopath, has some level of ethical knowledge. In order to illustrate this fact and in order to do a little ethical calisthenics or warm-up exercises, the following test cases have been provided below. Write a paragraph for each test case that has been assigned. Remember to provide *reasons* for a given response, not simply whether or not you would cheat or trade the company or whatever is the case.

Case #1:

You are a high school student in a tough physics course. You hope to get into a rather prestigious college, but you have not been doing very well in this class. You have asked the teacher for extra help, but she has insisted that you need to struggle with the problems yourself, that "the course is modeled on a college-level, self-directed course." Frankly, you don't believe she is a very good teacher; shouldn't she be helping the students if they ask for help? If you have a chance to get away with it and you feel your grade will suffer greatly otherwise, should you ever cheat on one of her tests? Why or why not?

Case #2:

You are a stockholder in a company named "Ace Combs." Your company has been doing rather well in this prosperous era. You are getting an annual return of 30% on every stock that you own. There is a proposal before the stockholders to merge with your nearest competitor, "Groovy Groomer Combs." The proposal is presented by the company president, a no-nonsense guy named Benton Baldright, who explains that the merger will yield better returns—about 50% on every stock within 10 years. The only problem is that the merger will mean that the company will have to lay off 25% of its current work-force, both management and labor, within a year after the merger. You know that the workers have performed superbly; honestly, they were the force behind the 30% return on the current stocks. Will you vote for the merger? Why or why not?

Case #3:

You are a priest who has been teaching at a high school for a number of years. One of the school's alumni comes to see you to ask your advice. He tells you he is gay. He does not want to live a promiscuous life, but he does feel the need for companionship. As a Catholic, he is troubled by the conflict between what he perceives as his needs and what is taught by the Catholic Church. What would you say to him?

Case #4:

You are a doctor. You have been helping an elderly woman who has tragically been afflicted with a severe case of multiple sclerosis. The disease has advanced to such a degree that she has been left with almost total paralysis, little control of her speech and bodily functions, and poor eyesight. She and her husband ask you to help her to end her life. You are aware of the deep suffering she endures. But, as a doctor, you also took the Hippocratic Oath which states, in part, "I will give no deadly drug to any, though it be asked of me, nor will I counsel such …" Additionally, you are a Christian, and you are aware that suicide has always been prohibited by your church. If you could administer a drug that would put this woman "to sleep" but would make her death appear to the coroner to be natural, would you meet the couple's request?

Case #5:

You are a student. After getting off the public transit line near your school, you walk toward your high school. Outside "Post Liquor," a homeless woman and her small child catch your eye. It's too late. You cannot act as if you didn't see her; she has seen you. In a polite voice, she asks, "Sir, could you please spare some money so my child can have something to eat?" On the one hand, you don't want to be rude, and you don't want anyone to starve. On the other hand, you know that she *is* outside a liquor store. Is that a coincidence? What do you say to her? Do you give her any money? Why or why not?

Case #6:

You have been dating someone for nearly a full year, and you are *positive* you are in love. You can't remember ever feeling this way about anyone before. Of course, making out has been great, but a side of you feels that the two of you are ready to pick up the pace a bit. Your friend has told you that he or she loves you, and you have echoed that declaration. You are committed to each other; you have an exclusive relationship. Getting caught is not the issue; his or her parents are out of town for the weekend, and your folks never bother to ask what you are doing as long as you are home before midnight. Do you have sex? Why or why not?

Case #7:

As a citizen of Texas, you have been called on for jury duty. Even though you have told the judge you are a Roman Catholic and do not believe in the death penalty, she determines that you are a prudent individual and that you are capable of determining what the law requires, as opposed to what your faith requires. The state prosecutors have sought the death penalty; if the man is convicted, he will probably receive a lethal injection. Death penalty aside, there is no question in your mind (or in the minds of the other jurors) that this man murdered two nurses in cold blood. However, a vote of "guilty" is also a vote for this man's execution. If you vote "innocent," you are certainly being dishonest, to some extent, but your vote could result in a hung jury. This man's execution would at least not be on your conscience. How do you vote? Why?

PART THREE:
RELATIVISM, THE MONKEY ON THE BACK OF ETHICS

In medieval Japanese culture, the warrior class—the Samurai—had a very interesting practice. When a Samurai warrior received a new sword, it was necessary for him to try it out to see if it worked properly. But the Samurai did not subject it to the kind of tests that one sees on television advertisements for Ginsu knives. The warrior did not try to cut a pipe with it or even try to slice through a watermelon; he tried out his new sword on any chance wanderer or traveler. If the Samurai was able to cut the unfortunate passerby in half—from the shoulder to the opposite flank—in one fell swoop, then the sword was a keeper. If he could not, his honor would be injured, his ancestors would be offended, and his emperor would be quite disappointed.

And the medieval Japanese people approved of this practice.

But one does not have to go back in history to witness cultures that accept practices of extraordinary cruelty. Today, in some countries of Africa and the Middle East, there is a practice that is, at least in theory, intended to prevent women from being promiscuous. At some time in their young lives, the women of these countries are "circumcised." However, the name given to this procedure is highly misleading. Male circumcision involves the removal of the male infant's foreskin from the tip of the penis; it is performed for hygienic reasons, and it in no way alters the level of sexual pleasure he will experience later in life. Female "circumcision," on the other hand, involves the removal of the clitoris, the organ that allows the woman to feel pleasure during intercourse. (Roughly speaking, there is nothing comparable that could be done to a man save, perhaps, the removal of the tip of his penis.) Now that the possibility of sexual pleasure is gone—so the reasoning goes—the possibility that one's wife will be unfaithful is gone as well.

And, to a large extent, the people (even the women) of these cultures approve of this practice. And there are people today, in America, who believe that we should *not disapprove* of this practice.

These people are called *relativists*; they maintain that *there are no moral rules that apply to all cultures or all people in one culture and that no country or person should "impose" their (or his) moral rules on any other culture or person.* In other words, relativists believe that there are no *universal* moral rules or rules *that apply to everyone.* This belief in relativism has become so pervasive in American culture that the slogans of relativism have almost become anthems for the current generation. Whenever someone openly disapproves of certain kinds of behavior—marital infidelity, lying, or self-indulgence—another person is guaranteed to reply with one of the following responses:

"Who are you to impose your morality on other people?"

"Why are you so intolerant of other people's opinions or ways of life?"

"You are so righteous/judgmental."

"Morality is a private affair. Keep your nose out of other people's business."

On an episode of the romantic drama *Melrose Place*, Jo, one of the female characters, found herself pregnant and unmarried—a fairly regular event on a romantic drama of this sort. While discussing with Amanda, another character, her decision whether to abort or keep her baby, Amanda tells Jo, with an air of moral authority, "Jo, it doesn't matter whether you keep the baby or not. What is important is that it is *your* decision."

Translation: Morality is a private affair. Any moral decision that is truly your own is *right for you.*

In fact, do the following experiment. Watch *any* talk show, "reality" program, or romantic drama for half an hour, and you will no doubt come across one of these cultural mantras. And if you are unfortunate enough to tune into a talk show, you can be guaranteed that the person who repeats one of these slogans will receive a standing ovation from the crowd.

Why is our culture so enamoured with relativism? If asked about the morality of cheating or the death penalty, most people will have a *very definite* opinion about these questions, and they will believe very strongly that they are correct. (Recall how confident you were about the responses you gave to the test cases in the previous section.) And then, a moment later, these same people will utter one of the catchy, mind-numbing phrases above. Why does our culture have such mixed opinions about morality? Why is relativism so appealing? What, if anything, is wrong with this ethical philosophy?

Before addressing these questions, however, it is necessary to understand why this philosophy is a threat to the *study* of ethics. To understand why, it will be necessary to learn a number of important terms.

A.   WHY RELATIVISM IS A THREAT TO THE STUDY OF ETHICS

Imagine the following scenario: A girl and a boy are standing outside a Ben & Jerry's ice cream shop. The girl is eating chocolate ice cream in a sugar cone with sprinkles and chopped up M&Ms, and the boy is eating vanilla ice cream in a cake cone without any toppings. Suddenly, an argument breaks out. "Chocolate is the best flavor of ice cream," the girl insists, with fire in her eyes. The boy, visibly disturbed, replies, "Anyone who doesn't believe that vanilla is the best flavor must be out of his mind." Later the argument moves on to the virtues of sprinkles and the great dispute between sugar and cake cones. Eventually, the punches start flying.

Obviously, most people do not behave this way. Ice cream flavors are simply not that significant, but more importantly for our purposes, people do not argue over ice cream because *there is no right or wrong in matters of taste.* In other words, people do not argue about what is "the best" flavor of ice cream because there is no best flavor. Everyone has his own favorite flavor; tastes are personal matters. What is considered the best ice cream is *relative* or *subjective; it varies from person to person.*

Relativism, in moral matters, is the attempt to put morality into the same category as ice cream flavors. For relativists, morality is not a subject that can be debated. One person has a set of moral rules by which he lives, and another person has her set of rules by which she lives. For a relativist, arguing about morality is like arguing about ice cream flavors; there are no correct answers to moral questions just as there is no best ice cream flavor.

If the relativist is correct in his beliefs, there can be no *study* of ethics because there will be no subject to study. Everyone could sit in a circle and tell her classmates how she *feels* about a certain issue—just as everyone could sit in a circle and discuss her favorite ice cream flavor—but there will not be any correct answer. For what makes an opinion correct is not that some—or even most—people think it is correct or believe in it sincerely. In order for a study of ethics to be possible, there must be something *objective* about ethics. To be *objective* means *"to exist or to be true independently of anyone's opinion."* In other words, an objective thing exists or an objective statement is true whether or not anyone believes in it. That a triangle has three sides is an objective matter; it is true whether or not anyone acknowledges it. That all people are mortal is an objective matter; it would be true even if all people believed they would never die. That chocolate is the best ice cream is a subjective matter; it is only the best for a person *if that person thinks it is the best.*

Unless there are objective elements to ethics—i.e., unless relativism is fundamentally wrong—there can be no course in ethics. Before analyzing the problems with relativism, however, a brief overview of the reasons why relativism is so appealing is necessary.

B. HOW THE MONKEY GOT ON OUR BACK: WHY RELATIVISM IS SO APPEALING

It is a very rare event in human history when a popular belief is *completely* wrong. Beliefs or ideas do not get to be popular or appealing unless there is at least something true about them. And relativism is no exception. Though some people who hold very strong moral and religious beliefs would love to eliminate relativism entirely, there are glimpses of the truth in moral relativism. Below, three of those glimpses will be discussed in an effort to determine why relativism has become so appealing to modern American culture.

B1. No Science, No Knowledge

As pointed out in the Introduction section "A Methodological Note," the study of ethics does not give the kind of precise answers that one receives in mathematics and science. In math, 2+3 *always* equals *exactly* 5; if people accepted any other answer, they would be fools. Likewise, in physics, the rate of acceleration of a falling body can be *precisely* calculated, and when an experiment is conducted, the falling body will be found to fall at almost the exact rate of acceleration that had been calculated.

But not everything that people study can have that type of precision. As previously mentioned, history cannot give the kind of precision that math or science can give. And even some branches of science such as biology, zoology, and psychology cannot provide the same degree of precision as physics or chemistry. However, for complex reasons, Westerners in general and Americans in particular tend to believe that science is the only area of human knowing that gives *any* answers. If science cannot deal with the issue, then it is merely a matter of opinion. No science, no knowledge. Because the answers that one discovers in an ethics class tend to be general and only applicable for the most part, some people tend to write them off as mere opinion, like discussions about the best flavor of ice cream. This urge, to write off everything that is not scientific, is understandable, considering how important science has been in human affairs. But the idea that scientific or mathematical knowledge is the *only* discipline that provides answers is false; e.g., one does not make a choice about a marriage partner based on science or math.

The fact is that there are many people who can give us types of knowledge that are not scientific. Historians give us knowledge that is not scientific or mathematical; fishermen can give us knowledge about how to catch trout that is different from the historian's knowledge; and good people can give us knowledge about how to be good that is different from the fishermen's knowledge.

B2. Circumstances Do Make a Difference

Another reason why relativism has taken hold so strongly is because it is so closely aligned to an idea that is indisputably true: *The circumstances surrounding an action often do make a difference.*[2] Relativism maintains that, in a sense, every person (or every culture) has his (or its) own moral rules; in other words, it implies that the morality of a given action can change with the person who performs it or that it can change depending on the circumstances surrounding the action. Both of these claims are often true.

A bachelor who is a lover of horror stories and spends all of his time alone in his room reading Stephen King novels is innocent of any wrongdoing (except perhaps wasting time), but a husband and father of five who locks himself in his study every night to read such novels while his wife feeds the children is certainly neglecting his family. These scenarios are similar to (but not identical with) relativism, the same action is transformed from good or innocent, in the case of the bachelor, to misguided and negligent, in the case of the family man. Circumstances can change the morality of an action—like reading a Stephen King novel.

And there are countless other instances in which the circumstances surrounding the person performing the action or the circumstances surrounding the action itself can change the level of responsibility of a person or the gravity of an action. A 14-year-old girl who is pressured into getting an abortion by her boyfriend and her parents is not nearly as responsible for her action as a 35-year-old lawyer would be if she decided to get an abortion to ensure that she would not miss out on a big promotion at the firm. Having a few beers with some friends (after one has reached the age of 21) is perfectly acceptable, but the same activity *while operating an automobile* is not.

Making love to your wife to whom you have promised to love and cherish "until death do you part" is a moral and loving action; making love to your best friend's wife is neither moral nor loving.

Given the complexity of evaluating moral actions, it is easy to understand why people could make the mistake that there is no objective right and wrong, that *every* aspect of morality changes as the circumstances change. At first glance, ethics is a gooey subject, one on which it is hard to get a handle. This complexity and lack of scientific precision often lead individuals to throw up their hands and say, "Ethics must be different for everybody; everybody must have his own moral rules." It is certainly understandable why someone might reach this conclusion, even if it is not true.

B3. The Virtues of Tolerance and Compassion

"Judge not, that you be not judged" (Mt. 7:1), Jesus taught the crowds who had gathered around him to hear his now famous Sermon on the Mount. Hypocrisy, preaching or teaching one thing while practicing another, was one of the worst offenses an individual could commit in Jesus' eyes, and His command not to judge others was part and parcel of His condemnation of this practice. Christians have taken this teaching to heart, and the virtue of showing compassion and reserving judgment of their neighbors has become a vital part of the Christian religion.

Tolerance and compassion are, indeed, admirable character traits, and in a distorted way, relativism preaches something like tolerance and compassion. Relativism preaches the idea that no country or person should impose its or his moral rules on any other culture or person. In a certain way, condemning or passing judgment on other people is similar to "imposing your moral rules on another culture or person." If an American politician makes a speech on the floor of Congress condemning the practice of female circumcision in some African country, she *is* passing judgment on that practice and that country. So, is not relativism, in a way, only preaching what Jesus taught in His Sermon on the Mount?

Relativism *does* somewhat share the message of the Sermon on the Mount, and it is for this reason, among others, that it commands respect; it is *close to* the truth. But there is a distinct difference between being a hypocrite, on the one hand, and believing that there are no moral standards that apply to all people and all cultures, on the other.

Jesus was hardly a relativist. After teaching that judging one another is wrong, He clarifies His teaching by asking the question "Why do you see the speck that is in your brother's eye, but do not notice the log that is in your own eye?" (Mt. 7:3). In other words, when Jesus is condemning the practice of "judging others," he is really condemning the practice of hypocrisy. A loving person, one who cares about the moral and spiritual well-being of his neighbor, *must* tell him his faults and try to correct him. As Jesus teaches later in the Gospel of Matthew, "If your brother sins against you, go and tell him his fault, between you and him alone. If he listens to you, you have gained your brother. But if he does not listen, take one or two others along with you, that every word may be confirmed by the evidence of two or three witnesses"(18:15-16). Not only does Jesus say that *you* should try to correct your brother's behavior, but also if that fails, you should involve *even more people* in your effort to teach him.

Trying to understand your brother or sister's special circumstances—trying to walk a mile in his or her shoes—is a Christian virtue. Trying to avoid hypocrisy at all times is a true Christian endeavor. Both of these virtues are *close* to the teachings of relativism—so close at times that one may even confuse the two. Relativism is very close to the truth, but sometimes, small differences make all the difference.

C.   WHY RELATIVISM IS WRONG AND UNAPPEALING

As a popular philosophy, relativism certainly has some glimpses or shades of truth, but as a whole, it must be rejected. As shown below, this ethical philosophy is both *self-contradictory* and wholly *impracticable*. Additionally, the relativist claim that every culture has wildly different codes of morality will be shown to be wildly exaggerated.

C1. Relativism is Self-Contradictory

Suppose someone held the following theory about government and freedom: All human beings should be free to choose whatever occupation they want (as long as it does not harm anyone) and that, to insure everyone has this right, all Hispanic men must become police officers to keep people from taking away other people's freedom. This position can be broken down into two distinct statements:

1.   All human beings should be free to choose the occupation they want.

2.   All Hispanic men must become police officers.

This position is "self-contradictory." *A statement or belief is said to be self-contradictory when one part of the statement or belief goes directly against another part of the statement or belief.* In other words, if Hispanic men must become police officers, obviously not all human beings are free to choose their occupation. One part of the belief makes the other part impossible.

Obviously, in order for a theory to be sound and worth keeping, it must not be self-contradictory.

But what does this have to do with moral relativism? As noted earlier, moral relativism states that there are no moral principles or rules which are universal or apply to everyone and that it is inappropriate or wrong for anyone to judge another culture's behavior based on its own moral rules. This position, as with the case of the theory of government above, can be broken down into two statements or beliefs:

1.   There are no moral principles or rules that are universal or apply to everyone.

2.   It is wrong or inappropriate for anyone to judge another culture's behavior based on his own.

Now, at first glance it may not appear that there is any conflict between the two statements, but a little thought shows that these two are incompatible. If the first statement is true, then the second statement cannot be true, i.e., *if there are no moral principles that apply to everyone, then the moral principle "it is wrong for anyone to judge another culture's behavior based on its own" cannot apply to everyone either.* This philosophical position wants to have its cake and eat it, too; it wants to first state that there are no rules that everyone must obey, and then, it puts forth its own rule that everyone must obey.

If, for example, an American stated that female "circumcision" is morally impermissible, a cultural relativist might argue, "Well, that is just a part of the American culture, and we have no right to impose our moral beliefs on the people of Africa (or whatever Muslim country)." If, however, all of the beliefs of Americans are *merely* a product of American culture, then why should anyone believe the cultural relativist? Why is what he has to say a universal moral rule when he has already stated that there are no universal moral beliefs? Could not someone say that cultural relativism *itself* is only an American set of beliefs that does not apply to any other country? If the relativist believes that there are no moral rules that apply to everyone, why does he feel comfortable giving his own moral rule? And if he allows that there is one moral rule, why not allow for other moral rules such as "No one should ever mutilate the sex organs of his neighbor" or "Thou shall not commit adultery"? As you can see, this philosophical position implodes; it folds in upon itself and collapses.

Additionally, because of the self-contradictory nature of this philosophy, relativists end up tying themselves in knots. Suppose that the vast majority of the people of Kuwait believed that the Iraqi government was wrong in its decision to invade their country. Also, suppose that the vast majority of the people of Iraq believed that its decision to invade was morally permissible. What would a cultural relativist have to say about this situation? Since the majority of Iraqis believe that invasion is the proper course, it is morally correct for them to invade, for such an action would be in accord with their cultural beliefs. Also, since the majority of Kuwaitis believe that an invasion is evil, then it is the cultural belief of the Kuwaitis that the invasion is wrong. Who is correct? A cultural relativist would have to say that both beliefs are correct, that the *very same action*—the Iraqi invasion of Kuwait—is both morally wrong and morally right at the same time.

C2. Relativism is Impracticable

Secondly, this position is wholly impracticable, i.e., *it commits the relativist to actions or attitudes that no sane person could ever carry out or hold.* If an individual believes she is a cultural relativist, she should think about what she really believes. Certainly, she does not believe that no one should have stood up to Hitler when he started to exterminate Jewish men, women, and children. Certainly, she does not believe that abolitionists should have remained silent about the issue of slavery. Certainly, she does not believe that she should not try to prevent future atrocities. Certainly, she does not believe that she should not prevent a friend from selling drugs or dropping out of high school, paths that will lead to personal destruction. In all these cases, is not "imposing your own moral rules on other people" the only moral thing to do? Do we not have a duty to try to help society and our friends to adopt the correct answers to life's problems?

This attitude does not mean, of course, that we treat people disrespectfully. It does not mean that we treat them as if they are small children who are incapable of making their own choices and listening to their own consciences. It doesn't mean that we presume that we have a right to check their sheets on Sunday mornings. But it does mean that the wrong actions of our brothers and sisters must be brought to their attention. Showing compassion is admirable, but when compassion degenerates into complete apathy about the behavior of those around us, civilization is in jeopardy. Walker Percy, a famous Catholic author, once stated, "Compassion leads to the gas chamber." In other words, if no one has the moral courage to stand up to atrocities and vicious dictators, then it will only be a short time before another Hitler, with his concentration camps, rises to power.

D. DIFFERENT CULTURES, DIFFERENT MORAL RULES?

One of the motivations behind relativism, in general, and cultural relativism, in particular, is the perception that different cultures throughout history have had drastically different moral codes. "How could ethics contain any objective elements when, obviously, every culture has had its own separate set of moral rules?" Most cultural relativists are fond of parading the fact that cannibalism was practiced by certain primitive South American tribes or that incest has not always been a forbidden practice. And though it is certainly true that there *have* been differences between the moral codes of different cultures, what is most striking about a survey of different cultures is not the slight differences but, rather, the remarkable similarities between their moral codes.

In the appendix to his *The Abolition of Man*, C.S. Lewis has compiled a list of these similarities between moral codes.[3] Below is a modified sampling of his compilation:

1.   The Golden Rule (And General Kindness to Neighbors)

✦   "You shall love your neighbor as yourself" (Jesus, Mt. 19:19).

✦   "You shall not take vengeance or bear any grudge against the sons of your own people, but you shall love your neighbor as yourself" (Ancient Jewish, Lv. 19:18).

✦   "Never do to others what you would not like them to do to you" (Ancient Chinese, *Analects of Confucius*, trans. A. Waley, XV. 23).

✦   "I have not brought misery upon my fellows. I have not made the beginning of every day laborious in the sight of him who worked for me" (Ancient Egyptian, *Confession of Righteous Soul. ERE* v. 478).

✦   "Utter not a word by which anyone could be wounded" (Hindu, Laws of Manu. Janet, *Histoire de la Science Politique*, vol. I, 6).

+ "Slander not" (Babylonian, *Hymn to Samas*. *ERE* v. 466).

+ "Men were brought into existence for the sake of men that they might do one another good" (Roman, Cicero, *De Off.* I. VII).

2.   Duties to Parents, Elders, and Ancestors

+ "Your father is an image of the Lord of Creation, your mother an image of the Earth. For him who fails to honor them, every work of piety is in vain. This is the first duty" (Hindu, Janet, I. 9).

+ "Has he despised Father and Mother?" (Babylonian, List of Sins. *ERE* v. 466).

+ "Honor thy Father and thy Mother" (Ancient Jewish, Ex. 20:12).

+ "To care for parents" (Ancient Greek, List of duties in Epictetus, III. VII).

+ "I tended the old man, I gave him my staff" (Ancient Egyptian, *ERE* v. 481).

+ "You will see them take care ... of old men" (Redskin, Le Jeune, quoted *ERE* v. 437).

+ "When proper respect towards the dead is shown at the end and continued after they are far away, the moral force of a people has reached its highest point" (Ancient Chinese, *Analects*, I. 9).

Against Stealing

+ "Has he drawn false boundaries?" (Babylonian, List of Sins. *ERE* v. 446).

+ "I have not stolen" (Ancient Egyptian, *Confession of Righteous Soul. ERE* v. 478).

+ "Thou shalt not steal" (Ancient Jewish, Ex. 20:15).

+ "Choose loss rather than shameful gains" (Greek, Chilon Fr. 10. Diels).

+ "If the native made a 'find' of any kind (e.g.,a honey tree) and marked it, it was thereafter safe for him, as far as his own tribesmen were concerned, no matter how long he left it" (Australian Aborigines, *ERE* v. 441).

+ "[A] man should treat common property as common property, and private property as his own" (Roman, Cicero, *De Off.* I. VII).

+ "Let the thief no longer steal, but rather let him labor, doing honest work with his hands, so that he may be able to give to those in need" (St. Paul, Eph. 4:28).

And the list goes on and on. Of course, it would be naïve to assume that the cultures mentioned in the foregoing lists had no influence over each other, that each culture was formed in a complete vacuum. Indeed, as Lewis states at the beginning of his appendix, "It is by no means certain that there has ever ... been more than one civilization in all history."[4] In other words, it makes more sense, in some respects, to say that there has only been one civilization and one history, the human. And so it should not be surprising that most branches of this one family tree should have a great deal in common, contrary to the assumptions of relativism.

E.   CONCLUSION AND TRANSITION TO SECULAR ETHICS

Despite its attractions and partial truths, the ethical philosophy of relativism must ultimately be rejected. In the foregoing pages, the attractions and partial truths of relativism have been discussed as well as its open and thoroughgoing errors. Morality is a reality, and this reality has been recognized and described by countless cultures since the beginning of human history.

In Chapter Two, a number of the classic ethical theories of different philosophers will be discussed, and all of these theories will have one thing in common: *Virtually none of them depend on a belief in God in any significant way.* These *secular* philosophies, like relativism, also will contain a great deal of truth; in particular, the "virtue ethics" of Aristotle will play an important role in the Catholic Church's understanding of human nature, virtue, and natural law. But, for Christians, these secular philosophies will only be part of the story.

SECTION HIGHLIGHTS

Relativism is the ethical philosophy which holds that there are no moral rules that apply to all cultures or all people in one culture and that no country or person should "impose" their (or his) moral rules on any other culture or person.

Relativism makes the claim that ethics is "subjective," i.e., that it varies from person to person. But if ethics is merely subjective, it cannot be a subject of study. It must contain "objective" elements, i.e., things that exist or are what they are independently of anyone's opinion."

Part of relativism's appeal is due to the false belief that science and math are the only fields that yield legitimate knowledge. But there are many fields of knowledge—from chemistry and physics to history and angling—and a study of ethics can yield a type of knowledge, as well.

Relativism is very close to the idea that the circumstances surrounding a person or an action can affect the level of responsibility of that person or the gravity of his action. Also, it resembles the virtues of compassion and tolerance. These similarities explain much of this philosophy's attraction.

Relativism is "self-contradictory"; i.e., one part of this theory makes the other part impossible (and vice versa). It also is impracticable, i.e., it commits its followers to actions or attitudes that no sane person could ever carry out or hold. Additionally, it can be shown that the claim that different cultures have drastically different moralities is a gross exaggeration.

QUESTIONS

Follow the directions for the following assignments. If a written answer is required, be sure to answer in complete sentences on a separate sheet of paper.

Assignment for Day One of Relativism:

Read pages 9-11, stopping at the section entitled "How the Monkey Got on Our Back." Be prepared for a reading quiz.

Your teacher will assign you a television program to watch tonight. Yes, believe it or not, you are *required* to watch television tonight. If there are *any* instances in which the philosophy of relativism is being used, write a brief (two paragraph) description of the instance of relativism, explaining *why* you believe it is an example of this philosophy. Use information from the reading to support your claim. If there are not any instances of this philosophy being used, you still must write a brief (two paragraph) summary of what happened in the television program.

Assignment for Day Two of Relativism:

In preparation for a debate, your teacher will divide the class into two teams, A and B. Each student on Team A should write two to three paragraphs explaining why he or she believes (or at least pretends to believe) that relativism is true. Each student on Team B should write two to three paragraphs explaining why he or she believes (or at least pretends to believe) that relativism is false. Be sure to use *reasoning* in these paragraphs; do not simply describe relativism or only use examples.

Assignment for Day Three of Relativism:

Finish reading the section on relativism (pp. 11-18) and answer the following questions:

1. What is the difference between the kind of "compassion and tolerance" taught by relativism and that taught by Jesus?

2. Do you believe that there are some actions that are wrong *every time they are done*, i.e., actions that can not change from wrong to right (or vice versa) with a change in circumstances? Explain.

3. What does it mean to be "self-contradictory"? Why does the author maintain that relativism, specifically cultural relativism, is self-contradictory?

4. Are you convinced by the author's arguments against relativism? Why or why not? Provide specific reason for your position.

CHAPTER TWO:
SECULAR ETHICAL SYSTEMS

PART ONE:
ARISTOTLE

Though philosophers and non-philosophers alike had been thinking and writing about ethics for many years before the fourth century BC, Aristotle (384/2-322 BC) was the first philosopher to put forward ethical reflections in a coherent, clear, and systematic fashion. Socrates, the famous wandering philosopher whose pursuit of the truth led to imprisonment and execution, never himself wrote anything. All that we know about Socrates comes to us through other writers, most notably his most famous pupil, Plato. And though Plato, Aristotle's teacher and friend of twenty years, certainly wrote volumes that dealt with the nature of the good life, his works were, for the most part, in the form of dialogues, i.e., conversations between various characters who were either real or fictitious or a combination of the two. Needless to say, it is often difficult—if not impossible—to identify clearly what exactly Plato himself believed about ethics, and more often than not, Plato's dialogues end without reaching any conclusion. Aristotle, on the contrary, tried to present a systematic, scientific treatment of the subject.

And this systematic treatment, found in his *Nicomachean Ethics* (named after his son, Nicomachus) is unquestionably the most important systematic treatment of ethics written in antiquity and, arguably, the most important philosophical treatment of the subject ever written. Famous philosopher and educator Mortimer Adler, for example, has stated, "In my judgment, Aristotle's *Nicomachean Ethics* is the only sound, practical, and undogmatic moral philosophy in the whole Western tradition."[1]

What exactly Aristotle believed about ethics will be covered in the following pages. But it is first necessary to understand his teachings about nature, most especially human nature. Why this is necessary will become clear in time.

SECTION ONE:
ARISTOTLE ON HUMAN NATURE

A. "TELEOLOGY"

When Aristotle looked out into the natural world, he observed that nearly everything in it seemed to have a purpose for which it was made or a goal towards which it strove. Though Aristotle did not believe in a creator God, as Christians do, he could not help thinking that things in nature were "built" for a certain purpose. An eye, for example, was obviously "made" for the purpose of seeing, an ear for the purpose of hearing, and a mouth for the purpose of eating. Likewise, he observed that things like acorns or animal embryos had goals as well; an acorn is meant to grow into an oak tree, and an animal embryo is meant to grow into a fully developed animal. Additionally, because of the way a natural thing is made, it very often only has one kind of goal or purpose; acorns do not have the option of becoming elephants, and eyes cannot be used for hearing. This goal or purpose toward which things in nature aim Aristotle called a "final cause" or "telos," and because of this, Aristotle's philosophy of nature is described as "teleological."

But Aristotle was also aware that things in the natural world sometimes fail to achieve the telos or purpose for which they were made. Sometimes, because of disease or an accident, an eye will not function properly; Aristotle would say, then, that that particular eye did not reach its telos or goal. Similarly, some seeds do not develop into fully developed trees but are, instead, eaten by animals or destroyed by adverse weather; they, too, have not reached their telos.

B. THE TELOS OF HUMAN LIFE: HAPPINESS OR "EUDAIMONIA"

By now, however, you may be asking yourself, "But what does teleology have to do with ethics?" Well, Aristotle not only observed natural things such as eyes and acorns, but he also included human beings in his study of nature. By observing his fellow citizens, Aristotle concluded that human beings also have a telos or goal for which they were made and toward which they strive, and this goal is happiness or *eudaimonia*. Happiness is *the* purpose for which a human being is made; it is the ultimate reason we do everything we do. And, even though people will give different answers to the question "What will make you happy?", Aristotle recognized that all people will still say that happiness is their goal in life and that what they are doing in life is done for the sake of happiness.

In order to demonstrate that happiness is *the* ultimate goal of human life and the reason why a person does *everything* he does, Aristotle would probably ask a series of questions like the following: Why did you catch the bus or the metro to school this morning (or however you arrived)? If you answered (as you should), "To get a high school education," then Aristotle would again ask, "Why do you want to get a high school education?" Many people would answer, "So that I can get into college." But again, "Why do you want to go to college?" "So that I can get a good job and make some money." And again, "Why do you want to make money?" "So that I can get married and support children," a number of people would answer. But if further asked, "Why do you want to get married and raise children?" most people would simply respond, "Because doing so will make me happy." No sane person would ask why people wish to be happy; they simply do. It is the bottom-line, the end of the *whys*, the ultimate reason people do the things that they do.

C. HAPPINESS AND OBJECTIVITY

But, even if everyone can agree that happiness is the telos of human life, there certainly seems to be no consensus as to what exactly leads to happiness. Indeed, if people disagree about anything, they disagree about how to lead a happy life. Some say that, in order to be happy, people need to be disciplined and live a "life of moderation"; others say that they should always follow their emotions and be impulsive.

Some say that the best way to be happy is to lead a moral life, and others say, "Why be good? Look at people like John Gotti. They have murdered people and led vicious lives, but they are very happy, rich, and have everything they could possibly want." Or, "Look at Hollywood movie stars. They have good looks, fame, all the women or lovers they could want, and truckloads of money. Aren't they the happiest people around?" Isn't it the case that everybody has her own path to happiness, and that the pursuit of happiness is not of any help in a discussion of morality?

Aristotle replied that, just like an acorn or an eye, a human being has its own goal or purpose, and also like an acorn or an eye, a human being can only reach its own specific goal, happiness, in a certain way. By saying that happiness can only be achieved in a certain fashion, Aristotle did not mean that all people should dress a certain way or have a certain job or anything of that nature. What he did mean is that a person *must* live in a certain way, and that way is the way of virtue. (In the next section, we will see what exactly Aristotle meant by "virtue.") Virtue is a *necessary condition* for happiness; happiness is not possible without it.

As people living in the twenty-first century, we find this idea that human happiness can only be achieved in a certain way to be quite foreign. Most people today believe that each person is free to choose whatever path to happiness she wants and that being happy is a *totally subjective* matter, that it varies completely from person to person. Now, of course, this is true to a certain degree. Some of us, for example, may wish to become painters or musicians, and others may want to become farmers or politicians. Likewise, some people may wish to relax with a leisurely day of fishing, whereas others may enjoy tending their gardens or building furniture. Yet, according to Aristotle, a person's character *must be* formed in a certain way if she is to be truly happy; she must be virtuous. In other words, happiness includes *objective elements*—things that are true for everyone independently of anyone's opinion of them.

An analogy may, perhaps, be of some help here. Suppose that everybody in the classroom were given a brand new automobile, and everyone wanted to keep his car in tip-top shape. Now, some might decide to paint their cars red; others may like orange; and still others may choose black. Some might want to have leather seats, and others may choose to have vinyl or suede. Things like the color of a car or the material of the seats are up to each person; they are purely subjective matters that depend on the whims or preferences of individuals. But there are other aspects to maintaining an automobile that are not *subjective* but are, rather, *objective*. For example, a certain kind of fuel and a regular maintenance schedule are *necessary* if an automobile is to function effectively. If someone wanted to put sugar water or vinegar in the tank, the car would simply not run. Even if this foolish person insisted, "Your opinion about fuel is your opinion, and mine is mine," he would still have a car that would not run.

What Aristotle is saying about human beings is similar to what we just stated about cars. There are certain things in life that we are free to choose, but there are other things in life that must be done a certain way if we are to be truly happy. Preferences like fishing over gardening or watching baseball instead of World Cup Soccer are matters that vary from person to person. But for Aristotle, a truly happy man must be virtuous; no matter what mobsters like John Gotti will tell you, it is impossible that they are truly happy. By making bad choices in life, they have become diseased and corrupted individuals, unable to achieve the telos for which they were created: happiness.

D.   "BUT IF I BELIEVE I'M HAPPY, AREN'T I HAPPY?"

At this point in the study of Aristotle, some student invariably and rightly asks, "But if John Gotti believes he is happy, isn't he happy?" Or, further, "Who is Aristotle to judge who is happy and who is not happy?" and "If I believe I am happy, aren't I happy?" These questions—which are more like assertions—express the popular understanding that people today have of happiness. How does Aristotle respond to these question-assertions?

In Book X of his *Nicomachean Ethics*, Aristotle gives his readers a number of clues to his answer. Early in this book, Aristotle writes, "[N]o one would choose to live with the intellect of a child throughout his life, however much he were pleased at the things that children are pleased at, nor to get enjoyment by doing some most disgraceful deed, though he were never to feel any pain in consequence."[2] And again, later in this book he adds: "Those [pleasures] which are admittedly disgraceful plainly should not be said to be pleasures, except to a perverted taste."[3]

In order to make sense of these quotes and to relate them to the question above, a number of examples and explanations will be given.

After eating all of his vegetables and behaving properly at the dinner table, a young boy is rewarded with a banana split. As he takes the sundae out onto the front porch of his house to savor it outside in the middle of a cool, summer evening, he is joined by his father. His father sees how much he is enjoying his sundae and how relaxed he is, and the father recognizes that this moment would be a good time to teach his son one of life's lessons. "Son," his father begins, "I know you *really* enjoy that dessert, but I want to tell you about what will happen when you get older." His son watches him attentively. "When you get older, things will change, and you will someday fall in love with a beautiful woman. The two of you will marry, have children, and grow old together. And you will be happier than you have ever been." To all of this his son responds, "But will I also get to eat my banana split?" Chuckling to himself, the father replies, "Well, I don't think you'll really be all that concerned with sundaes at that point in your life." Hearing this response, the boy concludes, "Well, if I can't have my sundae, then I think I'll just pass on all the other stuff."

The point of this rather belabored example is, of course, that the boy is in no position to judge what true happiness is, for he is just a child. Looking out from his fishbowl, so to speak, he has such a limited view of the nature of happiness. Though he might say he is happy and, indeed, might have a level of happiness appropriate to a small child, his conception of happiness pales in comparison to that of an adult. And a vicious man or a self-absorbed Hollywood star is somewhat like a child in the game of life; his life has become so distorted that he is no longer capable of understanding what true happiness is. In a way, a vicious person—a person with a diseased soul—is much like a sick person—a person with a diseased body. Very often, a person with a severe medical condition or addiction will crave something that really is not, by its nature, pleasant or she may shun something that truly is pleasant. A morphine addict may crave morphine or methadone, but these things are only pleasant to him because he is sick; no one who is healthy has any such cravings. Likewise, a woman who is suffering from a high fever may find some foods unpleasant because of the condition of her body, even though she had previously enjoyed them when she was healthy. Similarly, a vicious man will find the life of virtue to be painful, and he will shun it, along with the possibility of true happiness.

E.   ARISTOTLE AND RELATIVISM

As a concluding note, it is worth mentioning that Aristotle's insights into human nature may be used as a powerful antidote to the plague of relativism that has swept Western civilization.

Relativism, it will be remembered, is the philosophy that states that there are no moral rules that apply to all cultures or all people in one culture and that no country or person should impose their (or his) moral rules on any other culture or person. However, if Aristotle is correct in his assertion that *all* human beings share the same basic nature and that *all* human beings must live lives of virtue in order to achieve their goal or telos, then relativism must be fundamentally flawed. Cultures may differ—sometimes significantly—but they cannot alter the nature of the human. As C.S. Lewis observed in the foregoing section, as far as moral rules or codes of conduct are concerned, it makes more sense to speak of *one human history* with many divisions than several independent histories of various cultures and races. People come in different sizes, shapes, and colors, and they wear different clothes, speak different languages, and eat different foods. But it would be dishonest not to acknowledge the extent to which most human cultures share the same basic moral rules or codes of conduct.

If human nature crosses cultural boundaries, and human nature demands that certain rules of conduct and certain behavior must be followed, then morality—which offers certain rules of conduct and certain codes of behavior—crosses cultural boundaries, as well.

SECTION TWO:
ARISTOTLE ON "CHARACTER TYPES"

As we learned above, Aristotle believed that every natural thing has a telos or goal toward which it strives and that the telos or goal of human beings is happiness. We also learned that in order to achieve this goal, a human being must be virtuous; virtue is a necessary condition for true happiness. It is now time to investigate Aristotle's understanding of human nature and virtue in more depth.

A. CHARACTER

People act in predictable ways, and when we have known someone such as a best friend for many years, we know how that person will act in a given situation. In fact, the reason we love our true friends is because we know that they will almost always treat us in respectful and loving ways. If people acted one way one day and a completely different way another, it would be impossible to form friendships, and life would be chaos. Life is not a soap opera or television show; men are not faithful, loving husbands one week and, then, adulterers who beat or poison their spouses the next. Short of a miracle, there are no Scrooges in reality; no one is a greedy, selfish, and thoughtless person for seventy years and, then, one day miraculously becomes a loving humanitarian. People have set *characters*, i.e., *fairly stable sets of attitudes, opinions, and dispositions that result in fairly stable patterns or ways of acting and reacting.* Whether or not we find a person's character or personality appealing determines whether or not we choose to become friends with him or her.

When we look around us or back into history we see that there are and have been people of differing moral character. We know that people like Mother Teresa have the finest of characters and that they will nearly always do the right thing no matter what the situation. Other people, like John Dillinger, are almost always inclined to do the wrong thing. The rest of us, neither saints nor mobsters, find ourselves somewhere in between these extremes.

B. THE PARTS OF A HUMAN BEING

All of these observations about human behavior inevitably lead us to ask such questions as "How is a person's character formed?" and "How can I improve my character?" By closely observing human beings, Aristotle tried to figure out answers to these questions. "Ethos" is a Greek word for "character," and Aristotle's famous manuscript, *The Nicomachean Ethics*, is primarily a study of human character.

In the section to follow, more will be said about the nature of habit formation, in general, and the acquisition of "virtues," in particular. But before discussing these issues, some broad generalizations about character types will be given in order to help us understand why having a virtuous character is necessary for human happiness.

Aristotle's observations of human beings led him to conclude that each person has two basic parts, a rational and a non-rational, and that the non-rational part has two parts as well, a "vegetative" and an "appetitive":

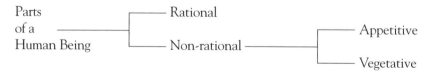

Parts
of a
Human Being
— Rational
— Non-rational
— Appetitive
— Vegetative

The rational part or "reason" thinks, deliberates and, most importantly for our purposes, judges what is right and wrong; it is the part that distinguishes human beings from the rest of the animal kingdom. The appetitive part is the various appetites, desires and emotions that a human feels, such as sexual desire, anger, fear, and pity. To a large degree, the human shares this part with higher animals such as dogs, cats, and monkeys. The vegetative part controls all of a person's involuntary functions, such as growth, breathing, heartbeat, digestion, and the fighting of diseases or infections. This part is called "vegetative," for it is the most plant-like of all human capacities; a plant is alive, but it does all of the things it does without willing to do so.

Because the vegetative part of a human being deals with involuntary functions, it is not of any concern to a person studying ethics. No one should be praised or blamed for what is completely out of his control. Ethics deals with choices, not heartbeat, growth, or breathing. If we want to develop good characters, we should concentrate on the parts of a human being we can change or control, and except for yogis or mystics, the functions of the vegetative part cannot be controlled by people.

C.   THE FORMATION OF VIRTUES AND CHARACTER

Our rational part or reason, however, can bring the appetitive part under its control with discipline and the formation of good habits. This notion, that our desires and emotions can be tamed and harnessed, might seem odd to us because we constantly hear phrases like "They're just feelings, don't judge them" or "I can't help the way I feel." And it is true that when we are having our desires and emotions, they do seem to be beyond our control, but as Aristotle observes, it is possible to form new habits.

Some things we learn by doing, and the virtues or good habits are such things. As Aristotle states:

> [T]he virtues we get by first exercising them, as also happens in the case of
> the arts as well. For the things we have to learn before we do them, we
> learn by doing them: e.g., men become builders by building and lyre-players by playing the lyre; so too we become just by doing just acts, temperate
> by doing temperate acts, brave by doing brave acts.[4]

People do not learn how to ride a bike by reading about it in books; they simply get on the bike and, many scrapes and bruises later, know how to ride a bike. By repeatedly doing a certain action, we become *habituated* to that type of activity. Through repetition we train our bodies to behave in a certain way, and the way we train our bodies will determine our behavior in the future.

Practice does not make perfect, as the popular slogan wrongly declares; practice makes permanent. If we train ourselves in a bad fashion, we will create bad states of character, and if we train ourselves in a good fashion, we will create good states of character. And this process of training applies to our appetites, too, such as anger, jealousy, and fear, as well as to skills such as riding a bike or playing a piano. By repeating certain types of behavior, we can change how we feel or react to certain situations.

For example, all of us have friends or at least know of people who are irascible or "hot under the collar," i.e., people who are constantly getting into fights and whose anger is aroused by the smallest things. Whenever these people get into a troublesome situation, their anger immediately overwhelms their rational part, and they find themselves getting into fights even when they know they should not. But, if they are able to control themselves one time (perhaps, with the help of counselors or friends), they may find that the next time they are in a tough spot, their anger may be just a little less overwhelming. If they can continue to abstain from fighting and stay away from potentially dangerous situations, they will find over time that their anger is much less powerful and much more manageable. In this way, they have begun to form a new habit; they have brought their appetitive part under the control of their reason.

When people have taught or habituated themselves both *to judge with their rational part* the appropriate way to behave or respond in a certain situation and *to feel or desire* in the appropriate way (i.e., in the manner prescribed by their judgment), then they have acquired a "virtue."

But, in the same way that a bad habit can be corrected or modified by discipline, a good habit or virtue can be corrupted by lax behavior or continued bad actions. For example, people who are trustworthy and honest can become liars by repeatedly lying. The more people lie, the more likely they are to lie in the future; after a while, the guilt starts to fade, and the urge to lie becomes overwhelming. In general, people's actions determine their character, and people's character determines their actions.

D.   THE FOUR MAJOR CHARACTER TYPES

Most people are constantly struggling to keep their emotions and desires under the control of their reason so that they will behave the right way in a given situation. Most people must fight the urge to eat too many sweets, to be lazy, to be overwhelmed with fear and flee a dangerous situation that calls for courage, to spend beyond their means, etc. Their rational part judges the appropriate course of action, but their appetites and desires just do not seem to follow reason's lead. If people characteristically win their battles with their appetitive part—i.e., their emotions and desires eventually, though reluctantly, follow the guidance of their reason—then they are *continent* or *enduring*, according to Aristotle. People are *continent* if they can ward off the desire for too much pleasure and *enduring* if they can withstand fear or painful emotions in difficult situations.

Others, unfortunately, lose their struggle with their appetitive part; they end up eating too much, being too lazy, being overwhelmed with fear and fleeing, spending too much, etc. These people, who characteristically lose these battles, Aristotle calls *incontinent* or *soft*. *Incontinence* is a state of character that is marked by an overwhelming weakness toward pleasure, *softness* by an overwhelming aversion to pain.

But there *are* some people who do not have to struggle because their appetites are in harmony with their rational part. This kind of person Aristotle calls *virtuous*. Whereas some people are mean-spirited and must fight against themselves to be kind, and other people are too milquetoast and wishy-washy and must struggle desperately to stand up for themselves, the *virtuous* person is able to show the appropriate mix of friendliness and self-respect without any struggle. Whereas cowardly people must strain every nerve to keep themselves from fleeing a dangerous situation, and other rash or foolhardy people must fight the urge to run blindly into such situations, the *virtuous* person is courageous, feeling the proper amount of fear and judging the proper course of action that the situation demands.

It is important to note, at this juncture, that the difference between virtuous and continent or enduring people is not that the virtuous do the right thing more often. The difference is *how* they do the right thing. Whereas continent or enduring people must struggle and experience some form of pain in doing the right thing, virtuous people experience much less pain and a great deal more pleasure, for their actions go along with the habits they have formed.

Another group of people are what Aristotle calls *self-indulgent* (in regard to pleasures) or *vicious*. Unfortunately, this type of moral agent has been so corrupted through bad actions and difficult circumstances that their rational part is no longer able to judge right from wrong. Unlike most of us, vicious people do not struggle with their emotions or desires but, rather, actively do the wrong thing without much remorse.

Unlike any of the other character types, vicious people are virtually incorrigible; they are almost beyond help. For when people counsel others, they usually appeal to their rational part; counselors offer arguments or reasons why people should modify their behavior. "The next time you feel anger welling up inside of you, make sure that you leave the room so that you can calm down," a friend or parent might advise a young person. But the vicious person's reason is corrupted as well, and it is pointless to try to counsel someone whose reason is corrupted. To what do you appeal? "When water chokes, what is one to wash it down with?" asks a proverb cited by Aristotle. According to Aristotle, these people are incorrigible, and he recommends they be executed or permanently isolated from society.

In our criminal justice system, we recognize the difference between a vicious and a weak-willed person. Very often law enforcement officials or lawyers will say things like "Sure, Johnny stole that television, but he is not a criminal," whereby they mean that, though Johnny was overwhelmed by his passion to steal, he still knows the difference between right and wrong.

Aristotle, then, saw moral agents as generally falling into one of four categories depending upon the relationship that they have between their reason and appetites.

The following chart illustrates the differences between these character types in a clear fashion:

Character Types	Is Reason Able to Judge Right from Wrong?	Are the Appetites in Line with Reason?	Does the Agent Do the Right Thing?
VIRTUOUS	YES	YES	YES
CONTINENT/ ENDURING	YES	NO	YES
INCONTINENT/ SOFT	YES	NO	NO
VICIOUS/ SELF-INDULGENT	NO	YES	NO

E.   WHY VIRTUOUS PEOPLE ARE THE HAPPIEST

From what has been stated above, it should be relatively clear why the life of virtue is the most pleasant and the most conducive for happiness. But for the sake of clarification, Aristotle offers the following insights:

> [T]hose who have done many terrible deeds and are hated for their wickedness even shrink from life and destroy themselves. And wicked men seek for people with whom to spend their days, and shun themselves; for they remember many a grievous deed, and anticipate others like them, when they are by themselves, but when they are with others they forget. And having nothing lovable in them they have no feeling of love to themselves. Therefore also such men do not rejoice or grieve with themselves; for their soul is rent by faction, and one element in it by reason of its wickedness grieves when it abstains from certain acts, while the other part is pleased, and one draws them this way and the other that, as if they were pulling them in pieces.[5]

Though wicked (vicious) people will most probably be friendless (for who would want to spend any time with a truly wicked man, a man who does not treat anyone justly or with the proper respect?), they are forced to seek friends in order to avoid themselves, for they have nothing admirable about themselves to enjoy. Indeed, it is said that Josef Stalin, the Soviet dictator who routinely executed his enemies and killed approximately 20 million Russian peasants with his collectivization of farms, could not stand to be alone; he always sought "friends" to distract him from himself. Likewise, *incontinent* people (and even *continent* people) are doomed to lives of anguish and turmoil. Their reason is not thoroughly corrupted, and so one part of their soul is pleased when they abstain from bad activities. But because their passions are so out of kilter, they suffer great emotional or psychological pain, as morphine addicts suffer gut-wrenching withdrawal symptoms even though they might be aware that this withdrawal is for the best.

But *virtuous* people live a life of harmony; their reason and passions act in unison, and they have their mind set on what is truly good. They are capable of a unique level of pleasure that is beyond that of children or diseased men. The pleasure of dealing with others justly or helping others in need that the virtuous enjoy has no parallels. For the most part, this fact is not something that Aristotle can prove on paper. It is the experience of living a happy life of virtue that is his ultimate "argument" against the other types of lives.

SECTION THREE:
VIRTUE AND MODERATION; ARISTOTLE AND CATHOLIC CHRISTIANITY

In our study of Aristotle's theory of character types, we learned that every human being has a rational and an appetitive part and that every person falls into one of four general categories of moral agency—the virtuous, continent (or enduring), incontinent (or soft), or vicious—depending upon the relationship that holds between these two parts. Yet, we still need to learn more about how a virtuous person makes moral decisions, for all we have really learned is that virtuous people have their emotions in harmony with their reason. But how exactly do virtuous people choose the right thing to do? How does one become virtuous?

A.   VIRTUE: THE GOLDEN MEAN

In the preceding section, "virtue" was defined in the following manner: a state of character that allows a person both to judge with his or her rational part the appropriate way to behave or respond in a certain situation and to feel or desire in the appropriate way (i.e., in the manner prescribed by his or her judgment). But it remains to be discovered how exactly the virtuous person judges the appropriate way to respond.

For Aristotle, the virtuous person strives for the middle course or what today we would speak of as "the golden mean." For *nearly every* passion and action, the virtuous person will try to steer an *intermediate* or *mean* course between two extremes. This intermediate way of feeling and acting Aristotle calls a "virtue," and the two extremes that flank this intermediate way he calls "vices." One of the extremes is an excess or a "too much," and the other is a deficiency or a "too little." For example, in regard to eating, it is possible for people to eat more than is necessary for their health; these people eat excessively, and this vice is called gluttony. On the other hand, it is also possible for people to eat much less than is necessary for their health, as is the case with someone suffering from anorexia nervosa; these people eat deficiently, and this vice is called, for lack of a commonly used term, "insensitivity." Virtuous people, however, find the mean, the action that is appropriate for the situation, and avoid either excess; virtuous people will practice temperance, the virtue in regard to food. Virtuous people know with their reason that only so much food is necessary for a healthy body, and because they are virtuous, they only desire that amount of food.

Also, because a virtue is the ability to find the middle course of action, it will be flanked on either side by a vice, a deficient or excessive course of behavior. Hence Aristotle states, "For men are good in but one way, but bad in many."[6] In other words, there are two directions in which a person may go astray, whereas the appropriate course of action is limited to the middle.

B.   THE MEAN IS RELATIVE TO EACH PERSON

Though, as we saw in Section One, Aristotle would be the first to reject the philosophy of *relativism*, he is the first to admit that the middle or mean has to be *relative* to each person. This fact is evident in regard to areas such as eating and exercise. What is a fitting diet for a six-foot-seven-inch man would obviously be excessive for a five-foot-two-inch woman. Likewise, what is a healthy exercise regimen for a teenager might kill an elderly man. What is moderate giving on the part of the middle class would be miserly on the part of the rich.

But to say that the middle is relative to each person is not to say that there is no objective right or wrong for each person. All people have a range of eating, spending, desiring, etc. that is objectively right for them, even though that objective range is relative to each person. A large man *can* eat too little, and rich people *can* give too little. These are objective matters.

C.   CHART OF VIRTUES AND VICES

Below is a list of several of the virtues and vices that Aristotle mentions in his *Ethics*:

ACTIVITY	VICE (EXCESS)	VIRTUE (MEAN)	VICE (DEFICIT)
Reacting to Injustice	Irascibility	Anger	Inirascibility
Claiming Honors	Vanity	Proper Pride	Humility
Being Pleasant/Amusing	Buffoonery	Ready-wittedness	Boorishness
Fearing Danger	Cowardice	Courage	Foolhardiness
Giving Money	Prodigality	Liberality	Illiberality
Eating, Drinking, And Desiring Sex	Gluttony, Self-indulgence	Temperance	Insensitivity
Interacting Socially	Obsequiousness	Proper Friendliness	Sulkiness

D. EXCEPTIONS TO THE RULE

The virtuous moral agent, then, will generally try to find the mean or middle course in a given situation or in regard to a certain activity, but "the golden mean of moderation" does not hold for all actions. As Aristotle observed, there are actions that are essentially evil and do not have excesses or deficiencies associated with them:

> But not every action nor every passion admits of a mean; for some have names that already imply badness, e.g., spite, shamelessness, envy, and in the case of actions adultery, theft, murder; for all of these and suchlike things imply by their names that they are themselves bad, and not the excesses or deficiencies of them. It is not possible, then, ever to be right with regard to them; one must always be wrong.[7]

A murderer, then, cannot take any consolation in the fact that his three murders are some type of a mean between a "deficiency" of no murders, on the one hand, and an "excess" of six murders on the other. Nor should a man who has cheated on his wife with *only* one woman for a number of years feel that he has avoided the vices of being "too faithful," on the one hand, and "too promiscuous," on the other. Murder and adultery are, by nature, disordered; they do not admit of corresponding deficiencies and excesses.

E. PRACTICAL ADVICE ON HOW TO FIND THE MEAN

Now, as Aristotle noted in his treatment of character types, most people are not virtuous but are either continent (enduring) or incontinent (soft). If Aristotle is right and people can only be truly happy if they are virtuous, then we should ask, "How can we become virtuous?" Aristotle's *Ethics* contains many helpful suggestions as to how a continent or incontinent person can become virtuous. (As noted above, according to Aristotle, vicious people are practically incorrigible or untreatable because they cannot be reasoned with and they have little desire to change themselves.) Indeed, many psychologists and counselors have found that his advice is often beneficial to their patients.

E1. The Virtuous Person is the Measure

In Book II of his *Ethics*, Aristotle states that a virtue is a mean or middle that is determined by reference to what the virtuous man would do. It is the virtuous man who has really discovered or determined what virtue is. It is not as though Aristotle locked himself in an ivory tower and cleverly devised a number of rules for becoming virtuous. His knowledge of virtue was acquired in the same manner everyone's knowledge of virtue is acquired: by observing virtuous people. Similarly, sports writers did not create the rules for becoming a great quarterback out of thin air; they observed great quarterbacks in action and, then, described the general traits that these men had in common.

And in much the same way that a budding quarterback should watch and imitate an expert quarterback or an aspiring golfer should watch and imitate an expert golfer, continent and incontinent people who wish to be virtuous should model their behavior on that of virtuous people. In a way parallel to that of the quarterback or golfer, virtuous people are experts in their field; they have, to a certain extent, mastered the game of life. And just as it would be wise to consult Brett Favre or Venus Williams on how to be a great quarterback or great tennis player, it would be wise to consult a virtuous man or woman on how to live well.

In addition to providing models of behavior, virtuous people may also help continent and incontinent people understand their situation. Very often non-virtuous people perceive their own situation in a distorted fashion, and so it is helpful to get the opinion of someone whom everyone regards as wise and good. In effect, incontinent and vicious people tend to shift the spectrum of actions (and emotions/desires) and to view *themselves* as occupying the median position and everyone else a deficient or excessive one. For example, a coward may actually believe that he is being courageous and that a truly courageous person is being rash or foolhardy, and a rash person may actually believe that a courageous person is behaving cowardly. Or, in a recently publicized study, interviewers found that women who had been prostitutes for a very long time came to view themselves as shrewd businesswomen and married women as dupes or fools who had been tricked into making love to men for free. A virtuous person, who possesses the virtue of prudence, can often help people such as these to see things in their proper perspective.

E2. Other Guidelines

Other rules that Aristotle suggests that may help us become virtuous and find the "golden mean" are the following:

Avoid the extreme that is more opposed to the mean.

Each virtue is usually flanked by two vices, one deficiency and one excess, but usually one of these vices is much more likely to ensnare a moral agent. Even though virtues are usually referred to as the mean or middle, very often one of the vices is closer by nature to the virtue. For example, in regard to food and sexual desire, most people are much more likely to fall into self-indulgence or gluttony than insensitivity. Indeed, not desiring food or sex enough is quite a rare event in human affairs, which is why there is not a common term to describe this phenomenon. Usually, the pleasure of overeating or overindulging in sex is so great that it makes the virtue very difficult to achieve, whereas insensitive people do not have as far to travel to achieve the virtue; their journey to the middle is less onerous and, perhaps, even pleasant. Hence, of the two vices surrounding temperance, gluttony is the "more opposed" to the mean; it is further from the middle and has less in common with temperance than insensitivity does. Likewise, cowardice seems to have less in common with courage than foolhardiness does. Overcoming a fear of danger that is quite strong is usually harder than toning down one's bravado or brazenness. Hence, of the two vices, cowardice is more opposed to courage and is to be *especially* avoided. If one must fall into vice, he or she should at least choose the better of the two.

Know yourself.

Even though cowardice might, in general or by nature, be more opposed to courage than foolhardiness, I might have a problem with foolhardiness. Or even though most people have a problem with being too stingy or illiberal, I might give my money too frequently or too recklessly. Like Thoreau who came after him, Aristotle recommended that one should strive to "know thyself" and, as a result, learn to avoid those vices to which he or she is particularly prone.

Always be wary of pleasure, for of all things, it is most likely to lead you astray.

Though there is nothing wrong with pleasure and the happy and moral life will certainly be, in large part, a pleasant one, the pursuit of pleasure *in itself* is usually the cause of most of our problems. If we think about why we did not study for the midterm examination or why we spent more money than our budgets allow, we usually find that the pursuit of pleasure is at the bottom of our failings. "I know that I should be watching my diet," we rationalize to ourselves, "but that chocolate cake tastes *so good*." Or "I know that I should give more money to the poor than I currently do, but imagine how good I'll look in those new pair of shoes."

Of course, these pleasures are pleasant for the moment, but in the long run, according to Aristotle, we pay the price. The pursuit of long-term happiness—and ultimately long-term pleasure—is somewhat like the pursuit of a cat. As anyone who owns a feline knows, most cats do not like to be handled very often, and if someone spends too much time trying to be affectionate with a cat, that cat will avoid that person like the plague. But if the cat is left alone, a great many times she will seek out a person with whom she does want to spend some time. Similarly, if people seek pleasure around every corner, they become self-indulgent and a slave to their passions. No longer are they in control. Their desires and hungers govern their every move, and ultimately, they are left unsatisfied and unhappy. But ironically, if people pursue the middle course—eating food and spending money moderately, for example— then they will find themselves enjoying life, even though they do not pursue pleasure directly. Oddly enough, pleasurable lives are lived only by those who do not directly pursue the life of pleasure.

The bent stick remedy.

Aristotle maintains that people whose emotions or desires are out of harmony with their reason are like bent sticks. If someone wishes to straighten out a bent stick, he or she will have to bend it all the way back in the opposite direction before it will straighten out. Likewise, people who are, for example, vain should try to be as humble as possible, and by so doing, they will hopefully find the mean, in this case proper pride. Or, again, people who spend extravagantly and recklessly should try to be miserly, and by doing so, they will hopefully find the mean, liberality or proper generosity.

The reason that Aristotle advocates such an extreme solution is that, as noted above, incontinent people are usually unable to properly judge where exactly they are situated in the spectrum of virtues and vices. For example, a glutton tends to view temperate people as prudes or sticks-in-the-mud. In order to compensate for this skewed perspective and to overcome the force of acquired habits, Aristotle recommends that a person should strain every nerve to reverse his or her behavior completely. In most cases, a complete reversal is impossible, and fortunately, the person in question will end up in the middle, exactly where he or she should be.

F.   ARISTOTLE'S ETHICS AND CHRISTIAN MORALITY

Now that we have become acquainted with Aristotle's virtue ethics, it will be helpful to conclude our study of his thought by looking at it through the lens of Christianity. To what extent should Christians, in general, and Catholic Christians, in particular, embrace this non-religious philosophy?

1.   Similarities between Aristotle's ethics and Christian morality

Though Christians should acknowledge that Aristotle's conception of ethics is incomplete and, at times, uncharitable, they also should acknowledge that it is more in keeping with the spirit of their religion than any of the other secular ethical systems we will cover in this chapter. In large part, the reason for this kinship in spirit can be traced to the fact that Aristotle's thought is more "pre-Christian" in character than "secular." As opposed to the other ethical systems we will cover in this chapter, Aristotle's virtue ethics appeared before the birth of Christ, and some of his teachings were incorporated into the thought of some Christian theologians. His teachings on everything from ethics and nature to God and the soul have been immensely influential in Catholic thought in particular, especially through the writings of the medieval theologian St. Thomas Aquinas. Indeed, Aristotle is even mentioned by name in the treatment of the human virtues in the *Catechism of the Catholic Church.*[8]

Yet even Protestant denominations that place less emphasis than Roman Catholics do on the role of tradition and philosophy in moral and theological matters can appreciate the similarities between Aristotle's thought and some Biblical teachings.

Perhaps the most striking similarity between Aristotle's thought and Christianity is the emphasis that both of them place on human happiness or flourishing. Whether or not they were acquainted with Aristotle's notion of "teleology," Christian theologians throughout the centuries have stressed the notion that God has implanted in every human being a desire for happiness, a desire that can only be fulfilled by eternal union with God in heaven. For example, in a justly famous passage of his *Confessions,* St. Augustine muses:

How do I seek you, O Lord? For when I seek you, my God, I seek the happy life. Let me seek you "so that my soul may live." My body lives by my soul, and my soul lives by you … Is not the happy life that which all men will to have, and no man entirely wills against it?[9]

Likewise, St. Thomas Aquinas argued that the goal toward which all human beings strive is happiness and that "[f]inal and perfect happiness can consist in nothing else than the vision of the Divine Essence."[10] Indeed, the message of Christianity itself could be summarized in the following passage from St. Ignatius Loyola, which uses the Aristotelian language of "goals" and "purposes":

God freely created us so that we might know, love, and serve Him in this life and be happy with God forever. God's purpose in creating us is to draw forth from us a response of love and service here on earth, so that we may attain our goal of everlasting happiness with God in heaven.[11]

Furthermore, the Bible itself, especially its wisdom literature, repeatedly emphasizes the Aristotelian notion that the good life is the happy life, i.e., that moral virtue is a necessary condition and essential component of human happiness. For example, Psalm 1:1-2 states that true happiness can only be found in obedience to God's law:

Happy those who do not follow
    the counsel of the wicked,
Nor go the way of the sinners,
    nor sit in company with scoffers.
Rather, the law of the Lord is their joy;
    God's law they study day and night.

And in a similar spirit, Proverbs 11:18-19 proclaims:

The wicked man makes empty profits,
    but he who sows virtue has a sure reward.
Virtue directs toward life,
    but he who pursues evil does so to his death.

Whether through divine intervention or through the natural consequences of their actions, the virtuous or righteous are always depicted in the wisdom literature of the Bible as eventually enjoying a happy life, and the wicked or vicious always eventually suffer a miserable fate.

Moreover, the influence of Aristotelian ideas on Christian thought is evident in the specific ways that virtue itself is characterized in Scripture and other Christian writings. For example, The Book of Sirach 18:30-33 describes the virtuous life as one in which one's appetites are kept under control:

Go not after your lusts,
>
> but keep your desires in check.

If you satisfy your lustful appetites
>
> they will make you the sport of your enemies

Have no joy in the pleasures of the moment
>
> which bring on poverty redoubled;

Become not a glutton and a winebibber
>
> with nothing in your purse.

Additionally, Proverbs 30:8-9 advocates moderation in regard to money:

[G]ive me neither poverty nor riches;
>
> provide me only with the food I need;

Lest, being full, I deny you,
>
> saying, "Who is the Lord?"

Or being in want, I steal,
>
> and profane the name of my God.

And in this same vein, the *Catechism* offers the following definition of "human virtues," a definition that, except for its reference to "faith," would be perfectly at home in Aristotle's *Nichomachean Ethics*: "*Human virtues* are firm attitudes, stable dispositions, habitual perfections of intellect and will that govern our actions, order our passions, and guide our conduct according to reason and faith."[12]

Finally, Aristotle's reflections on the role of reason in the life of the virtuous person have had a tremendous impact on the formation of what the Catholic Church calls "natural law." In chapter five, we will discuss this pivotal concept, and at that time, the Aristotelian influence of this concept on Catholic thought will become evident.

2.   Differences between Aristotle's ethics and Christian morality

However, as striking as some of these similarities between Christianity and Aristotle's virtue ethics are, it must be acknowledged that Aristotle was not a Christian, and as such, his conception of the moral life is often incomplete and sometimes simply incompatible with the Christian message.

Though Aristotle certainly believed in a god—indeed, he even offered a philosophical proof for its existence—his god was not the personal God of the Jews and Christians, a God Who is in charge of the course of history and Whom we are instructed to call "Father." Aristotle's god was the highest of all beings and certainly worthy of contemplation, but his god did not create human beings out of nothing, did not have any concern for human beings, and did not offer hope for eternal salvation. Obviously, since Aristotle was unfamiliar with the Jewish faith and lived before Jesus, he could not have espoused the theological virtues of faith, hope, and charity; he could not have realized that the true *telos* of a human being is to be eternally united with Christ.

Because Aristotle did not have a fully Christian conception of the divine, he did not have an appreciation for many Christian moral virtues. In particular, because Aristotle did not believe in a personal Creator, he saw no need for the Christian virtue of humility in his conception of the good life. For Aristotle, human beings might recognize the greatness of god, but they had no reason to be grateful to him or to expect good things from him. In contrast, the Judeo-Christian tradition has always emphasized that "fear of the Lord" is the beginning of holiness and an integral part of virtuous living. For example, when commanded by Pharaoh to murder all the male offspring of the Jews, the Hebrew midwives refused to do so for they feared the Lord, and as a result, "God dwelt well with the midwives" (Ex. 1:15-21). Additionally, Jesus taught his followers that they should trust and depend on God, as children trust and depend on their parents, if they wish to enter the kingdom of God:

> At that time the disciples approached Jesus and said, "Who is the greatest in the kingdom of heaven?" He called a child over, placed it in their midst, and said, "Amen, I say to you, unless you turn and become like children, you will not enter the kingdom of heaven. Whoever humbles himself like this child is the greatest in the kingdom of heaven" (Mt. 18:1-4).

And, as the *Catechism* notes, "humility is the foundation of prayer."[13] With humble and contrite hearts, Christians offer up praise and thanksgiving to God, ask for forgiveness of their sins and the wisdom and courage to carry out His divine plan. In contrast, Aristotle would never have described his virtuous person as someone with a "humble and contrite heart." For him, humility is either a vice—a failure to recognize that one rightfully deserves honors and goods that he or she has not claimed—or a sad but true recognition that one is not virtuous, that one is actually inferior to other people.

Additionally, Aristotle seems to have had little concern for the welfare of those outside his own circle of friends or, at most, his own city-state. In contrast, Jesus commanded His followers, "You shall love your neighbor as yourself" (Mt. 22:39), and by "neighbor," Jesus meant "every human being, both Jews and Gentile"; in other words, Jesus expressed and commanded His followers to adopt a *universal* concern for humanity. Though Aristotle certainly advocated helping friends in need, he could not have embraced such a broad commandment, for he did not embrace a God with such a broad concern for humanity. Jesus explains to his followers that they are to obey this commandment because God is the Father of all human beings, and we are called to be God-like and show concern for all people. In the Gospel of Matthew, Jesus states:

> But I say to you, love your enemies, and pray for those who persecute you, that you may be children of your heavenly Father, for He makes his sun rise on the bad and the good, and causes rain to fall on the just and the unjust ... So, be perfect, just as your heavenly Father is perfect (Mt. 5:44-45,48).

Again, later in that same Gospel, Jesus offers another rationale for loving your neighbor as yourself: Whatever you do for your neighbor, you do for God (Mt. 25:31-46). Thus, Christ not only identifies each human being—both the just and the unjust—as a child of God, but He also identifies each one *as God Himself*; in some mystical way, our neighbor *is God*. Needless to say, these theological insights were not available to Aristotle, and thus, he did not see the need for caring for anyone outside the boundaries of his city-state.

Further, because Aristotle did not believe all human beings were made in the image and likeness of God, he had little concern for the poor and marginalized in society. Solidarity with the poor, the oppressed, the widow, the orphan, and the sojourner in a foreign land is just not a component of the good life as far as Aristotle is concerned. Indeed, like Plato, Aristotle allowed for abortion as a way to limit the population of a city-state, as well as infanticide in cases in which the baby is deformed. And as was noted above, he also advocated execution for the truly vicious members of society, a practice that has been virtually abandoned by the magisterium of the Catholic Church.

Nonetheless, it must be acknowledged that, for the most part, Aristotle's influence upon Christianity has been both profound and positive. For Catholics in particular, Aristotle's conceptual framework has helped to illuminate many truths of the moral life. And even Protestants, who historically have rejected the influence of Aristotle in Christian thought, must at least acknowledge the extent to which Aristotle's conception of the good life resembles their own.

SECTION HIGHLIGHTS

Aristotle maintained that all things in nature have a goal or purpose for which they strive; he called such a goal or purpose a "final cause" or "telos."

The goal of human beings, according to Aristotle, is happiness or "eudaimonia." It must be the goal of human life, for it is always the ultimate reason why any person does what he does.

Aristotle observed that human happiness contained both "subjective" and "objective" elements. Some elements of happiness vary from person to person; fishing may relax some and bore others. But other things, such as living a virtuous life, must be the same for all people because of the way human beings are built.

Believing that one is happy is not sufficient proof that one is truly happy. Like a small child or a diseased person, a vicious person lacks the proper perspective on happiness. He may settle for "childish" goods or, in his diseased soul, crave pleasures that are not truly pleasures—as a heroin addict may crave heroin or methadone.

Aristotle's ideas regarding human nature are a healthy corrective to the errant views of relativism. If all human beings share one, basic nature, then a difference in cul-

ture cannot override the fact that all people are built in the same way and fundamentally require the same things.

Character is the fairly stable sets of attitudes, opinions, and dispositions of a person that result in fairly stable patterns or ways of acting and reacting. In general, our actions determine what our character will be, and our character determines what our actions will be.

For Aristotle, the human being is "divided" into three different parts: the rational, the appetitive, and the vegetative. The vegetative, which deals with involuntary functions, is not important for ethics, which deals with choices. A person's character type is determined by the relationship between his rational and appetitive parts.

When people have taught or habituated themselves both to judge with their rational part the appropriate way to behave or respond in a certain situation and to feel or desire in the appropriate way (i.e., in the manner prescribed by their judgment), then they have acquired a "virtue."

Habits and character states are produced by performing like activities; "we become just by doing just acts, temperate by doing temperate acts, brave by doing brave acts."

Aristotle recognized at least four character types: the virtuous, the continent (or enduring), the incontinent (or soft), and the vicious.

Virtuous people, who live a life of harmony, are the only type capable of reaching their goal as humans: happiness. Continent and incontinent people are torn apart by the struggle within their souls, and vicious people find themselves friendless (but in need of friends) and incapable of experiencing the higher pleasures.

For most actions and passions, the virtuous person will try to find the mean, the middle ground (or virtue) between two extremes (or vices), one of which is an excess and the other a deficiency.

In most cases, the mean or virtue will be relative to the individual and to the circumstances. This is not to say that Aristotle was a relativist, in the sense explained in the previous chapter. There is a proper and objective way for each person to desire, judge, and act, but that standard is dependent on the person's situation.

The golden mean of moderation does not hold for all actions or desires. Some actions, such as murder, or feelings, such as envy, are by nature bad and do not become good by being performed or felt in moderation.

The desires, judgments, and actions of the virtuous person are the standard by which all desires, judgments, and actions are measured. In particular, the virtuous person can help provide moral counseling, for he or she can help correct the skewed perspective of incontinent people, who usually misjudge where they stand in regard to virtue.

Aristotle offers many guidelines for becoming virtuous. Among them are avoiding the extreme that is most opposed to the mean; knowing oneself; being wary of pleasure; and the bent stick remedy.

Aristotle's virtue ethics has a great deal in common with Christianity, in general, and Catholicism, in particular. Like Aristotle, Christians believe that the telos of human life is happiness, that the good life is also the happy life, and that many virtues are accurately described as a kind of moderation. However, Aristotle's historical situation made it impossible for him to appreciate some basic Christian values, such as respect for all life, especially the most vulnerable in society.

QUESTIONS

To show that you comprehend what has been presented about Aristotle's understanding of virtue and moderation, answer the following questions in paragraph form. Write your answers on a separate sheet of paper.

1. Do you think that natural things have a goal or purpose toward which they strive, as Aristotle claims? Why or why not? Explain your answer.

2. What would Aristotle say to a moral relativist who said, "What makes you happy might be one thing, but what makes another person happy could be *entirely* different, so do not impose your lifestyle on other people"?

3. Do you think Aristotle is correct when he claims that a person must be virtuous in order to be happy? Why or why not?

4. Even though we have not yet discussed what revelation and Church tradition have to say about human nature or ethics, try to think of how Christians would interpret the notion that a human being has a purpose or "telos" for which he or she was made. Write out your answer.

5. Do you think that Aristotle's analysis of the human being and his understanding of character are accurate? Why or why not? Explain your answer.

6. Choose a literary character or a movie/television character and explain which character type you believe he or she embodies. Give episodes or incidents from this character's life to support your claim.

7. Do you believe that there are any people who are *so* vicious that they are *completely* beyond help, as Aristotle seems to imply? Why or why not? If so, what should be done with them?

8. One of Aristotle's predecessors, Socrates, taught that nobody ever *knowingly* does what is wrong, e.g., when somebody steals, he only does so because he is ignorant of the fact that stealing is wrong. In other words, for Socrates, all

wrongdoing is simply a form of ignorance. Having read this section, how do you think Aristotle would respond to Socrates' position? Explain your answer.

9. Many segments of American culture advocate living a life of excess or a life "on the edge." Do you think that Aristotle is right to champion a life of moderation, or do you believe that "living life to the extreme" is the best road to pursue? Why or why not? Illustrate your answer with an example.

10. What is the "bent stick remedy" that Aristotle prescribes for incontinent people? What other guidelines or advice, in addition to those proposed in this section, would you give to a person who was trying to become virtuous?

11. In the reading, the author suggests that pursuing pleasure is somewhat similar to pursuing a cat. What does he mean by this comparison? Is this observation about pleasure true? Illustrate your answer with an example from your own life.

12. Do you think Jesus would have agreed with Aristotle that the virtuous course of action usually consists in finding a mean or middle course between two extremes? Explain your answer using examples from Jesus' life or from His teachings.

PART TWO:
IMMANUEL KANT'S ETHICAL THEORY

A. HISTORICAL BACKGROUND

Between the time of Aristotle and the Enlightenment, the era in which Immanuel Kant (1724-1804) constructed his ethical theory, many great moral philosophies arose throughout the Western world. For example, during the first and second centuries, the Stoics formulated an austere and demanding code for living based on "following nature" that helped to pave the way for the development of what Catholics would later call "natural law" ethics. Also, during the Middle Ages, numerous Catholic authors such as St. Augustine of Hippo (354-430) and St. Thomas Aquinas produced their own moral theologies, weaving together original strands of thought with Scriptural wisdom and insights from their predecessors. Furthermore, earlier in the same century as Kant produced his moral theory, a number of philosophers, most notably David Hume (1711-1776), advanced the notion that human beings could tell right from wrong by means of a "moral sense"—just as people have eyes to sense the color of things and ears to hear the sounds given off by things, they also have something like a "sense" to perceive the good or bad qualities of a thing or action. However, with the possible exception of "utilitarianism" (which we will cover in Part Three), Immanuel Kant's ethics stands out as the most influential secular system of moral thought produced since the birth of Christ. As will become clear, the American way of thinking about ethics has been heavily influenced by Kant.

However, to say that Kant was a "secular" or "non-religious" figure may be a bit misleading. Raised in a strict Protestant household, Kant certainly believed in God and maintained a lifelong appreciation for Christian morality, though he had little to no interest in prayer or a formal church structure. Indeed, one of the formulations of Kant's moral law that we will study bears a striking resemblance to the Golden Rule of Christianity—"Do unto others as you would have them do unto you." However compatible Kant's moral theory is with Christian principles, though, it is important to note that he was not inclined to cite Jesus, Scripture or any church as an authority. Rather, he attempted to ground his claims in the reflections of *reason alone*, and in this regard, he was certainly a product of his time.

Kant developed his ethical system during the Enlightenment or the Age of Reason. During the 17th and 18th centuries, the discoveries of the sciences, especially in the areas of astronomy and physics, began a revolution in the way people viewed their place in nature and their relationship to religion. Almost everyone before Galileo believed that the sun and the other planets revolved around the Earth, but Galileo showed that, in fact, the Earth revolved around the sun. The Earth and human beings could no longer be seen as the center of the universe, as the Catholic Church once believed. The Church threatened Galileo, demanding that he recant his views, and he did. However, Galileo's views were true and ultimately won over public opinion, and people began to question statements that rested only on authority. Reasoning and observation seemed to be much more effective and fruitful tools than faith for discerning scientific matters. Following the spirit of his times, Kant believed that moral questions should also be kept separate from matters of faith, and in this spirit, he put forth a moral theory that was grounded in reason alone. However, as we will see below, Kant's moral theory is often similar to the teachings of Jesus.

B.   KANT'S CASE AGAINST ARISTOTLE

As we learned in Part One of this chapter, Aristotle argued that the "telos" of a human being is to achieve happiness. Ultimately, happiness is the foundation and goal of the moral life. Indeed, for Aristotle, human beings acquire virtue in order to achieve happiness; the good life is the happy life. And, furthermore, it is the faculty of reason that is designed to guide us toward virtues and happiness; the good and happy life is the life lived in accord with reason.

Immanuel Kant disagreed with these basic claims of Aristotle's system. He did not dispute the fact that everybody *does, in fact, desire to be happy*. What he did dispute is the notion that the purpose of our lives here on earth as rational creatures, who can make choices based upon reason, *should be* to achieve happiness. In other words, he believed that human beings have been given reason and a will for a purpose other than to achieve happiness. In short, Kant believed that the pursuit of the happy life was distinct from—and often quite opposed to—the pursuit of the moral life. But why did he deny Aristotle's claims about reason and happiness?

1.   The life of reason is not necessarily a happy one

In reply to Aristotle's position that the goal of our rational part is to direct us to happiness, Kant objected that if nature had given men and women reason to make choices for that purpose, then she really fashioned the wrong tools for getting the job done. If she intended people to be happy, he argues, she surely would *not* have given them reason or the ability to make choices. All of the natural disasters and diseases in the world cannot compete with human free will when it comes to producing misery. How many people in the world have made a complete mess of their lives by making bad choices? Don't we sometimes wonder, when reading the newspaper or watching the news, why in the world people are allowed to run their own lives? If anything, doesn't it seem like the people who are the happiest are the ones who live closest to their instincts or animal drives and the ones who are the most miserable are those who "think too much"? Isn't it fairly common for those who have a powerful intellect or a philosophical bent to envy those whom they perceive to have a much simpler life, one unburdened by worries and endless deliberations? In this regard, Kant is very much like the author of the Biblical book of Ecclesiastes who declares, "Much wisdom, much grief, the more knowledge, the more sorrow"(1:18). In short, if nature had intended happiness as the end or goal of a human being, she would have left everything to instinct, for it is a far surer guide in practical matters. So, for Kant, nature must have given human beings a reason and a will for another purpose.

2.   "Categorical imperatives" vs. "counsels of prudence"

Kant argued that, contrary to what Aristotle maintained, doing one's moral duty is a different kind of activity than striving for one's own happiness. For Kant, to do one's duty is to follow moral *rules*, and moral rules are always *absolute commands*.[14] For Kant, moral rules are commands that apply to *everyone* in *every situation*. If "treat one's neighbor with respect" is, indeed, a moral rule, then *everyone* must treat his neighbor with respect. And every person must do this *in every situation* that presents itself. Every person must abide by this moral rule even if her neighbor is a vile creature who tortures cats and refuses to brush her teeth regularly and even if she does not feel like treating this neighbor with respect. Moral rules are what Kant calls "categorical imperatives," i.e., they are commands that must be followed by everyone in every situation.

Thus, according to Kant, it follows that Aristotle's "moral philosophy" is not really about morality at all. Aristotle's *Nicomachean Ethics* has few, if any, absolute commands or "categorical imperatives." In Kant's view, Aristotle only puts forward "counsels of prudence" or general rules of thumb that experience has shown commonly result in human happiness. Aristotle, as noted earlier, had maintained that a person *must* acquire virtue if he wanted to achieve happiness. But is it true that virtue will *always* lead to happiness? How does one know that being virtuous will not result in the loss of one's job, leaving the virtuous person destitute and homeless? How does one know that treating one's neighbor with respect will lead to happiness? What if one's neighbor not only tortures cats but also people, and the one who tries to treat his neighbor decently ends up severely beaten or even murdered, as has happened to countless Christian martyrs in the past? And might it not be the case that being vicious, at least on an occasion or two, will actually make a person happier in the long run? Human happiness is just too uncertain to provide grounds for moral rules. No one knows beyond a doubt what will make him happy, let alone what will make the entire human race happy. How many lottery winners eventually end up broke and miserable? And how many cancer patients oddly enough end up describing their illness as one of the best experiences of their lives? One would have to be God to know precisely what steps he would have to take at every turn in his life to achieve happiness. Therefore, Kant argues, moral rules cannot be the same things as rules that make a person happy, as Aristotle had argued. Moral rules confront us with the demand "Everyone must follow me, no questions asked!" But guidelines for becoming happy make a much milder claim, "Sometimes some of you should follow me, but not always, for every person and every situation is a little different." Thus, says Kant, moral rules are a wholly different creature than Aristotle's counsels of prudence.

3.   Happiness cannot be the foundation of morality

But even if reason *were* a reliable guide for achieving happiness, Kant further argues, and even if we *were* sure enough of the path to our own happiness to be able to issue absolute rules for being happy, we would still have to ask ourselves a number of questions: Is happiness *always good in itself*, as it would have to be in Aristotle's system?

Is happiness really the foundation or basis of the moral life? Do we really regard the happiness of other people *regardless of how they have achieved it* as being good? To all of these questions, Kant would respond, "No!" As he observes, "The sight of a being who is not graced by any touch of a pure and good will but who yet enjoys an uninterrupted prosperity can never delight a rational and impartial spectator."[15] Happiness *itself* is not always a good thing; indeed, it seems to make evil people even more evil if they are enjoying themselves while they perform their wicked deeds. For example, following the terrorist attacks on the World Trade Center and the Pentagon, the press released a video of the mastermind of the attacks, Osama bin Laden, laughing with his fellow terrorists about the destruction and death he helped to orchestrate. No one of good will would view this man's happiness as a good thing; indeed, the fact that he has taken pleasure in his deeds almost makes him diabolical.

For Kant, then, happiness cannot be the anchor that secures the laws of morality. For Aristotle, happiness or human fulfillment is the greatest good, and everything else, like courage or friendship, acquires its goodness because it leads to, facilitates, or partially comprises human happiness. Courage, for example, is of value in Aristotle's system in large part because human fulfillment does not seem to be possible without it.[16] Difficulties and even tragedies are an unavoidable part of life, and if one is not equipped with courage, he will be easily *dis*couraged and overrun by misery. In other words, courage is necessary for happiness, but in Aristotle's theory, it does not seem to have value apart from happiness. Courage only shines by reflected light; happiness alone is luminescent. Within Kant's system, however, if a moral agent performs a courageous act, that act is good in itself, whether or not it lead to happiness.

So, if Kant is correct that happiness is not always a good thing, then there must be a different source of goodness in the world. But, if it is not happiness, what could the source of all goodness be?

C.   A GOOD WILL IS THE BASIS OF MORALITY

"There is no possibility of thinking of anything at all in the world, or even out of it which can be regarded as good without qualification, except a *good will*,"[17] writes Kant. Whereas Aristotle believed happiness to be the end of the moral life and that toward which all of our actions should be directed, Kant maintained that having a good will is the only thing of intrinsic worth anywhere in the cosmos...or even beyond it. When Kant states that a good will is "good without qualification," he means that a good will is always good in itself, regardless of what might follow from it. For example, Aristotle believed that courage is a virtue, but according to Kant, courage is not good "without qualification" or not good in itself. For example, a terrorist who undertakes a suicide mission is all the more dangerous if he possesses courage, and thus, courage is only good *if* it exists in a person with a good will. Likewise, a tyrant, such as Adolf Hitler, could only have come to power and maintained his position *if* he had intelligence and charisma, and thus, intelligence and charisma are only good *if* they exist in a person with a good will. Indeed, as the example of bin Laden above illustrates, happiness can even enhance wickedness, and as such, happiness itself is only good if it exists in a person with a good will. But unlike these character traits or states, a good will is good regardless of its surroundings or who possesses it; its goodness does not depend on any *if*, which is what Kant meant by describing it as good "without qualification."

According to Kant, a good will is the source of all goodness, and to use the imagery from above, it alone of everything that exists shines by its own light; everything else, such as courage, intelligence, and happiness, only shines by reflected light, that is, from the light of a good will. In themselves, courage, intelligence, happiness, wealth, etc. are morally neutral. One cannot tell whether these attributes are good or bad until one knows who possesses them; if a man with an evil will possesses them, then they are evil, and if a man with a good will possesses them, then they are good.

D.   WHAT MAKES A WILL GOOD

1.   Obeying the moral law "for the sake of the moral law itself"

For Kant, then, the end of the moral life and the reason that human beings have been given reason and will is to acquire a good will. But as of yet, we do not have any clear or concrete sense of what exactly Kant means by a "good will." What makes a will good? Or to put the question in a more practical way, how do we go about acquiring a good will?

A person has a good will, according to Kant, if he chooses to obey the moral law *for the sake of the moral law itself*. This position needs a great deal of explanation, for among other things, we do not yet know what this moral law is or what it commands us to do. But before we try to tackle Kant's notions about the moral law, we must first make sense of the italicized phrase in the first sentence of this paragraph. What does it mean to obey the moral law *for the sake of the moral law itself*? What Kant means here is similar to what we mean when we tell children, in the popular Christmas song "Santa Claus is Comin' to Town," "to be good for goodness' sake." "To be good for goodness' sake" is not to be good because we expect something from being good—like a pat on the back or a feeling of accomplishment—or because we fear being punished if we do not do good. Rather, "to be good for goodness' sake" is simply to be good because being good is the right thing to do. We should obey the moral law because, as Kant phrases the matter, we have "respect" for it.

In order to clarify further what Kant means, it will be helpful to draw some contrasts between obeying the moral law for the sake of the moral law (or what he calls "doing one's duty") and obeying the moral law for other reasons. Though we have yet to analyze what Kant means by the moral law, let us suppose that it forbids a man from cheating on his spouse. Now, imagine that one husband, Lloyd, finds himself attracted to another woman at his workplace, and she has made it clear to him that any advances would be quite welcome.[18] Lloyd's wife is an unbearable nag, and she has done nearly everything in her power to make life miserable for him. In addition, she is quite suspicious and vindictive; she often reads through his e-mails, checks his wallet for receipts, and has threatened to hire a divorce lawyer if he misbehaves. In this situation, Lloyd finds himself pulled in several different directions: The moral law is commanding him to stay faithful to his wife; his desire for his officemate is pulling him in the opposite direction of the moral law; and his fear of being caught and, perhaps, raked over the coals by a bloodthirsty attorney is pushing him in the same direction as the moral law. For Kant, the important question to ask is not so much *what* Lloyd ends up doing but *why* he ends up doing it. Obviously, if he a) gives in to his passions and commits adultery, he has broken the moral law, and his action is morally blameworthy. But for Kant, if he b) decides to stay faithful to his wife merely because he fears the possible consequences of being caught, then his action has no moral worth. Only if he c) decides to remain faithful because he knows that he must do his duty does his choice acquire any moral worth. In the cases b) and c), Lloyd remained faithful to his wife. But in case b), he did what the law commanded, but he did not do it for the sake of the law itself. In other words, he acted *in conformity with* the law but not *from duty or out of respect for* the law.

Most people would probably agree with the Kantian position that, if Lloyd only refrained from infidelity because he feared the legal and financial repercussions, then he did not do anything worthy of praise. But Kant's position, that a good will is one that obeys the moral law for the sake of the law itself, is actually much more radical than this example would lead one to believe. Indeed, his moral philosophy is more rigorous and exacting than the standards by which most people live. Another example will hopefully show this character of his thought and further elucidate what he means by "doing one's duty."

Suppose this time that a different husband, Clarence, also works with a woman who is interested in him and has made her intentions known. However, Clarence is not married to an unbearable nag; Clarence's wife is a beautiful and compassionate woman who is head-over-heels in love with him. And he, in turn, is passionately in love with her. In this situation, Clarence's emotions are pushing him in the same direction as the moral law. The law demands that he remain faithful to his wife, and his passions make him want to remain faithful, as well. In order for Clarence's choice to be morally praiseworthy, however, he would have to choose to stay faithful to his wife out of respect for the law, not because his emotions compelled him in that direction. Here, then, one can see the stringency of Kant's demands; one must have the purest intentions, wholly free from the influence of any emotion, in order to be truly good.

Indeed, Kant's standards are so high that he states it is impossible to tell without a doubt whether *any* action that *anyone* has ever performed has been a truly good one, i.e., has been chosen purely out of respect for the moral law. Even in the case where a person does what the moral law commands and there does not *appear* to be any emotion or desire pushing or pulling him to act in conformity with the moral law, Kant warns us that one can never be sure that he has not deceived himself and actually acted out of some unrecognized desire. For example, even if Lloyd, who is smitten with his co-worker and repulsed by his wife, had *no fear* of being caught, his choice to stay faithful to his wife might not be morally praiseworthy. Perhaps, Lloyd did not act out of duty but, rather, chose the path he did to inflate his own sense of worth or convince himself that he is truly a splendid and self-sacrificing creature. As Kant observes, "We like to flatter ourselves with the false claim to a more noble motive; but in fact we can never, even by the strictest examination, completely plumb the depths of the secret motives of our actions."[19] Who can ever be sure that he has acted solely out of respect for the moral law, and not for some other reason that is less noble and, therefore, unpleasant to acknowledge?

"But why," one might naturally ask at this point in the study of Kant, "does he hold such impossibly high standards? What is so wrong with doing the right thing for some reason other than out of respect for the moral law? Isn't it good, for example, to tutor children or work in a soup kitchen not out of respect for the moral law but, rather, *because one enjoys doing so*? Indeed, isn't it a mark of virtue, as Aristotle had argued, to take pleasure in virtuous acts?" Though Kant's moral theory might seem counterintuitive at this point, he does have good reasons for holding up such exacting and rigorous standards. In short, his rationale in this regard is quite simple: *A person should only be praised or blamed for something that is within the power of his will.* Just as people should not be praised or blamed for their height, skin color or sex—all of which are outside of the control of the will—they also should not be praised or blamed for the way they feel or do not feel or for what they like or do not like. Why, Kant asks, should a person who is naturally inclined to help others be given moral praise when she really did nothing to deserve praise? If one woman has been endowed with a special gift for empathizing with the suffering of others and another is naturally grumpy and reclusive, why should the first be praised for following her natural incli-nations and not the second? For Kant, neither woman should be given any moral credit for following her inclinations, for neither *chose* her inclinations. However, no matter what a person's inclinations might be, she is still capable of choosing to follow the moral law out of respect for the moral law. In effect, Kant is arguing that the moral playing field is a level one. Every rational being has a free will, and everyone is equally capable of doing her duty for the sake of duty. Any other natural gifts a person may or may not have are not part of the game.

2.   Good consequences do not make an action good

And this notion, that a person should only be praised or blamed for something that is within the power of his will, is also behind Kant's insistence that an action should not be considered good simply because it happens to have good consequences. Just as a person does not choose to feel the way she does or like the things she likes, she also does not have complete control over the consequences of her actions. As such, these consequences should not be factored into an evaluation of a given action. Of course, by making this claim, Kant is not trying to open the door for excuses, such as "I didn't intend to crash my car when I was driving drunk, so I am not responsible for it" or "It's not my fault that my girlfriend got upset because I lied to her." Instead, Kant is arguing that, if a person abides by the moral law, then the consequences that follow from his action do not enhance or detract from its worth. For example, suppose that one man, Rex, were to find a wallet filled with hundreds of dollars, and instead of returning the wallet to the owner—whose driver's license was in the wallet—he kept the money and threw the wallet away. Even if it turned out that the owner of the wallet was later captured by the FBI for drug dealing and confessed that he recently lost money he intended to use for a drug deal, Rex's action would still not be morally praiseworthy, even though it had good consequences. Likewise, if Rex had decided to return the wallet to its owner, his action would still be good even if the owner of the wallet bought drugs with it and sold those drugs to children. For Kant, only the action itself is worthy of praise or blame, for only the action itself is actually willed.

Indeed, following this line of reasoning to its logical conclusion, Kant argues that, even if for some reason a person were prevented from carrying out his intentions—perhaps because he was being imprisoned or was particularly stupid or clumsy—he should still be praised *simply for his decision to act*. Why? Because the decision itself is the only thing that is truly and completely under the control of his will. As Kant states, "[W]hen moral worth is being considered, the concern is not with the actions, which are seen, but rather with the inner principles, which are not seen."[20] And just as a person should not be held accountable for his passions or the consequences of his actions, he should also not be held accountable for paralysis or a natural inability to execute his plans. If, in the midst of trying to save a drowning victim, a person were suddenly incapacitated by a stroke, his will would still be as worthy of praise as it would have been if he had not suffered this misfortune.

3. A good will is one that follows the "categorical imperative"

Kant, then, believed that a will was good if it chose to follow the moral law; whether or not that choice was accompanied by warm and fuzzy feelings or resulted in pleasant consequences is irrelevant. Yet, to this point, we still have not said anything about Kant's understanding of the moral law itself. Just what is this moral law? What exactly are we commanded to do?

The first thing to be stated about the moral law that Kant describes is that it is not a series of specific and concrete commands like one would find in the sacred books of Western religions. When Kant speaks of the moral law, he does not mean particular laws like "Thou shall not steal" or "Thou shall not covet thy neighbor's wife." Kant's understanding of the moral law, or what he calls the "categorical imperative," is much more general or formal than any of the Ten Commandments. Indeed, one could say that Kant's categorical imperative is more like a test that a proposed action must pass than an actual directive to do such-and-such or abstain from such-and-such.

According to Kant, there is really only one categorical imperative—one general test that any proposed action must pass to be deemed good. However, this imperative can be formulated in numerous ways that highlight its different aspects. Leaving aside the controversial and complicated question how these various formulations are related to one another, we will simply look at the two most famous "formulas" of the categorical imperative, the "formula of universal law" and the "formula of the end in itself."

3a. The formula of universal law

Kant's first formulation of the categorical imperative is as follows: "Act only according to that maxim whereby you can at the same time will that it should become a universal law."[21] What *exactly* Kant means by this phrase is controversial and difficult to say, but the general gist of the formula of universal law is easily understood. Leaving his technical terminology aside, we can say that an action is only moral if our reason for performing it could be a reason that everyone could have. Or, to phrase it in the form of a question, the formula of universal law might read: "Is my reason for doing what I am about to do a reason that everyone could have or am I making a special exception for myself?" An ethical decision is one that has a universal or exceptionless character for Kant.

In order to understand this formula more precisely, it will be helpful to examine a couple of examples, for what Kant means here is far from obvious. This first example will be supplied by Kant himself:

> [A] man in need finds himself forced to borrow money. He knows well that he won't repay it, but he sees also that he will not get any loan unless he firmly promises to repay it within a fixed time. He wants to make such a promise, but he still has conscience enough to ask himself whether it is not permissible and is contrary to duty to get out of this difficulty in this way. Suppose, however, that he decides to do so.[22]

Is this action moral? According to Kant, we need to ask whether this man's reason for doing what he is doing is a reason that everyone could have. Is it? This man reasons, "If I am in need of a loan but know that I cannot pay it back, it is permissible for me to make a false promise to secure the loan." Now, what if everyone were to adopt this line of reasoning? Could this be made into a "universal law" that would hold for everyone? As Kant notes, it would be impossible even to conceive of such a law, for the very practice of loaning money would cease if this reasoning were adopted by humanity. In other words, there could never be a law "If anyone is in need of a loan and knows he cannot pay it back, it is permissible to promise to repay that loan," for the practice of loaning itself presupposes that virtually all people will repay their loans in difficult situations. To fool someone into loaning you money that you cannot repay, you must convince him that, despite your circumstances, you will pay him back. But if *everyone* were to think as you do in this matter, then it would be impossible to devise such a plan, for no one would loan money to anybody. Hence, according to Kant, this action would be a violation of the categorical imperative, for it could not even be *conceived of* as a universal law. What would it mean "to promise" something in a world in which no one kept promises?

Thus, for Kant, one way in which a proposed action could fail to pass the "test" of the categorical imperative is if it could not be conceived of as a universal law. But Kant also maintains that the formula of universal law has a broader application. Sometimes a proposed action is immoral, even though it can be conceived of as a universal law. Again, Kant offers an example:

> [A] man finds things going well for himself but sees others (whom he could help) struggling with great hardships; and he thinks; what does it matter to me? Let everybody be as happy as Heaven wills or as he can make himself; I shall take nothing from him nor even envy him; but I have no desire to contribute anything to his well-being or to his assistance when in need. If such a way of thinking were to become a universal law of nature, the human race admittedly could very well subsist ...[23]

As Kant acknowledges in the last sentence, a world in which no one helped another human being in need would certainly be conceivable. Unlike a world of promise-breakers, which is not possible, a world of stingy self-centered people is certainly possible. But Kant claims that a man who reasoned in this way would violate the formula of universal law in another way: He could not will that his reasoning be adopted by everyone, for by doing so, he would also be willing a world he would not be willing to inhabit. As Kant puts it, his will "would contradict itself," for by willing a world in which no one took care of anyone else, this man also would be willing a world in which no one would take care of *him* if he were to fall on hard times. And no one would will such a thing. Likewise, a world of people who throw their trash out of their car windows is certainly conceivable, but nonetheless, a woman who chooses to litter would not also choose to live in a world in which every person throws his trash wherever he pleases (especially in her front yard). Thus, for Kant, the formula of universal law demands not only that we should be able to *conceive of* our way of reasoning as a universal law but also that we should be able to *will* that our way of reasoning should become a universal law.

Though initially Kant's formula of universal law might sound somewhat foreign, in his defense we need to acknowledge that at least some of our moral language certainly has this exceptionless character. When the nagging schoolmistress chides a gum-chewing student by asking, "Did you bring a piece of gum for everyone?" or when she asks a student who has his feet up on a desk, "Would you put your feet up on a desk in your own home?", she is drawing attention to the fact that the guilty student is making an exception for himself. Likewise, Jesus himself taught his disciples to follow the Golden Rule, "Do unto others as you would have them do unto you," a principle that is strikingly similar to Kant's formula of universal law. More generally, whenever one person rebukes another by saying "How would you like it if someone did that to you?", he is highlighting this universal character; a bad man believes he should be able to treat others one way yet be treated by them in another. Furthermore, is it not the case that many of our moral failings occur when we try to exempt ourselves from a general rule? "I know that adultery is immoral, but this case is different—you don't understand what I have to put up with in my marriage," one might rationalize to herself or others. "I have never cheated on an exam before, and so if I cheat just this once, it will not be a big deal," one might say to himself as panic begins to set in during a tough midterm.

3b.   The formula of the end in itself

Kant's second formula is not nearly as subtle or difficult to understand as his first, and moreover, it is much closer to our commonsense understanding of right and wrong. The formula of the end in itself is the following: "Act in such a way that you treat humanity, whether in your own person or in the person of another, always at the same time as an end and never simply as a means."[24] If I treat someone as an "end," I treat her as *intrinsically valuable*—valuable in herself, not for some purpose she might serve. On the other hand, if I treat her "simply as a means," I treat her like an instrument or tool that only has value insofar as it can further my purposes. The reason people should be treated with respect and dignity is because they are creatures with reason and a will. People stand above or outside of the natural world of inanimate things, plants, and animals, and as such, they deserve to be treated in a way that reflects their unique status. As Kant would put the matter, human beings are "self-legislating" creatures; they govern themselves by their own reason. The behavior of all other things in the universe is wholly governed by the laws of nature, and as such, these things can be used to meet our needs. So, Kant's formula of the end in itself is basically a command to treat every human being like a human being, viz., like a being with reason and a will.

As a test case for the formula of the end in itself, we can use the example above of the man who secured a loan with no intention of paying it back. According to Kant, this man was guilty of treating his lender "simply as a means." To use someone simply as a means is to treat him as an object or a thing that does not have a will. Or, to put the matter in the words of one Kant scholar, "To use someone as a *mere means* is to involve them in a scheme of action to *which they could not in principle consent*."[25] In this scenario, the lender was not aware of this man's plans not to repay the loan, and so, when he agreed to give him the money, he was not really capable of making an informed choice. In other words, he was not able to consent to what was really transpiring at that moment. Had he known of the lendee's intentions, he would never have given him the money.

And for this same reason, we can see why, for example, there is nothing wrong with "using" a mechanic or plumber but why there is something wrong with "using" a person for sexual pleasure alone or to get back at an ex-boyfriend or girlfriend. Though, in a sense, a person who hires a mechanic is using him—i.e., treating him like a living instrument—the mechanic has consented to be used in exchange for a fee. The terms of the contract are clear to both parties, and both members have entered into the contract freely. If, however, a young man pretends to have amorous feelings for a young woman simply because he wants to gratify himself sexually or irritate his ex-girlfriend (who, for example, might be friends with this woman), then he is using her simply as a means. He has hidden his true intentions, and so, the woman is not able to consent to what he is *really* proposing. Hopefully, she will not fall for this ruse, but if she does, it is clear that she has not consented to his true intentions; no healthy person wishes to be reduced to an object for someone else's purposes.

Unlike the formula of universal law, which is somewhat foreign to our commonsense notions of right and wrong, the formula of the end in itself should strike the reader as a true reflection of much of our moral language. No talk show, romantic comedy, Harlequin romance, or high school dance would be complete without someone accusing her partner of using her for whatever purpose. Likewise, many—if not most—Americans subscribe to the notion that any activity between adults is morally permissible as long as both adults are consenting. In the same spirit, at least one of the reasons Americans champion democracy so fervently is because, in this type of government, the people who are ruled have, to a certain extent, consented to be ruled by their leaders. Even if a king were benevolent and furnished his people with protection, adequate material goods, health care, a solid infrastructure, etc., we would still be wary of such a government because of our deep-seated Kantian convictions.

E. KANTIAN ETHICS AND CHRISTIANITY

As should be clear from the preceding paragraph, Kant's ethical theory has certainly been influential in shaping the way we Americans understand morality. But has this influence been a positive one? More specifically, to what extent should someone who is a believer in Christianity embrace this moral philosophy? These are questions that the reader must really assess for herself, but before concluding this chapter, some brief analysis of Kant's ethical theory will be given to stimulate the reader to thoughts of her own. (What a Kantian way of proceeding!)

As noted above, Kant's categorical imperative, specifically in its formula of universal law, is strikingly similar to Jesus' Golden Rule, and in this respect, it is certainly compatible with Christian teachings. More generally, Kant's notion that an immoral person is one who makes an exception for himself—one who wishes to treat others in one way while being treated in another—is certainly a Biblical one. In his "Parable of the Unforgiving Servant," for example, Jesus uses a line of reasoning of which Kant would have approved. In this parable, a servant who has amassed a huge debt is forgiven this debt by his master, but then, this servant refused to forgive a debt that is owed to him by another servant. In response to this refusal, Jesus has the master offer the following rebuke: "You wicked servant! I forgave you your entire debt because you begged me to. Should you not have had pity on your fellow servant, as I had pity on you?" (Mt. 18:32-33). Except for, perhaps, hypocrites—who say one thing and do another—Jesus seems to reserve his fiercest rebukes for those with double standards.

Moreover, Kant's emphasis upon the privileged position of human beings within the natural world is also compatible with a Christian outlook. As described above, Kant argued that, of all of the creatures that inhabit the earth, human beings alone possess reason and a will, and as such, they are to be treated accordingly, viz., with dignity and respect. Though, as a philosopher, Kant would not be willing to speak of humans as "made in the image and likeness of God," as Christians do, his emphasis upon their unique place in nature is certainly compatible with the Biblical understanding of man. In Genesis, God gives human beings, who are created in His image, "dominion over the fish of the sea, the birds of the air, and the cattle, and over all the wild animals and all the creatures that crawl on the ground" (Gen. 1:26). Similarly, Kant wrote, "Animals are not self-conscious and are there merely as a means to an end. That end is man."[26]

However, there are certain tendencies in Kant's thought that should put a Christian on guard. As noted above, many Americans believe that any act is morally permissible as long as consenting adults commit it. Though Kant himself would not endorse this overly simplistic view, there is no question that he is one of the intellectual fathers of this notion. And this notion is certainly not a Christian one. Prostitution involves two consenting adults but is nonetheless an immoral perversion of human love. More generally, a person could conceivably consent to become a slave, to sell some of her body parts, or to give up all her possessions to a fraudulent televangelist, but none of these actions would be moral, despite the fact they were consensual. Often, the absence of consent can, indeed, render an action immoral, but the mere presence of consent is not always enough to render an action moral.

And perhaps most importantly, there is a tendency in Kant's thought that is opposed to the very heart of the Christian message. For Kant, reason alone is the source of all sound moral principles, and as creatures that have reason, human beings would seem to be equipped with everything they need to live a moral life. In fact, Kant argues that any principle of morality that originates outside the will or outside reason is "spurious" or counterfeit. The natural outgrowth of such ideas is the emergence of a radical distrust of authority of any kind, including the authority of God. Though, as we will see in later chapters, Catholics certainly do believe that reason can be helpful in discerning God's will, the notion that reason is *the sole source* of our moral principles is incompatible with a Christian conception of life. Christians believe that the wisdom revealed in the Sacred Scriptures is necessary for good and holy living and that the wisdom in these books in some sense *goes beyond human reason*. Indeed, one could say that the overarching principle of the Christian life is submission to the will of God, while the overarching principle of the Kantian life is submission to the dictates of reason. Yes, on many occasions, the Christian and the Kantian will end up carrying out the very same actions. But Kant's system does not prepare a person to endure virtuously the suffering that tragedy—e.g., terminal cancer—visits unexpectedly on so many people. Often, the only "reason" for submitting nobly to the mysterious will of God in such instances is *faith* in the goodness of God and *faith* in Jesus and His teachings.

Neither does Kant's system supply the same inspiration for the practice of heroic virtue that a Christian finds in a loving contemplation of Jesus' heroic sacrifice for the human race. Who, if anyone, has been truly moved by a "sheer respect" for the abstract moral law? Kant's categorical imperative may challenge the human conscience, but it hardly moves the human heart! Throughout the ages, however, the model of moral perfection provided by Jesus has inspired countless Christians to devote their lives to building the Kingdom of God here on earth.

SECTION HIGHLIGHTS

Immanuel Kant's moral theory emphasizes the rightness or wrongness of acts or intentions themselves, regardless of their consequences.

Kant set forth his moral theory during the Enlightenment, a time of great scientific accomplishment as well as growing distrust of religious authority. Though Kant was raised a Christian and had sympathies for Christianity, his moral theory is based on reason alone, not divine revelation.

Kant rejected Aristotle's notion that a life lived in accord with reason was the happiest; often it is the people who are guided by instinct, not reason, who are happiest.

Whereas Aristotle's guidelines for acquiring virtue only hold for the most part, Kant argued that a true moral law is one that has no exceptions: It must be followed by everyone in every situation.

Unlike Aristotle, Kant held that happiness cannot be the true anchor of morality; happiness is not good in itself, and the way to happiness cannot be known with any degree of certainty.

Kant believed that a good will is the only thing in the whole world "that can be regarded as good without qualification." Courage, intelligence, wealth, health, and every other potentially good thing are only good if possessed by a person of good will.

In order for an act to be good, according to Kant, it must be done out of respect for the moral law. The mere fact that an act happens to have good consequences does not mean that it is moral. In short, for Kant, a person should only be praised or blamed for things that are under his control or within the scope of his will. And things like consequences or a person's feelings are not within that scope.

For Kant, a good will is one that follows the "categorical imperative," and this imperative can be formulated in a number of ways, most importantly (for our purposes) as "the formula of universal law" and "the formula of the end in itself." The formula of universal law states that an action is only moral if a person's reason for performing it could be a reason everyone could have. The formula of the end in itself states that one must always treat human beings as intrinsically valuable, never simply as means.

Kant's ethical theory is often strikingly similar to Christian teachings; e.g., his formula of universal law is virtually identical to Jesus' Golden Rule. However, Kantian eth-

*ics is incompatible with Christianity's insistence that divine revelation is an au-
thoritative source of moral principles, and Kantian ethics lacks the inspirational
power found in the virtuous life and death of Jesus.*

QUESTIONS

To show that you understand what has been presented about Kant's ethical theory,
answer the following questions in paragraph form. Write your answers on a separate
sheet of paper.

1. Explain the difference between what Kant calls a "categorical imperative" and a
    "counsel of prudence."

2. Do you believe that the good life is also necessarily the happy life, as Aristotle
    maintained, or do you side with Kant, that the two are not necessarily joined
    together? Give reasons for your answer.

3. Explain what Kant means when he states that a good will is the only thing that
    can be regarded as "good without qualification"? Why does he maintain this
    position?

4. In an American court, if one man—drunk driver A—were found guilty of fall-
    ing asleep at the wheel and killing a pedestrian on the sidewalk, he could be
    charged with involuntary manslaughter and sentenced to many years in prison.
    If, though, another man—drunk driver B—were found guilty of falling asleep at
    the wheel on the very same road at the very same time of day but he did not hit
    anyone, he could merely be charged with reckless driving, would not spend any
    time in jail, and might not even lose his license. Would Kant agree with this
    ruling? Explain. Do you agree with this ruling? Explain.

5. Apply the "formula of the universal law" that you read about in this section to
    the following scenario:

    Having landed a job in an area of the country without decent public transporta-
    tion, Sheila decides to buy a new car. She is immediately attracted to sport
    utility vehicles (SUVs) because of their spacious interior and safety features.
    They are so sporty, and she loves the experience of driving so high off the ground.
    They could fit an army of her friends, and if she had an accident with another
    car, she would fare better than she would have in a smaller car. On the other
    hand, she knows that SUVs get horrible gas mileage, emit more pollution and
    environmentally damaging CO_2 than smaller cars, block the visibility of other
    drivers, and are more likely to hurt *other* people in the case of a wreck. After
    weighing the pros and cons, she decides to buy an SUV.

6. Given what you have learned about the ethical theories of Aristotle and Kant,

as well as what you know about Christianity, which of these ways of thinking about right and wrong do you find is most in keeping with your own way of thinking? Are you an Aristotelian, a Kantian, or a Christian? Give reasons for your answer.

PART THREE:
UTILITARIANISM

A few decades after Immanuel Kant set forth his ethical theory, a radically different approach to morality surfaced in the West, an approach that continues to exert considerable influence on the way we understand right and wrong. In the early 19th century, an English philosopher named Jeremy Bentham (1748-1832) put forward a moral philosophy called "utilitarianism," and later that century, another English philosopher named John Stuart Mill (1806-1873) presented a more polished and palatable version of this same philosophy. Though utilitarian ways of thinking can be traced back to Epicurus (341-270 BC) and even Plato, it was Bentham and Mill who first presented this philosophy in a precise and systematic form. Since then, utilitarianism has been refashioned and defended in countless ways, and today, many philosophers and non-academics continue to find it appealing.

Like Kant's philosophy, utilitarianism is based solely on human reasoning and observation; it does not rely on revelation for its principles. However, unlike Kant's philosophy, which is often difficult to understand and counterintuitive, utilitarianism is easy to grasp, and it resonates much more deeply with our commonsense notions of right and wrong.

Utilitarianism is a "consequentialist" moral philosophy. As opposed to ethical theories like Kant's which argue that an action (or intention) is itself good or bad, consequentialist theories argue that the morality of an action is a function of what follows from it. Roughly speaking, an action is good if it has good consequences, and an action is bad if it has bad consequences. (Kant, it will be remembered, argued that consequences are not relevant when one is determining whether a given action is good or bad.)

In this section, John Stuart Mill's version of utilitarianism will be discussed, and comparisons will be drawn between utilitarianism in general, on the one hand, and Kantian ethics as well as Christianity, on the other.

A.   THE BASIC TENETS OF JOHN STUART MILL'S UTILITARIANISM

Though the word "utilitarianism" certainly looks intimidating, it actually names an ethical theory that is easy to understand. In particular, John Stuart Mill's version of this theory can really be boiled down to three basic notions, none of which are as subtle or convoluted as notions one regularly encounters in Kant's thought.

1.   The "principle of utility"

Utilitarianism gets its name from what Mill and Bentham call the "principle of utility" or the "greatest happiness principle." Quite simply, this is the notion that, when a person has a variety of options in a given moral situation, the right choice is the one that results in the greatest amount of happiness for the greatest number of people.

Setting aside for the moment what exactly Mill means by "happiness," we can see that this principle is commonly used as a basis for moral decisions, especially ones that affect a large number of people. Those who form public policy frequently use this type of reasoning, and more dramatically, it has often been the rationale for decisions in war. During the beginning of World War II, for example, the British succeeded in breaking the code the Germans used to communicate among themselves. Through a secret intelligence operation code-named "Ultra," the English were able to interpret and decipher radioed German messages and gain crucial information. Of course, they did not wish to let the Germans know of their advantage. This put them in a serious moral dilemma in November of 1940, when they learned that the Germans planned a heavy air raid on the densely populated city of Coventry. If they had warned the citizens there of what was coming and had helped to save their lives, the Germans would have figured out that they had broken the code, and they would have been unable to save other lives in the future and retain their intelligence advantage over the Germans. Winston Churchill decided not to warn the citizens of Coventry to evacuate. In the devastation of that raid, four hundred people died, and thousands of others were injured and rendered homeless. In this instance, Churchill's rationale was clearly utilitarian: Though the British would initially suffer some causalities, he calculated that, in the long run, more lives and the well-being of more people would be preserved if the British did not immediately alert the public.

2.   Hedonism

If, then, we are to be good utilitarians, we must try to provide the greatest possible number of people with the greatest possible amount of happiness. But what exactly did Mill mean by "happiness"? "By happiness is intended pleasure and the absence of pain," Mill writes, "by unhappiness, pain and the privation of pleasure."[27] Whereas Aristotle defined happiness more specifically as a human type of flourishing connected with virtuous activity and the life of reason, Mill defines happiness very broadly, in such a way that animals and even insects could be understood as enjoying "happiness." For Mill, happiness is pleasure and the absence of pain, and surely every sentient creature is capable of experiencing either of these.

But Mill wanted to maintain an even stronger thesis than the mere notion that happiness is pleasure or the absence of pain. Mill argued that, indeed, pleasure and the absence of pain is the only thing that is desirable or good. "The utilitarian doctrine is that happiness is desirable, and the *only* thing desirable, as an end; all other things being only desirable as means to an end." Thus, for Mill, only pleasure itself or the absence of pain is to be considered good in itself, and everything else that is called good is only good insofar as it leads to pleasure. This doctrine is called "hedonism," the notion that pleasure is the only good that exists.

Now, in order to do justice to Mill's position, it is necessary to distinguish this philosophical sense of "hedonism" from the sense that this word has in everyday language. If, outside of philosophy, someone calls another person a "hedonist," she means this person is a "pleasure-seeker," one who has a ravenous desire for bodily or sensual pleasures—such as food and sex. To call someone a hedonist in everyday language is not a compliment; a hedonist is a depraved creature who neglects the higher goods in life and merely seeks the instant gratification of his basest desires.

Mill, on the other hand, emphasized that there are various types of pleasures, and some types of pleasures are superior to others. As he states, "It is quite compatible with the principle of utility to recognize the fact that some kinds of pleasure are more desirable and more valuable than others."[28] Pleasures can differ in their duration, their intensity, and also in their kind. For example, the pleasure of reading a novel is of a different kind than the pleasure of eating a steak, and unless one is a world-class glutton, the pleasure of eating cannot be sustained for as long a period of time as the pleasure of reading. According to Mill, those people who have had experience of the whole range of pleasures that life has to offer ultimately end up preferring the higher pleasures—such as helping others in need, pursuing the truth, or creating a work of art. Those who have tasted these higher pleasures will never set them aside to pursue the lower ones, even if their attainment is more difficult. "It is better to be a human being dissatisfied than a pig satisfied; better to be Socrates dissatisfied than a fool satisfied," Mill argues. "And if the fool, or the pig, are of a different opinion, it is because they only know their side of the question."[29]

3.   The viewpoint of "a disinterested and benevolent spectator"

The utilitarian, then, not only seeks to produce the greatest *amount* of pleasure for the greatest number of people but also the highest *kinds* of pleasures for the greatest number of people. To say the least, this is a tall order to fill. Ordinarily, people are only concerned with their own well-being, but utilitarianism demands that we strive for the greatest good for the greatest number of people possible. If taken seriously, then, utilitarianism is an extremely demanding philosophy, one that often requires the subordination of one's own happiness to the good of the whole. As Spock of the popular television series *Star Trek* put the matter, "The good of the many outweighs the good of the few." And often, "the few" may include you!

Mills emphasizes this selfless character of this philosophy when he states that a true utilitarian should "be as strictly impartial as a disinterested and benevolent spectator."[30] What Mill means here is that, when evaluating the various choices that one has in a given situation, the moral agent should give equal consideration to each person affected by this decision, *including himself*. We should not give special consideration to ourselves or our loved ones; we should make the decision that a "benevolent spectator"—someone of good will who is not connected to the situation—would make. The happiness of each person is to be given the same weight, and thus, a true utilitarian will often be called upon to make sacrifices—even great ones, such as giving up his own life—for the good of the whole.

According to Mill, this principle of morality is the same one taught by Jesus of Nazareth, and so, Christians should feel comfortable embracing it. "'To do as you would be done by,' and 'to love your neighbor as yourself,'" Mill argues, "constitute the ideal perfection of utilitarian morality."[31] If one truly loved everyone else to the same extent that he loved himself, then he would have to seek the happiness of everyone equally, and he would not give special preference, for example, to himself or a family member. Utilitarianism, then, Mill argues, is a truly noble and beautiful moral philosophy, one that has been embraced by great moral teachers like Jesus and one that demands the highest standards of conduct from its adherents.

B.   UTILITARIANISM AFTER MILL

Mill's ethical system is only one form that utilitarianism has taken throughout the history of philosophy. For example, other utilitarian philosophers have defined happiness in a different way than Mill did, and others still have rejected his hedonism. Another highly influential English philosopher named G.E. Moore, for example, argued that the contemplation of natural beauty or artistic creations, the possession of knowledge or friends, and many other qualities or states of affairs are good as well, regardless of whether or not they bring pleasure.

Yet, however much utilitarian philosophers may disagree about the finer points of their systems, they all have a common way of viewing ethical decision-making. In their *Ethics: Theory and Practice*, Cynthia Rostankowski and Manuel Vasquez have described this common essence in the following way:

> All utilitarian theories claim that the morality of an action depends on the amount of goodness the action produces, although utilitarians hold considerably different views concerning what goodness consists of. Some, like John Stuart Mill, hold that pleasure or happiness (or satisfaction of some other pleasant state of consciousness) is the only basic good; others hold that there are many things besides pleasant states of mind that are intrinsically good, such as friendship, knowledge, love, courage, beauty, and so on. ... Regardless of their views on what constitutes goodness, utilitarians all agree that only *intrinsic or ultimate* goods should be taken into account when evaluating the morality of an action. Intrinsic goods are things we value for themselves, and not merely because of what they will give us.
>
> Utilitarians also agree that in order to determine the morality of an act, one must measure the amount of good the act will produce, and subtract from this the amount of evil it will produce. The net result is the 'utility' of an act.[32]

All utilitarian philosophies, then, see ethical decision-making as a process similar to mathematics. First, they determine what things are to be considered intrinsic goods, i.e., things that are good in themselves and not merely because they lead to other goods. John Stuart Mill, as we noted above, considered only pleasure and the absence of pain as intrinsically good things, but other philosophers, like G.E. Moore, maintained that such things as the possession of knowledge or the contemplation of beauty are also good in themselves. Second, whatever things are chosen as good in themselves are then given a value or ranked on a scale; a human life may be placed higher on a scale of intrinsic goods than the aesthetic appeal of a landscape, which in turn might rank higher than the life of a cow. Third, the utilitarian philosopher tries to determine the choices he has and the consequences that follow from each. In the example above, for instance, the British government concluded it had two options: to notify the public of the impending German bombing or not to notify them. The first option, they reasoned, would have short-term benefits, but ultimately, this loss of an edge in intelligence would lengthen the war, causing more deaths and greater destruction. The second option would have short-term losses, but ultimately, the edge in intelligence would shorten the war and help the Allies end the Nazis' reign of terror. In the end, the good utilitarian—whether he is a hedonist like Mill or not—will choose the option that produces the greatest amount of intrinsic good.

C.   UTILTARIANISM AND KANT

Given this basic introduction to this ethical theory, one should immediately recognize that a conflict is bound to arise between the way utilitarians and Kant see morality. Whereas Kant did not believe that the consequences of an action had any moral relevance whatsoever, utilitarians believe that the consequences of an action are the only morally relevant factor in any decision. Needless to say, this is not a minor dispute, and thus a true Kantian would undoubtedly behave in a very different fashion from a true utilitarian. For example, Kant's formula of the end in itself commands that no one may ever be treated simply as a means, regardless of the good consequences that doing so might produce. However, for a follower of someone like Mill, there would certainly be situations in which the good of the whole would require the treatment of someone as a mere means.

To use a gruesome example, suppose three men find themselves trapped on a desert island after their ship has been struck by lightning. Because of the sudden nature of the accident, no distress signal was sent. Luckily, the men were able to float to shore on parts of the broken ship. One of these men badly broke his leg in the accident and is considerably weaker than the other two. Of those who were not injured, one is a Kantian and the other a utilitarian. With no food on the island, the three quickly realize they are going to starve to death if they are not rescued fairly soon. After several days pass without any signs of a rescue attempt, the utilitarian would have to propose that he and his Kantian mate kill the third man and eat him. If all three simply continue to wait for help, they will all die in a very short time. However, if the third man is killed and eaten, the remaining two will at least buy a few more days, time in which a rescue might occur. Because of his feeble and precarious state, the third man is the most logical candidate to be killed and eaten; he could be killed most easily, and with a broken leg, he is the least likely to survive anyway. Though the utilitarian might appear to be acting selfishly in this regard, a benevolent spectator would certainly finger the third man as the best candidate, as well. Further, such a decision would minimize the pain for the greatest number of people and open up the possibility for a rescue, as well.

The Kantian, however, would most probably advocate that he and his utilitarian mate simply wait for help and, if no help arrived, starve to death rather than defile themselves in such a manner. If killing someone and eating him is not an example of using a person simply as a means, then nothing is. Who would consent to being killed and eaten? Furthermore, it is fairly clear that no one would be willing to make the utilitarian's reasoning in this matter into a universal law. Though a person might be willing to take the life of another person in a dire situation, he would not be willing to have his own life taken if the shoe were on the other foot. Would the utilitarian be willing to be killed and eaten if *he* were the injured third islander? And as for the possibility of being rescued, the Kantian would probably argue that this possibility is ultimately outside of the scope of our will. Whether or not they will be rescued is ultimately outside of their control. Making the moral decision is not a crapshoot; it is not a matter of calculating the probabilities of various possible outcomes. It is our actions or intentions themselves that are right or wrong, regardless of what happens to result from them.

D. UTILITARIANISM AND CHRISTIANITY

And Kantians are not the only ones who would fervently disagree with the utilitarian approach to morality. Despite Mill's belief that the Golden Rule of Jesus of Nazareth is "the ideal perfection of utilitarian morality," Christianity is fundamentally incompatible with this type of moral approach. This is not to say that there are not aspects of this philosophy that resemble Christian teachings. Yet, in the final analysis, this way of approaching decision-making is foreign—and in many ways, hostile—to the Christian approach.

As opposed to Kant—and in keeping with utilitarian thought—the Catholic Church, for example, has always emphasized that the consequences of an action must be taken into account when one is determining the morality of an act. As we will see in Part Four of Chapter Four above, the Church states the consequences are part of the "circumstances" of an act, i.e., part of the secondary elements of an act that can increase or diminish its goodness. However, according to the Church, no act that is evil in itself can be made good by having good consequences. Even if, by some bizarre sequence of events, it would be possible to rid the world of cancer simply by murdering one innocent person, the Church would never sanction such an act. Following St. Paul (Rom. 3:8), the Church teaches that one can never do evil so that good may come of it.

Indeed, for a true utilitarian, there is no such thing as an act that is evil in itself; given the right circumstances, any act would be permissible if it satisfied the principle of utility. Thus, one finds a utilitarian philosopher such as Peter Singer arguing that there is nothing inherently wrong with abortion, infanticide, or voluntary euthanasia. If a child is born with severe birth defects and her parents do not want her, why shouldn't the state take her life? Wouldn't such an act relieve the child of a painful existence and save others the burden of caring for her? And similar reasoning has been given to justify abortion and voluntary euthanasia. However, for Christians in general and Catholics in particular, there are certain categories of actions that are always forbidden, no matter what consequences are alleged to follow from them. For example, the *Catechism of the Catholic Church* lists blasphemy, perjury, murder, adultery, fornication, and abortion as acts that are wrong regardless of the consequences that may follow from them.[33]

And most importantly, the Christian teaching that *each and every* human being is sacred and possesses dignity is ultimately irreconcilable with the utilitarian way of making decisions. On the surface, Mill's insistence that a moral agent should take the perspective of a "disinterested and benevolent spectator," i.e., that he should give each person involved in a moral situation equal consideration, bears some resemblance to Christian teaching. If, in the process of doing my utilitarian calculations, I give no preference to any given individual—including myself—then I am, in a certain sense, treating my neighbor as I am treating myself, as the Golden Rule teaches. Yet, giving everyone equal consideration when calculating the greatest good for the greatest number of people is quite different from loving one's neighbor as oneself. In certain situations, for example, a utilitarian would have to conclude that the lives of certain people are expendable for the good of the whole, whereas no true Christian could ever view her neighbor's life as expendable precisely because she could never view *her own* life as expendable. We are called by Christ to treat others as we would like to be treated. And because each person is made in the image and likeness of God, every person possesses dignity, and no person's life can be dispensed with even if, somehow, doing so would produce the greatest good for the greatest number of people.

That utilitarians dismiss the Christian notion that each and every human life is sacred and possesses dignity can be seen quite clearly in their writings. For example, one utilitarian philosopher, John Harris, has actually proposed that a "survival lottery" should be instituted. Each year, many people die waiting for organ transplants, but Harris has conceived of a way to remedy this problem. Every person in the country would be given a number, like a lottery number, and then:

> [w]henever doctors have two or more dying patients who could be saved by transplants, and no suitable organs have come to hand through "natural" deaths, they can ask a central computer to supply a suitable donor. The computer will then pick the number of a suitable donor at random and he will be killed so that the lives of two or more others may be saved ... With the refinement of transplant procedures such a scheme could offer the chance of saving large numbers of lives that are now lost. Indeed, even taking into account the loss of lives of donors, the numbers of untimely deaths each year might be dramatically reduced, so much so that everyone's chance of living to a ripe old age might be increased.[34]

Because a single person could provide healthy organs to many other people—a heart to one, a kidney to another, another kidney to a third, a liver to a fourth, etc.— this system could ultimately increase the life span of the average human being, Harris argues. (Later in the article, he offers various ways in which the terror involved in the lottery process could be removed: euphemisms for murder, such as "giving life," could be employed, perhaps statues could be erected as memorials to those healthy people who gave their lives for others, etc.)

Needless to say, any orthodox Christian thinker would reject this indecent proposal. Human beings are made in the image and likeness of God, and for this reason, this practice would be forbidden because it treats human beings like living refrigerators, not beings endowed with reason and freedom. This is not to state that a human being should not be permitted to donate his organs after his death or even to donate a kidney while he is alive. But such voluntary actions are quite distinct from the murder of an innocent human being. The fact that a computer randomly selects "a suitable donor" does nothing to change the fact that an innocent person has been killed; a randomly selected victim is still a victim. And just as my own healthy self-love would cause me to fight tooth-and-nail if a government official came to take my organs, my love of my neighbor as myself would cause me to fight tooth-and-nail if a government official came to take his organs.

Yet, on a more positive note, utilitarianism should be praised for its insistence that the welfare of the human race as a whole—not just one's family, town, state, or nation—should be the concern of every human being. Just as Christians have always emphasized that love of one's neighbor extends beyond the boundaries of one's family or friends, utilitarianism also emphasizes a global perspective. So, to his credit, utilitarian philosopher Peter Singer has written at length about the disparity in wealth that exists between many Western countries and those in the Third World, and he reportedly gives half of his income to various charities. Like Saint Thomas Aquinas, who argued that "whatever certain people have in superabundance ought to be set aside ... to help the poor,"[35] Singer has argued that we affluent Westerners have a moral duty to give up our luxuries and give our extra income to the poor so that they can meet their basic needs. At least in this respect, then, utilitarians like Singer and Christians can agree; both would endorse the slogan "Live simply so that others may simply live."

Unfortunately, however, this concern of utilitarians such as Singer for the welfare of others does not extend to innocent individuals like unborn children and "useless" humans such as the retarded, the handicapped, or the elderly. In many cases, Singer and his associates would be willing to sacrifice these folks on the altar of utilitarian eugenics. It is this overall disregard of the rights and the worth of society's "useless" people that marks the major divide between utilitarian and Christian moralists.

SECTION HIGHLIGHTS

Utilitarianism is a consequentialist moral philosophy, i.e., one that judges actions in terms of the goodness or badness of their results.

Like Aristotle and Kant, utilitarian John Stuart Mill based his moral theory on reasoning and observation alone, not divine revelation.

The "principle of utility" is the principle that the right action will be the one that produces the greatest amount of happiness for the greatest number of people.

Mill was a "hedonist"; he believed pleasure or the absence of pain is the only thing that is good in itself. However, Mill believed that some pleasures, such as those arising from intellectual pursuits, were higher than others, such as bodily ones.

According to Mill, the true utilitarian approaches a decision from the perspective of a disinterested and benevolent spectator, i.e., someone of good will who is not connected to the decision and thus gives each party involved equal consideration.

Utilitarianism has taken many forms throughout the last two centuries, but all forms of utilitarianism involve a process similar to mathematics—a process in which the utility of an act is calculated by subtracting its anticipated evil from the good that it will supposedly produce.

The Catholic Church agrees with the utilitarians that the consequences of an action must be factored into an ethical decision and also that a truly moral person must make the welfare of society as a whole part of his concern. However, like Kant, the Church emphasizes the inherent worth and dignity of every human being, and thus, they reject the utilitarian notion that the lives of some people may be taken for the good of the whole.

QUESTIONS

To show that you understand what has been presented about utilitarianism, answer the following questions in paragraph form. Write your answers on a separate sheet of paper.

1.   What is the "principle of utility"? Do you think this principle should be followed? Explain your answer.

2.   John Stuart Mill argued that the utilitarian should give equal consideration to every person affected by a given decision. Is this a good principle to follow, or should people give special consideration to themselves, their children, or their friends? Explain your answer.

3. In an episode from the popular television series M*A*S*H, the following scenario was presented:

    Surgeons Hawkeye Pierce and BJ Honeycutt overhear an officer, who is visiting the 4077th, bragging about his military accomplishments and prowess. In addition, they hear that he plans to ignore the recent commands of his superiors and advance upon enemy troops in the area. The officer reveals that he plans to draw fire from the enemy and then use this fire as an excuse to engage in battle. If questioned about the ensuing battle, he will merely claim that his troops were acting in self-defense. Furthermore, Hawkeye and BJ learn that this officer has quite a bad track record when it comes to casualties; he seems to be quite cavalier when it comes to putting his troops in harm's way. In order to stop this reckless officer, Hawkeye hatches a plan: He will make the officer think he has appendicitis. By performing unnecessary surgery on the officer, Hawkeye will be able to prevent him from carrying out his plans, and the officer will merely be losing one unnecessary organ. As a result, dozens of lives will be saved. BJ, however, rejects Hawkeye's plan. He argues that such an action would violate the Hippocratic Oath that all doctors take. The oath states that, first and foremost, one must never do harm to any patient, and unnecessary surgery is certainly some form of harm. BJ argues that, no matter what good consequences might follow from this surgery, an oath of this sort cannot be broken.

    How would Mill and Kant evaluate the plans or arguments given by Hawkeye and BJ? With whom would you side in this debate? Explain your answer.

4. Explain the difference between the Golden Rule and the utilitarian principle that each person should be given equal consideration in an ethical decision. Use an example to illustrate the difference.

5. Explain what you find appealing or unappealing about this school of thought. Do you agree with the objections that Christian moral philosophers bring against utilitarianism? Why or why not?

6. Your instructor may decide to show the last 30 minutes of *Extreme Measures*, a dramatic film about the ethics of conducting medical experiments on unwilling human beings in order to cure paralysis. If your instructor does show the end of this film, describe the Kantian elements in Dr. Luthan's (Hugh Grant's) ethical arguments in this film, and then describe the utilitarian elements in Dr. Myrick's (Gene Hackman's) ethical arguments.

PART FOUR:
RIGHTS AND ETHICS

So far in this chapter, we have learned about various ethical systems that do not rely on Scripture or Church authority in any meaningful way—viz., Aristotle's virtue ethics, Immanuel Kant's rule-based ethics, and John Stuart Mill's utilitarianism. Hopefully, our study of all of these systems has shed light on the way we understand morality in the 21st century. In some fashion or another, all of these systems have influenced the way we evaluate moral choices in the West, yet perhaps, the most influential secular ethical system of all remains to be examined. No study of secular ethical systems would be complete without an examination of rights theories, and this is especially true for people who live in the United States, the land of rights.

"The right to vote!" "The right to privacy!" "The right to free speech!" "The right to bear arms!" "The right to life, liberty, and the pursuit of happiness!"

In nearly every situation in our lives as Americans, we use the language of "rights" to express what is most dear to us. Our Constitution contains a "Bill of Rights" which adds to this charter document ten rights that we believe should be the law of the land. For instance, we believe that, even if people hold an unpopular position on a particular issue, they should still be permitted to voice their opinion if they do so in a rational and responsible manner, for we know that an argument that is unpopular might, nonetheless, be true. We express this belief with the language that all adults should have the "right to free speech." In fact, our very system of government, a representative democracy, is built on the notion that it is vital to the health of our nation as a whole that every person who has reached adulthood should be permitted to vote. We express this belief with the language that all adults should have the "right to vote." Indeed, every area of our lives—from the courtroom to the classroom, and from the lunch counter to the kitchen table—is saturated with rights talk.

As Americans, we not only speak about legal matters using rights language, but we also couch our moral concerns in the same terms. For example, if a person were to learn that a friend of hers was being deceived by her unfaithful boyfriend, she might reason that "her friend has a *right* to know what is going on behind her back." Of course, when she reasons in this way she does not mean that it is written into local law or the U.S. Constitution; no law reads: "All duped girlfriends shall have the right to know what their boyfriends are doing behind their backs or else their negligent friends can be sued, jailed, or flogged." What she means is that it would be *morally wrong* to keep this information from her friend.

But even though most Americans speak about the concept of a right as if it were self-evident, the concept as we currently understand it did not come into existence until around the seventeenth century. Neither Socrates, Plato, Aristotle, Jesus, St. Paul, nor St. Thomas Aquinas ever spoke the language of "rights." And moreover, the concept of a right is far from unproblematic. Though rights language permeates so much of our lives and seems so ordinary, the concept is surrounded by a host of philosophical difficulties or questions. Therefore, as educated citizens and Christians seeking the moral course in life, we need to investigate this pivotal concept and evaluate its strengths and weaknesses.

A. WHAT IS A "RIGHT"?

Like most philosophical or theological concepts, the concept of a "right" is extremely difficult to explain in a clear and precise manner. Though this concept is a part of the vocabulary of virtually every Westerner, there is no general agreement as to what rights people (or animals) actually have, and as will be seen below, this lack of agreement makes a rigidly bounded definition of the concept problematic. Additionally, it is often difficult to distinguish the difference between a right understood in a legal sense and a right understood in a moral sense. For example, someone might argue that people have a right to view pornography, but he also might argue that viewing pornography is wrong. So, in this case, he would be advocating that people have a right to do something wrong. But, then, what type of right is this? Simply a legal one granted by a government or is it somehow or another a moral one, as well? As this example hopefully demonstrates, formulating a definition of the concept of a right is far from easy.

One fairly mainstream definition of a "right" has been proposed by Ronald Dworkin, a famous philosopher and law professor. Dworkin writes:

> In most cases when we say that someone has a 'right' to do something, we imply that it would be wrong to interfere with his doing it, or at least that some special grounds are needed for justifying any interference. I use this strong sense of right when I say that you have the right to spend your money gambling, if you wish, though you ought to spend it in a more worthwhile way. I mean that it would be wrong for anyone to interfere with you even though you propose to spend your money in a way that I think is wrong.[36]

According to this definition, *to have a right to something is to have a sphere of activity or an area of one's life protected from outside interference.* On this account, having a "right to spend money," as Dworkin explains, means being able to do as you please with your money without outside interference. Similarly, having a "right to free speech" means being able to speak one's mind without outside interference.

This notion of a right, though, is too narrow; there are many rights that Westerners claim to have that do not fit his definition.[37] For example, many people in the United States and elsewhere claim that every human being has a "right to affordable healthcare." By making this claim, these people are not simply stating that no human being should be prevented from entering a clinic or hospital. They are arguing that society as a whole should make healthcare available to everyone at a reasonable price. To say the least, if there is such a right, it demands *action* on the part of many people, not merely a willingness to refrain from interfering in someone else's business. Doctors, nurses, hospital administrators, and taxpayers in general would have *to do* many things to insure this right. In short, for better or for worse, this right places a burden on many people besides the rights bearer himself, and Dwokin's definition above cannot account for this aspect of some rights. In this same vein, the "right to vote," the "right to a just wage," the "right to affordable housing," as well as many other rights require action on the part of someone besides the rights bearer. For example, if people have a right to vote, then the government has to do many things to facilitate this right. If there is only one voting booth in the whole country and it sits on the top of a very high mountain, then it is sheer folly to say the citizens' right to vote has been insured simply because there are no man-made obstacles to ascending the mountain. A genuine right to vote would require the establishment of many easily accessible voting centers throughout the country and, perhaps, government-funded ways to facilitate voter registration and to assist the elderly or disabled.

Thus, *"having a right" seems to mean a) "having an activity or an area of one's life protected against outside interference" and, in some cases, b) "having a claim on another person or society as a whole to deliver a particular service or facilitate a certain activity."* It should be noted, then, that it follows from b) that some rights only exist inside a developed society and, further, that some rights only come into existence over time. For example, it makes little sense to state that every member of a primitive South American tribe has a "right to affordable healthcare" when their society does not really have anything that could be properly called "healthcare." Nor does it seem reasonable to believe that the first human beings who emerged on the planet really had a "right to affordable housing." Observations such as these inevitably lead philosopohers to ask, "Where do rights come from?" And as will be seen, this question is inextricably linked to the question "What rights do people (and animals) really have?"

B.   WHAT RIGHTS DO PEOPLE (AND ANIMALS) HAVE, AND WHAT IS THEIR SOURCE OR GROUND?

Though there is certainly agreement in the Western world that people have rights, there is much disagreement about the specific rights they do have and about the source or ground of these rights. For example, gun advocates argue that Americans have the legal and moral right to own guns for self-defense or sport, whereas some gun control advocates argue that gun ownership should be limited to certain authorities and that the Second Amendment to the Constitution relates to the outdated notion of militias, not individual citizens in modern America. Moreover, more religious people tend to argue that our rights are "God-given," whereas many people of a more secular bent argue that our rights are due to our rational capacity or arise from a contract of some sort. In this section, we will briefly present three different theories about the kinds of rights that people (and animals) have and/or the sources or grounds of these rights.

1.   John Locke's theory of natural rights

"We hold these truths to be self-evident that all men are created equal, that they are endowed by their Creator with certain inalienable rights, that among these are life, liberty and the pursuit of happiness." Though most Americans know these words are part of the Declaration of Independence, fewer know that the ideas can be directly traced to the thought of the British philosopher John Locke (1632-1704). No figure in the history of political thought has had as profound an impact on American society as this pivotal figure, and thus, it is proper to begin with his views on rights.

To a certain extent, it must be acknowledged that John Locke is somewhat out of place in a discussion of "secular" ethical systems, for as will be seen, Locke maintains that our natural rights are "God-given." Though he rarely uses Scripture in any substantial way and the role of God in his arguments is often peripheral, Locke was certainly a Christian, and it would be a mistake to believe that his faith did not influence his philosophical views. However, today, most of Locke's philosophical descendents do not believe God, Scripture, or Church authority plays any significant role in rights theories; indeed, many modern rights theorists are aggressively atheistic. Yet, Locke is unquestionably one of the great forefathers of rights theory, and any treatment of the subject that ignored him would be suspect, to say the least.

According to Locke, even before the establishment of a government, all people are endowed by God with a number of basic rights, most notably the right to life, liberty, and the pursuit of property. In his *Second Treatise of Government*, Locke offers the following reasons why all human beings have the right to life and liberty:

> The *state of nature* has a law of nature to govern it, which obliges every one: and reason, which is that law, teaches all mankind, who will but consult it, that being all *equal and independent*, no one ought to harm another in his life, health, liberty, or possessions: for men being all the workmanship of one omnipotent, and infinitely wise maker; all servants of one sovereign master, sent into the world by his order, and about his business; they are his property, whose workmanship they are … : and being furnished with like faculties, sharing all in one community of nature, there cannot be supposed any such *subordination* among us, that may authorize us to destroy one another, as if we were made for one another's uses, as the inferior ranks of creatures are for our's.[38]

In this one monstrous sentence, Locke puts forward a number of related reasons why human beings have a right to life and liberty. If people follow their reason or what Locke calls the "law of nature"[39]—which God has given to them to guide their actions—they will see that all human beings have roughly the same type of faculties or capacities—e.g., five senses, a memory, reason, an imagination, etc.—and, thus, that no person is naturally under the control of another. No person is naturally the property of another, and thus, no one is authorized to take the life of another; all human beings have a "right to life." And in the same vein, God has not placed any adult under the control of any other adult; all human beings have a "right to liberty."[40] Ultimately, God is the owner of every human life, and if someone murders or enslaves another human being, he or she is taking God's property and defying His wishes that all of His creatures be free to carry out His business. Locke's reasoning in this regard, then, is in large part theological. Human rights are grounded in the authority of God and the laws of nature that He has instilled in human beings.

In addition to life and liberty, the right of securing and holding private property is fundamental to Locke's political theory. In his *Second Treatise*, Locke defends the right of private property in the following way:

> Though the earth, and all inferior creatures, be common to all men, yet every man has a *property* in his own *person*: this no body has any right to but himself. The *labour* of his body, and the *work* of his hands, we may say, are properly his. Whatsoever then he removes out of the state that nature hath provided, and left it in, he hath mixed his *labour* with, and joined to it something that is his own, and thereby makes it his *property*.[41]

Locke begins this passage with the sound observation that God gave everything in the natural world to humanity *in general*; no tree, cow, or plot of land comes with an ownership tag. However, from this observation, Locke does not conclude that people should be socialists and own everything in common. Rather, he argues that when someone adds his labor to something in the natural world, that something—be it a tree, a cow, or a plot of land—becomes his private property. As Locke argues in the first sentence, there is a sense in which every person owns his own person and his own freedom. And when a person puts his labor into, e.g., a plot of land, he puts something of *himself* into that land, and thereby, it becomes his own.

"But," someone might respond to Locke, "why does the person who merely puts labor into something in nature thereby become its owner? Did this person make the plot of land out of nothing? Of course not! God did. Then, why shouldn't the land remain common property, available for everyone to use, as God seems to have intended?" Locke's response to this argument is that, prior to the addition of human labor, a plot of land and nearly everything else in the natural world is virtually useless. When God gave the world to people in common, He did so with the intention that they would transform it into something of value in their lives, and what gives value to something in nature is the labor that a human being puts into it. A plot of land that is uncultivated is of little use to a person, as is a cow that is not milked or slaughtered or a tree that is not cut down for lumber. To be sure, there is some value in these raw materials, but as Locke argues, "[O]f the *products* of the earth useful to the life of man nine tenths are the *effects* of labor."[42] In short, the person who puts labor into a thing gives it nearly all of its value. By putting his labor into a product of the earth, a person becomes, as it were, the majority stockholder of that product; though nature owns some of that stock, he owns the vast majority and is, therefore, the controlling interest.

In addition to life, liberty, and property, Locke also insisted that people possessed other rights, such as the right to restrain and punish criminals, and a fuller account of his theory would have to include a discussion of these rights, as well as a discussion of the pivotal role government plays in protecting and limiting the exercise of these rights. But this section has at least given the reader a look at the way Locke derives three of his fundamental rights. As should be clear, some of the reasoning that he gives is theological in nature, though much of it could probably stand on its own without theological support. For example, an atheist could probably accept the brunt of Locke's argument for private property; he could agree that, by adding labor to something in the natural world, a person transforms it into private property without agreeing that God bequeathed the natural world to human beings. Nonetheless, the theological character of Locke's theory should not be denied; Locke repeatedly incorporates God into his arguments for natural rights.

2.   Tom Regan's theory of rights

Though John Locke's theory of God-given rights has been extremely influential in American thought, many—if not most—contemporary rights theorists do not follow Locke in putting forth theological grounds for their rights claims. Today, many theorists argue that human beings (and, in some cases, animals) have rights *because of some distinctive ability or capacity they possess* and not because God is the owner of human beings or because He has bequeathed them the natural world. According to these theorists, an analysis of the abilities or capacities of human beings themselves is enough to reveal the foundations of our rights claims; one need not make recourse to God.

One such theorist is philosopher and animal rights activist Tom Regan. Regan argues that human beings, as well as many non-human animals, have rights because they are what he calls "experiencing subjects of life." An experiencing subject of life is "a conscious creature having an individual welfare that has importance to us whatever [its] usefulness to others."[43] Like Kant, who argued that human beings should never be treated merely as means, Regan argues that human beings and many nonhuman animals have what he calls "inherent value," i.e., value in themselves, quite apart from the use they may have for other beings. But unlike Kant, who argued that human life is distinctive because it is *rational*, Regan argues that the mere ability to experience life—to be a conscious, desiring, feeling being—is what grounds our rights claims.

But why does Regan zero in on this capacity of human beings (and animals), and not their ability to think abstractly, make choices, or communicate? Regan begins his argument by claiming that *all* people have the same inherent value and the same rights. As Regan states:

> The genius and the retarded child, the prince and the pauper, the brain surgeon and the fruit vendor, Mother Teresa and the most unscrupulous used-car salesman—all have inherent value, all possess it equally, and all have an equal right to be treated with respect, to be treated in ways that do

not reduce them to the status of things, as if they existed as resources for others.[44]

Now, if this claim is correct—as most Americans would agree it is—then, Regan argues, we must ask what quality all of these human beings have in common that makes them inherently valuable and confers upon them the status of rights bearer. It could not be reason or intelligence, for in that case, the genius would be more valuable and have more rights than the retarded child. Nor could it be strength of character, for in that case, Mother Teresa would be inherently more valuable and have more rights than the unscrupulous used-car salesman. At bottom, Regan argues, what ties all of these inherently valuable rights-bearing people together is the fact that they are all experiencing subjects of life. All of these people are conscious beings who have preferences, interests, beliefs, and desires. Regan rejects the notion that the basis of our rights claims could be any other capacity, like the ability to reason or make moral choices. For he believes that, if we were to ground our rights claims on any other ability or capacity, such as the ability to reason or make choices, we would have to conclude that certain groups of people who do not have this ability or capacity—such as newborns, the mentally ill, or the handicapped—do not have rights, either. And most people, Regan asserts, would find such a conclusion unacceptable.

Furthermore, Regan argues, if human beings have inherent value and rights precisely because they are experiencing subjects of life, then one must acknowledge that animals, as experiencing subjects of life, must have inherent value and rights as well. Animals, it is true, cannot do many of the things that humans can do; they cannot think abstractly, make moral judgments, or design cathedrals. However, many human beings cannot do these things either, and yet, we do not deny that they have inherent value and possess rights. As experiencing subjects of life, animals should be given the respect they deserve, and the human practice of using animals as resources must end. In particular, Regan calls for "the total abolition of the use of animals in science, the total abolition of commercial animal agriculture, [and] the total elimination of commercial and sport hunting and trapping."[45]

Regan's theory is only one of the many theories that attempt to ground rights claims in a distinctive characteristic or ability of human beings (and, in Regan's case, animals). Yet, however much these theorists may argue over which ability or capacity is the foundation of our rights claims, all of them maintain that rights claims do not need a theological foundation.

3.   John Rawls' theory of rights

Before concluding this section on the kinds and foundations of rights, it will be worthwhile to survey a theory of rights that has received considerable attention in the last thirty years, viz., that of the late Harvard philosopher John Rawls (1921-2003). The imaginative way in which Rawls derives his basic rights has captured the attention of many a student and teacher and has made his book A Theory of Justice a modern classic in political thought. In particular, Rawls sees our basic rights as arising from a "social contract," and though the idea of a social contract is not new, Rawls presents his contract in a novel and engaging way, viz., as a thought experiment that can be carried out by his readers.

As its title indicates, Rawls' A *Theory of Justice* is an attempt to answer the question "What is justice?" or, more specifically, "What rights and duties should people have, and how should power, authority, opportunities, and other social goods be distributed?" In order to arrive at an answer to these questions, Rawls presents a thought experiment or a purely hypothetical (and, indeed, physically impossible) situation for his readers to contemplate. Rawls invites his readers to imagine a number of free and rational persons who decide to join together to form a society for their mutual benefit. Now, throughout history, it is clear that those who have created governments have had a tendency to write laws or adopt principles that advanced their own interests, often to the grave disadvantage of other groups. The British enacted corn laws that starved the Irish; the white slave owners in America enacted laws that reduced black slaves to the status of animals; and men in many countries enacted laws prohibiting women from voting. How, then, can these free and rational creatures avoid this pitfall and adopt just principles?

As a remedy to such biases, Rawls insists that these free and rational persons formulate their principles from behind a "veil of ignorance." Behind this veil, "no one knows his place in society, his class or social status, nor does any one know his fortune in the distribution of natural assets and abilities, his intelligence, strength, and the like."[46] Like Lady Justice, who wears a blindfold so she cannot see any of the physical characteristics of the disputants in a court case, the participants in this hypothetical situation also wear a blindfold of sorts to insure that justice prevails. They cannot see *their own* race, sex, and class nor *their own* natural strengths and weaknesses. Because these agents cannot see these things, it is in their best interest to adopt principles that do not favor one set of characteristics or conditions over another. If people do not know their race, they will be very careful to adopt fair principles, for if they do not, they just might find themselves the victims of their own bias when the veil is lifted. The veil of ignorance, then, insures that the founding principles of a society are the result of a fair agreement or social contract. Before the veil is lifted and the participants get to see the results of nature's lottery, they have already agreed to the principles upon which their society will be founded and, therefore, cannot complain if these principles do not always work in their favor.

What principles, then, should these free and rational agents adopt? According to Rawls, the participants in his hypothetical situation would adopt the two following principles:

First Principle

Each person is to have an equal right to the most extensive total system of basic
    liberty compatible with a similar system of liberty for all.

Second Principle

Social and economic inequalities are to be arranged so that they are both:

a.   to the greatest benefit of the least advantaged ... and

b.   attached to offices and positions open to all under conditions of fair equal-
       ity of opportunity.[47]

The first principle echoes a common one that is widely accepted in American
life: People should be able to do whatever they choose provided it does not interfere
with other people's ability to do whatever they choose. More concretely, Rawls explains that these basic liberties or rights would include the right to vote; the right to
be eligible for public office; the rights to free speech, thought, and assembly; the right
to property; and the right to due process (e.g., one cannot be arrested or held in prison
without cause). Everyone behind the veil of ignorance would choose these liberties,
for regardless of one's station in life, the free pursuit of one's goals is a necessary part of
a fulfilling life.

In regard to the second principle, one might suppose that the participants behind the veil of ignorance would choose a socialist system in which everyone is given
the same level of social and economic goods, regardless of her natural gifts or talents.
Would it not be safer to agree that everyone should receive the same amount of wealth
and prestige, just in case, when the veil is lifted, one discovers she does not have the
natural abilities that a capitalist system would reward?

Rawls, however, does not go the traditional socialist route. He argues that it
would better serve the interests of everyone if social and economic inequalities were
permitted *as long as* these inequalities are to everyone's advantage and they arise from
positions and offices open to everyone. For example, as long as everyone is free to
pursue a career in medicine, it is in the interest of everyone in society that doctors
receive more money and prestige than, say, workers in a fast food restaurant. Even
though nature does not give everyone the brains, focus, or desire to be a doctor, everyone benefits from the fact that doctors are respected and well-compensated. Such a
practice insures quality medical care for everyone, including the fast-food worker. A
society in which some enjoy greater social and economic benefits raises all people
above the level they would be in a society where there were no social and economic
inequalities. Recognizing that some inequalities are necessary for the benefit of everyone and acknowledging that these inequalities were agreed to before the veil was
lifted, even the people who end up in a lower social class will be willing to accept and
participate in this just society.

For Rawls, then, all of the rights that a person enjoys arise from a social contract,
which is itself an agreement between free and rational people.

C.   RIGHTS IN CONFLICT

Different rights theorists, then, disagree about what a right is, about the particular rights that exist, about the types of beings who have these rights, and also about

the origin or foundation of these rights. But perhaps the most hotly debated issue between rights theorists is how conflicts between rights or between rights and other goods should be resolved. If an unborn baby has a "right to life," as pro-life advocates claim, and a woman has a "right to her own body" or a "right to privacy," as pro-choice advocates claim, which right should win out if a woman wants an abortion? How is one to assess the rich American's claim that he has a right to private property when over 40,000 people in developing countries—all of whom have the "right to life"— die of hunger and its consequences *every day*? Just how far does a captured terrorist's right against self-incrimination (i.e., "taking the fifth") or right to legal counsel extend when the safety of thousands of people is at stake? Is the right to free assembly absolute, or can it be nullified in certain cases, as, for example, when neo-Nazis decide to have a parade in a Jewish town? Questions like these present a serious challenge to any rights theorist. What principles should be used to resolve such conflicts?

As one would expect, philosophers have dealt with these kinds of conflicts in many different ways. One popular and intuitively appealing way of addressing these conflicts is to argue that all rights are not on the same plane. Not all rights are absolute, and some rights are prior to or more fundamental than others. For example, though citizens have both the right to life and the right to free speech, the former is more fundamental; life is *the* most basic good, for without it, no other goods are possible. Thus, when the exercise of free speech poses an imminent danger to life—as it would if someone yelled "Fire!" in a crowded theatre—the right to free speech needs to be limited, for the right to life, as it were, trumps this right. Using this line of reasoning, pro-life advocates have argued that, whatever the concerns an expectant mother might have about a pregnancy, none of them are grave enough to override the unborn baby's right to life.

Other philosophers, most notably those inclined to support abortion rights, have attempted to resolve these conflicts by arguing that, in many cases, what appears to be a conflict of rights is not really a conflict at all. In general, such philosophers argue that one of the parties in the alleged conflict has misunderstood what a given right entails; in other words, one of the parties believes that having a right to something means much more than it actually does. For example, in the abortion debate, pro-choice philosophers —noting that pro-life advocates often argue that an unborn baby has a right to life and, therefore, has a right to use his or her mother's body—contend that, even if an unborn baby does have a right to life, that right does not entitle the baby to the use of the mother's body. So, in the case in which a woman wants to terminate a pregnancy, there is no real conflict of rights; the baby's right to life is quite separate from the mother's right to use her body as she wishes.[48]

The foregoing account has hopefully given the reader some indication of the importance of this area of rights theory, as well as the different ways in which philosophers argue over how to resolve rights conflicts.

D.   RIGHTS AND CATHOLIC CHRISTIANITY

1.   Catholic Christianity's agreements with the theory of rights

Unlike utilitarianism—which has largely been rejected by orthodox Christians, including Catholic Christians—rights theories have generally been well received by Christian communities. Indeed, the language of "rights" has been adopted by many Christian denominations, including Catholicism. For example, the *Catechism of the Catholic Church* makes the following statement, which is thoroughly Lockean in character:

> Respect for the human person entails respect for the rights that flow from
> his dignity as a creature. These rights are prior to society and must be
> recognized by it. They are the basis of the moral legitimacy of every au-
> thority: by flouting them, or refusing to recognize them in its positive leg-
> islation, a society undermines its own moral legitimacy. [49]

In this passage, the Church uses the modern language of "rights" to express the ancient Biblical notion that men and women are made in the image and likeness of God and, therefore, must be treated with respect and dignity. And, like Locke, the Church argues that government does not and cannot confer these rights on people; these rights are "prior to society," i.e., they are given by God in the very act of creating men and women. The role of government is much more modest, viz., to protect these rights from being violated.

More generally, the Christian adoption of the language of "rights" has been a · powerful weapon against the abuses of more utilitarian approaches to life. As opposed to thinkers like Peter Singer who sanction abortion if it leads to the greatest happiness for the greatest number of people, Christians insist upon the *inalienable* right to life of every innocent human being, a right that cannot be taken away by anyone for any reason. Citing the *Congregation for the Doctrine of the Faithful*, the *Catechism* declares, "[H]uman rights depend neither on single individuals nor on parents; nor do they represent a concession made by society and the state; they belong to human nature and are inherent in the person by virtue of the creative act from which the person took his origin."[50] In this case, as in many others, the notion of a right acts like a protective shield around a person, safeguarding him or her from the abuses of the powerful and overly pragmatic.

And in a similar fashion, the Christian use of the language of "rights" has proved to be an effective way of securing basic goods for oppressed or vulnerable people. In some cases, having a right to something means more than simply having a certain arena of life protected against abuse. Some rights claims function as demands, forcing people in positions of authority or privilege to meet the basic needs of others. For example, in his encyclical *Peace on Earth*, Pope John XXIII made the following decla-ration:

> [E]very man has the right to life, to bodily integrity, and to the means

which are necessary and suitable for the proper development of life; these are primarily food, clothing, shelter, rest, medical care, and finally the necessary social services. Therefore a human being also has the right to security in cases of sickness, inability to work, widowhood, old age, unemployment, or in any other case in which he is deprived of the means of subsistence through no fault of his own.[51]

As this passage makes clear, respecting the rights of others often means taking active steps to secure certain basic goods for them. If a person has lost her job through no fault of her own, she still has a right to the material goods necessary for survival, and society must provide her with them or else they are not respecting this right. Likewise, those who are too poor to pay for shelter or medical care still have a right to these basic goods, and thus, they can legitimately demand these things of their government.

2.   Catholic Christianity's disagreements with the theory of rights

As beneficial as the adoption of the language of "rights" has been, however, Christians must be aware of the dark side of this language. Mary Ann Glendon, a Catholic philosopher and Harvard law professor, has drawn attention to this dark side in her *Rights Talk: The Impoverishment of Political Discourse*. Glendon observes that the rise in the number of rights claims has not been accompanied by a similar rise in the acknowledgement of duties; indeed, the rise in rights claims might actually be blinding us to our moral responsibilities.

For example, in the United States, there are virtually no "Good Samaritan Laws," i.e., laws requiring a person to come to the aid of a stranger, even if doing so would require a minimum of effort. One judge whom Glendon cites even goes so far as to lay out the following scenario and make the following claim: "I see my neighbor's two-year-old babe in dangerous proximity to the machinery of his windmill in his yard, and easily might, but do not, rescue him. I am not liable in damages to the child for his injuries ... because the child and I are strangers, and I am under no obligation to protect him."[52] Though, in this passage, the judge in question is only making a point about the law, not about morality *per se*, one would think that, in a civilized society like America, some level of legal responsibility for the well-being of one's fellow citizens would be required. Of course, it would be unreasonable to demand heroism of all citizens—e.g., to penalize someone for not risking life or limb for a stranger—but in the scenario in question, the slightest effort would have saved the child from harm. Though the concept of a right is useful when we are demanding certain basic goods from our government or demanding that certain areas of our lives be left alone, this concept only covers part of the moral and legal terrain. In short, if a moral or legal language, such as the language of "rights," does not accommodate such basic duties as the duty to take a two-year-old out of harm's way, then it is clearly inadequate.

In this same vein, Glendon has noted that the American understanding of rights has led to "a neglect of the social dimension of personhood, and a consequent carelessness regarding the environments that human beings and societies require in order to flourish."[53] What Glendon means by this phrase is that human flourishing requires the support of many different levels and kinds of community but that the language of "rights" neglects this social dimension of human life. Historically, rights theorists have depicted human society as a group of atomistic individuals who have no significant forms of association outside of their relationship with the state. The state insures the rights of these individuals, and then, they are free to go about their business and engage in consensual contracts. But the fabric of human relationships is much richer and more complex than it is depicted in these theories. Children depend upon families; families depend upon churches; churches depend upon families; families and churches depend upon towns; towns depend upon districts; etc. And the types of relationships that exist between these people or groups is not that of strangers engaged in a social contract. For example, there is something truly perverse about describing the basic relationship between a mother and her unborn child in terms of rights. The language of "rights" cannot capture the richness and complexity of human relationships; instead, it reduces nearly everyone to the status of strangers. And as the case of the two-year-old above illustrates, any system of law or morality that fails to recognize the various bonds that tie human beings together is grossly deficient.

Despite these shortcomings, however, the language of "rights" has been incorporated into the lexicon of the Catholic Church, as well as that of other Christian denominations. Christians in general recognize the utility of this language, but they also recognize that rights are only part of the story. As shown above, Catholics have adopted this language, but they have incorporated it into a larger conceptual framework, one that is capable of curbing its excesses and making up for its shortcomings. In the chapters to follow, this larger conceptual framework will be mapped out.

SECTION HIGHLIGHTS

The concept of a "right" is difficult to define in a precise or rigidly bounded way. In some cases, having a right means having an activity or an area of one's life protected against outside interference. In other cases, having a right means having a claim on another person or society as a whole to deliver a particular service or facilitate a certain activity.

The authors of the Declaration of Independence and the Constitution of the United States were greatly influenced by the British philosopher John Locke. He maintained that human beings possessed the "God-given" rights to life, liberty, and the pursuit of property. To some extent, Locke provided theological grounds for these rights.

Tom Regan and many other modern philosophers argue that rights do not need a theological foundation. Instead, these philosophers argue that human beings (and animals) have rights because of some distinctive capacity or trait they possess, such as consciousness, self-consciousness, or reason.

John Rawls argues that rights are actually the outcome of a social contract between free and rational beings. Rawls argues that the participants in this contract need to derive their principles from behind a "veil of ignorance," which prevents them from knowing their sex, race, class, and natural strengths, weaknesses, and proclivities.

Any serious rights theory must provide criteria for dealing with rights conflicts, such as the conflict between the right to life of an unborn baby and the right to privacy of an expectant mother. Some philosophers try to resolve such disputes by arguing that some rights are prior to or more fundamental than others. Other philosophers attempt to resolve these disputes by showing that someone in the dispute is mistaken about what a given right actually entails.

Christians, in general, and Catholics, in particular, have embraced the language of "rights," for this language has been a powerful weapon against the abuses of utilitarianism. Also, by adopting the language of "rights," the Church has been able to help the oppressed and vulnerable people of the world secure basic goods and services. However, Christian groups are aware of the shortcomings of rights theory, especially its tendencies to blind us to our moral responsibilities and to misrepresent the nature of human relationships.

QUESTIONS

To show that you comprehend what has been presented about rights theories, answer the following questions in paragraph form. Write your answers on a separate sheet of paper.

1. According to Ronald Dworkin, having a right often entitles a person to do something wrong. Do you believe people should have the right to do immoral things, such as view pornography or procure a late-term abortion? Why or why not?

2. Why does Tom Regan believe that animals, as well as humans, have rights? Do you believe that animals have rights? Why or why not?

3. Psychologist Lawrence Kohlberg invented a scenario known as "Heinz's Dilemma." The dilemma is roughly as follows:

   A woman is diagnosed with a fatal form of cancer. Her husband, Heinz, discovers that the local druggist has discovered a cure for this form of cancer. Unfortunately for Heinz and his wife, the druggist is charging an exorbitant amount of money for this cure—much more than the amount he expended in his research. After many pleas to the druggist and numerous failed attempts to obtain the money legally, Heinz decides to break into the pharmacy and steal the drug.

   Given what you have learned about John Locke's theory of rights, how do you think he would evaluate this situation. Did Heinz violate the druggist's rights? Do you think Heinz did the right thing? Why or why not?

4.   Imagine that you are behind John Rawls' "veil of ignorance" and did not know your own race, sex, class, or natural strengths, weaknesses, or proclivities. What principles would you adopt if you wanted to found an ideal society?

5.   Read endnote 48 under "CHAPTER TWO: SECULAR ETHICAL SYSTEMS" at the back of this book. Explain how Judith Jarvis Thomson attempts to resolve the conflict between an unborn baby's right to life and an expectant mother's right to her own body. Do you agree with her reasoning in this matter? Why or why not?

6.   Should the United States have "duty-to-rescue" laws, i.e., laws that would require people to provide some minimum level of assistance to strangers who are injured or in danger? Why or why not?

7.   Do you think there is a difference between respecting the rights of your neighbor and following the Golden Rule, as advocated by Jesus? Use an example to illustrate your answer.

CHAPTER THREE:
TRANSITION
TO CATHOLIC ETHICS

PART ONE:
WHAT DIFFERENCE DOES GOD MAKE TO THE GOOD?[1]

A. THE QUESTION

Now that you have learned about four respected and influential approaches to ethics—Aristotle's virtue ethics, Kant's rule-based ethics, Mill's utilitarianism, and various rights theories—which, in no real significant way, make any reference to God, you might be asking yourself, "Why do I need to believe in God in order to have a sound moral character or to make good moral decisions? What difference does faith or the Church or Mass attendance make to ethics?" Indeed, when we look at our neighbors we sometimes see little correlation between the behavior of avowed Christians and that of agnostics or even atheists. Indeed, the newspapers regularly reveal the hypocrisies of television evangelists or some priests who *espouse* Christian values, such as being chaste and living simply, but *live* like monsters, dwelling in gaudy mansions, entertaining mistresses, or abusing children. Conversely, we often see that some of our atheist friends are most active in community service, tutoring, or feeding the poor. And as we just read in the previous chapter, it seems possible (and reasonable) to maintain a coherent ethical system without making any reference to God. In short, why bother with God? Can't we be followers of Aristotle, for example, without being Christian? Aristotle didn't seem to be in need of Christianity (of course, he came before Jesus), so why are we?

B. CLUES TO AN ANSWER

The first thing that must be acknowledged is that there is a great deal of *truth* to the notion that a person can have a fine moral character and perform virtuous actions without any faith in God. Indeed, the *Catechism of the Catholic Church* clearly states that "[t]he moral virtues are acquired by *human* effort"[2]; in other words, by hard work and proper habit formation, human beings who are left to their own devices, can—without any conscious reliance on God—achieve a certain degree of virtue and carry out virtuous activities. Unlike certain groups of Christians who maintain that only Christians are capable of doing good works, the Catholic Church readily acknowledges the quite obvious fact that non-Christians are very often good people, too. But this fact is not a stumbling block to the Catholic Church; in fact, it is exactly what is to be expected from an institution that has such a strong belief in *natural law*.

B1. Natural Law

Though we will study natural law in a much deeper and detailed way later on in this book, it will be sufficient at this time to understand belief in natural law as *the belief that God has implanted in all human beings an "original moral sense which enables [them] to discern by reason the good and the evil.*"[3] In other words, God has given to all men and women the natural ability to discover what is right and wrong *using their reason alone.* By reflecting on decisions and observing the way that the world and nature operate, men and women should be able to discern what is right and wrong.

This belief is present in Scripture, especially in the thought of St. Paul. When he writes to the new community of Christians that has arisen in Rome, Paul chastises the Romans for their wicked behavior—indulging in greed, lust, jealousy, etc. Evidently, some Romans were trying to excuse their behavior by pleading that they were ignorant of the right way to behave because no one explicitly taught them God's Laws. But Paul does not buy it: "Those people have no excuse at all" (Romans 1:20). Paul maintains that God has clearly laid down his plan for things by building the world the way that He did; anyone who reflects on the way things are built will be able to figure out the moral course of action. Later on in the same letter, in the course of describing how the Gentiles (non-Jewish people) and the Jews will be judged by Jesus Christ in the end times, Paul states that, even though the Gentiles have not been taught the Law of God, they sometimes do what the Law commands "by instinct" because "what the Law commands is written in their hearts" (Romans 2:14-15).[4]

In fact, Fr. Karl Rahner, a 20th century Jesuit theologian, recognized that people from non-Christian religions, as well as people with no religious affiliation at all, often do what God's Law commands even though they do not acknowledge or realize that that is what they are doing. Rahner called these virtuous people "anonymous Christians," for they were doing what they could to bring about Christ's Kingdom on earth though they were not doing so in the name of Christianity.

But we still have not really addressed the question at hand. So what if good people who are not Christians can be considered honorary Christians? In fact, does this not just highlight the point that Christianity does not add anything to ethics? If there is no difference between the behavior of Christians and non-Christians, then it seems to be the case that Christianity does not make any difference to morality.

B2. Natural[5] vs. Theological Virtues

The most important distinction to understand in order to answer the question "What difference does God make to the good?" is the one between *natural* and *theological virtues.*

As we learned in our study of Aristotle, a virtue is a state of character or firm disposition to do good that a person acquires through proper habit formation; virtues make individuals *desire and judge* what is appropriate or fitting in a given situation. For example, liberality is the virtue that deals with money matters. To be liberal is to be able to *judge* the proper amount of money to give away (e.g., not so much that one cannot feed his family and not so little that one is selfishly hoarding goods), how to give it away (e.g., anonymously so that one does not bring attention to oneself), to whom to give it (e.g., to those truly in need, not those who will squander it on gambling), etc., and to *desire* to give this amount away in this manner to this person, etc.

Natural virtues such as generosity, temperance, fortitude, justice, and prudence are of course important for Christians, but these virtues are only part of the story.

Everything in nature has a goal or purpose toward which it strives, according to Aristotle. The *telos* or *final cause* of an eye is to see, and the telos of an acorn, whether it achieves it or not, is to become an oak tree; these things are built for the sake of these goals or purposes. As Aristotle also pointed out and as all people are obviously aware, human beings, as a part of nature, also have a goal or purpose: *happiness*. But for Aristotle, who was a pagan, *this* life was the end of the story; for him, only the human species, not individual human beings, were eternal.[6] Hence, the virtues that he identified—the moral or natural virtues—were only concerned with the earthly existence of a human being; he was not aware of a heaven or Jesus or Holy Spirit to complicate matters.

But as Jesus has revealed to the Apostles directly and to us through Scripture, *earthly* happiness is not our ultimate end or calling. Anyone who has been to or watched a sporting event has probably seen fans holding signs reading "John 3:16." Such signs refer to a passage in the fourth Gospel that summarizes the Christian view of life: "For God loved the world so much that he gave his only Son, *so that everyone who believes in him may not die but have eternal life.*" Eternal life, one of friendship and communion with God, is the ultimate end or calling for a human being in the Christian understanding of things. Just as the moral or natural virtues are directed toward perfecting our lives as earthly creatures, the theological ones are directed toward perfecting our lives as spiritual creatures, sons and daughters of God.

An analogy might help to clarify the difference. Suppose people were like caterpillars. Through experience, caterpillars learned how to manage their lives well. Some caterpillars had the virtue of liberality and shared their scraps of leaves with their neighbors so no fights would break out and everybody would be well fed. Others had the virtue of temperance; unlike some of their neighbors, they knew how many and which kinds of leaves to eat. They lived longer, healthier lives, and they could move from leaf to leaf much quicker than their bloated comrades. In general, some caterpillars learned how to govern their lives well and live in peaceful coexistence. These virtues would be like natural virtues of the caterpillars, for they perfect the lives of these creatures *as caterpillars*. But suppose a group of a dozen of these critters were visited by a butterfly who told them that if they live their lives in a certain fashion, one day they too may fly. No more moving along on stubby little legs at one foot per hour! They could float on the air and have magnificent colors, too. So, this group of caterpillars re-arranges their lifestyles in order to prepare for this new level of existence. They continue to share their food and eat moderately, but they also start grooming themselves in a certain way, participating in certain ceremonies, or doing whatever they were instructed to do by the butterfly. (The other caterpillars might even begin to wonder what was going on with these "radicals." "What does grooming yourself in this manner have to do with being a good caterpillar?" some might ask. "Can't one be a good caterpillar without being a follower of Butterflianity?") These new rituals and practices would be for the caterpillars like the "theological virtues" (discussed below), for they are preparations for the lives of these creatures *as butterflies*. The caterpillars have been shown that, in addition to being mere caterpillars, they were called to participate in a higher level of existence.

In an analogous way, then, natural or moral virtues can only bring a person a certain degree of mortal or earthly happiness, but all men and women are called to live a higher, divine, and immortal life. The theological virtues are a necessary preparation for that life.

B3. The Theological Virtues

In his First Letter to the Corinthians, St. Paul discusses the various gifts that the Holy Spirit, the third person in the Christian Trinity, bestows upon men and women. In addition to various special gifts, such as the ability to teach others or the ability to preach the Good News, Paul mentions three primary gifts or virtues: faith, hope, and love (charity). Traditionally, these virtues have been known as the "theological virtues." In his *Summa Theologica*, St. Thomas Aquinas explains why they are given this title:

> [C]ertain additional principles must be given by God to man by which he can thus be ordered to supernatural happiness. ... These additional principles are called theological virtues: first, because they have God as their object, inasmuch as by them we are rightly ordered to God; secondly, because they are infused in us by God alone; and finally, because these virtues are made known to us only by divine revelation in Sacred Scripture.[7]

First, unlike the natural virtues, such as temperance or justice, the theological virtues are ordered to God; broadly speaking, they are faith *in God*, hope *in God*, and love *of God*. When we have attained them, we are beginning our preparation for our eternal existence with Him.

Second, we cannot simply attain these virtues in the way we can attain the natural ones. One does not acquire faith in God in the way one learns how to eat moderately or to give money in the proper way, viz., by human effort or habituation. The theological virtues require God's grace as well as a human willingness to accept this grace. St. Thomas and the *Catechism* use the word "infuse" to indicate that God puts these virtues into people who are willing or suitably disposed to accept them.

Third, these virtues are "theological" because no one would have known about them unless God had revealed them to human beings. This is why pagans, such as Aristotle, did not include them in their list of virtues. Why would anyone hope for eternal life unless God had revealed this reality to believers? The natural world does not give anyone conclusive evidence for such a possibility.

B3a. Faith

Despite what some television evangelists might proclaim, Heaven and Hell are not physical locations, like Wentworth, Ohio, or Washington, DC. God the Father is not Someone we are liable to bump into in McDonalds, and the possibility of ever-lasting life is not something that scientists are going to be able to confirm or deny, contrary to what *The Weekly World News* might proclaim. If we could visit Heaven or Hell, we would no longer have faith that they exist; we would have seen them with our own eyes. Likewise, if we could sit down and have a Big Mac with God, the way we could with one of our friends, then we would no longer have *faith* that He exists; we would have seen Him with our own eyes. But because we are physical creatures, limited in knowledge and trapped in space and time, we are not capable of having direct knowledge of any of these things. In this life, we can only have faith in them.

As St. Paul states, "Faith is the assurance of things hoped for, *the conviction of things unseen*" (Heb. 11:1). Faith is the belief and conviction that God created us out of nothing, that Jesus was the Son of God, that he rose from the dead, that this life need not be the end of our lives, and that all that God has revealed to us through Scripture and the Church is true.

Faith is always listed as the first of the theological virtues because it is the *beginning* of our journey to our ultimate good, an eternal and loving union with God. We cannot love or put hope in something unless we first believe that that something exists; only after Jesus has revealed that eternal life awaits His followers and we have accepted this promise *on faith* can we actively hope for this future outcome and begin to plan our lives accordingly. God has provided us with a spiritual roadmap that provides directions on how to live our lives and how to prepare ourselves for the gift of eternal life and union with Him. But in order to follow, we must have *faith* that this map charts out the actual lay of the land.

B3b. Hope

In a sense, faith is an issue of the head; through our will and our intellect, we *choose* to believe in the promises that Jesus has given us in Sacred Scripture. But a human being is not a Vulcan, like Spock on the television show *Star Trek*. Human beings are more than pure intellect; they have desires and aspirations that motivate them, as well. With the theological virtue of hope, the abstract promises laid out by the Church and Scripture begin to take hold of our hearts and motivate our activities.

Some people believe that there is life on other planets or that ghosts haunt houses, but neither of these beliefs really has any bearing on the way those people live their lives. Unless a person is performing seances in her living room in order to contact her dead relatives or is laboriously trying to build an interplanetary communicator in her garage, her life is completely unaffected by her faith in these sensational claims. Likewise, many Christians (as well as many non-Christians) are familiar with the Nicene Creed and, in particular, its last statement of faith: "We look for the resurrection of the dead, and the life of the world to come." If asked whether or not they believe or have faith in this statement, many will reply that they do believe in eternal life, but their reply may not have any emotional commitment behind it, like the belief many people have in ghosts or aliens. For Mother Teresa, however, who loved and cared for the victims of leprosy, AIDS, tuberculosis, and any number of deadly and contagious diseases in the poorest parts of the world—i.e., who was sur-rounded by death every moment of her life in a way most of us cannot even imag-ine—*belief in eternal life was as much of a motivation for her as a weekly paycheck is for most workers*. "People ask me about death and whether I look forward to it," she says in her book *A Simple Path*, "and I answer, 'Of course,' because I am going home. Dying is not the end, it is just the beginning."[8] As her life and work clearly demonstrated, Mother Teresa did not merely believe in an abstract way; she had real *hope*, granted to her by the grace of God, which breathed life into her every action.

B3c. Charity

"If I ... have not charity," says the Apostle Paul in his First Letter to the Corinthians, "I am nothing," and later in the same chapter of this letter, he adds, "[T]he greatest of the [theological virtues] is charity." Apparently, Paul thought char-ity was the greatest of all gifts one could possess. But what did he mean (and what does the Church mean) by "charity"? Why is it so important, more important than anything, even faith?

Today, whenever anyone hears the word "charity," he or she immediately thinks of giving away money or possessions to the poor, and though the word "charity" cer-tainly does have this meaning, the theological virtue of charity is much more than simply giving to the poor. Indeed, St. Paul even states that a person may give away everything that he owns and still not have the virtue of charity (I Cor. 13:3).

The theological virtue of charity is first and foremost "the virtue by which we love God above all things for his own sake."[9] In a sense, it is a type of friendship and love of God that is infused into and accepted by a person; as such, it is *the* real goal of human life and the source of eternal human happiness. If the word is understood in this sense, it is clear why St. Paul believes a person is nothing without charity and why charity, though the last in the order of the theological virtues, is the most important.

First, if charity is the true source of human happiness and the spiritual end of humanity, then a person who does not accept or strive for this virtue is like a man who plays the game of bowling thinking that the object of the game is to miss all of the pins. Charity is the object of the game of life. And secondly, though faith and hope come before charity in the order listed by St. Paul, they are only prior to charity in the order of generation, not in the order of importance. In other words, one must first have faith, before he can have hope, and hope before he can have charity. But faith and hope are *for the sake of* charity. A boy may know that an attractive young girl has moved into the house at the end of the street, and he may even have reason to hope that she likes him, too. But that knowledge and hope is nothing compared to a date with the girl or even becoming her boyfriend; his knowledge and hope is *for the sake of* acquiring a friendship with her.

If St. Paul is correct, the friendship and love that one can share with God is far greater than any relationship one could have with a person, even one's parents or that girl down the street. No one person in this life can possibly fulfill all of one's hopes and desires, but we believe by faith that friendship with God will ultimately lead to supreme and everlasting happiness, a happiness beyond our wildest dreams. As Paul states, "[N]o eye has seen, nor ear heard, nor the heart of man conceived, what God has prepared for those who love him" (I Cor. 2:9).

B4. Theological Virtues and Ethics

After becoming familiar with the nature of the theological virtues, however, one may still be baffled or, at least, unclear as to the relationship between the theological virtues and the natural ones. "So Christians have this extra set of virtues that deal with God. So what? What difference do these extra virtues make to our everyday lives? Couldn't it even be the case that Christians, who have their head in the clouds, are less moral than other people who have both of their feet squarely on the ground?"

According to the Catholic Church, not only is charity an extra virtue, alongside all of the other virtues like faith, temperance, courage, etc., but it is also *the form of all the virtues.*[10] What the Church means by this statement is that once a person acquires a genuine and loving relationship with God, all of the other natural virtues become perfected; charity purifies all of the natural virtues, puts them in their proper order, and creates harmony between them. (Indeed, the real question we, as Christians, should be asking is *not* "What difference does a relationship with God make to ethics?" but, rather, "What difference does ethics make to our relationship with God?" In other words, charity is the ultimate goal of human life, and the natural virtues are only important because of the role they play in this relationship.)

In order to illustrate this rather abstract idea that charity and the other theological virtues "perfect" the natural virtues, three concrete examples of this "perfecting" ability will be given.

B4a. Faith, Hope, and Temperance

One of the most popular slogans of the late eighties, made famous by Bo Jackson of the Los Angeles Raiders and the Kansas City Royals, was "Just Do It!" And in many areas of life, sheer willpower and guts is enough to overcome laziness and get the job done. But Christians recognize the power of sin in life, and very often, a person acting alone is not able to do what she needs to do. People become enslaved by their habits and passions, and sometimes, the gravity of sin is simply too much for a person left to her own devices to overcome. Such is the problem with alcoholics.

For most people, the ability to achieve the virtue of temperance (the virtue in regard to food, drink, and sex) is the result of good habit-formation; from their days as a self-indulgent little baby to their years as an adult, most people have fought the temptations that bombard every adult in a pleasure-saturated culture. But alcoholics, for whatever reason, have become enslaved by their desire for alcohol; they cannot stop drinking on their own.

What is interesting to note is that Alcoholics Anonymous, the most successful organization in the world that deals with treating alcoholism, centers its 12-step recovery programs around the notions of faith and hope. After admitting that they are "powerless over alcohol—that their lives had become unmanageable," members of AA acknowledge that "a Power greater than [them]selves [can] restore [them] to sanity." Then, they turn their wills and lives over to the care of this "Higher Power" and pray for continued strength, understanding, and perseverance.

B4b. Hope and Courage

One of the natural virtues that Aristotle mentioned and that everyone recognizes is courage. Aristotle understood it as a mean between cowardice—i.e., having too much fear—and foolhardiness or rashness—i.e., having too little fear. Of course, there have been a great many courageous people in the world who have not been religious, but it seems to be indisputable that the theological virtue of hope can strengthen or perfect the natural virtue of courage. Indeed, many libraries could be devoted to the extraordinary courage that saints and martyrs have shown in the hope that God's promises of love and eternal life are true. St. Stephen, one of the seven helpers chosen by the Apostles, was stoned to death for preaching Jesus' message, but we are told that he never stopped preaching the message, even as the stones reigned down upon him (Acts 7:56-60); St. Edmund Campion, a Jesuit scholar at Oxford University in the 16th century, was persecuted, mocked, beaten, and eventually drawn and quartered but never lost his hope that Christ's promises of eternal life would be fulfilled; nor did St. Peter ever discontinue preaching the gospel of Jesus Christ even though he was imprisoned in Rome and eventually, as legend has it, crucified upside down during the reign of Emperor Nero.

But one does not need to go so far back in history to see feats of courage motivated and sustained by Christian hope. Fr. Richard Malloy, SJ, who teaches anthropology at St. Joseph's University in Philadelphia and also preaches at Holy Name parish in Camden, New Jersey, had a confrontation with drug dealers in 1994. After a young drug dealer was murdered in Camden, some of his friends—who were also dealers—commissioned an artist to paint a mural of this young man on the side of a building near the Church. Though in some misguided way the young men were trying to grieve for the loss of their friend, Fr. Malloy recognized the danger in such a mural; the children of Camden, who live in poverty, do not need to have the life of drug dealing glorified. He feared that, without much hope of bettering their situation, many children might believe that dying in a gun fight and having a mural devoted to them may be the best life (and death) they could expect. But Fr. Malloy knew otherwise. Armed with a roller and a can of paint, he covered up this mural, with full knowledge that he was putting himself in great danger. Indeed, shortly afterward, a death threat appeared overtop of Fr. Malloy's paint job. In the end, he met with the young men, and they figured out an appropriate way to mourn the loss of their friends and all of the people who have lost their lives to drugs in Camden. Such courage is rarely found, but Fr. Malloy's was certainly bolstered by his faith and hope in Christ's message that love conquers everything.

B4c. Charity and Loving One's Neighbor

In the foregoing section, "charity" was defined as first and foremost "the theological virtue by which we love God above all things for his own sake," but moreover the *Catechism* states that it is also the virtue "by which we love … our neighbor as ourselves for the love of God."[11] What in the world does it mean to "love our neighbors … for the love of God"? Understanding what this means also helps one understand why "charity" is almost always meant as "helping our neighbors" or "giving to charity."

A Sister Dolores of Mother Theresa's Missionaries of Charity explains this further meaning of charity in the following manner:

> There is only one love and this is the love of God. Once we love God deeply enough we will love our neighbor to the same extent because, as we grow in our love for God, we grow to respect all that He has created and to recognize and appreciate all the gifts He has given us. Then naturally we want to take care of all of them.[12]

In some way, Sister Dolores is able to love all people *because* she loves God. Likewise, Mother Teresa speaks about the unborn children of the world in these words:

> Unborn children are among the poorest of the poor. They are so close to God. I always ask doctors at hospitals in India never to kill an unborn child. If there is no one who wants it, I'll take it. I see God in the eyes of every child—every unwanted child is welcomed by us. We then find homes for these children through adoption.[13]

Again, through charity, understood as the love of God, Mother Teresa is able to give charity, understood as the love of one's neighbor.

Does this love of neighbor, which is obviously very real in these women, make sense? One good way to understand how the love of God can result in the love of God's children is to look at human relationships. Though it may not be easy to explain, our love for certain people does naturally spread onto other people with whom those people are associated. "Any friend of so-and-so's is a friend of mine." When a woman has a baby, everyone in her family immediately loves and cares for this child *because the child belongs to their sister/daughter*. When good friends, who have known each other for decades, get a chance to meet each other's children, a natural love for those children arises simply *because the child belongs to the good friend*. Indeed, imagine how much respect, attention, and devotion all of humanity would receive if each person regarded every other person as the child of his or her sister or best friend. This is the way Sister Dolores, Mother Theresa, and countless other Christians view their neighbors, and it is this way of seeing people, through charity as God's children, that allows them to have the highest *moral* character.

C. CONCLUSION

Hopefully at this junction, the reader will have some knowledge of how the Catholic Church and other Christian churches understand the relationship between the natural virtues and ethics, on the one hand, and the theological virtues, on the other. In the sections of this chapter to follow, the lives and philosophies of a number of Christian theologians and saints will be studied in order to illustrate how deeply the theological virtues influence and perfect the natural virtues. Through a study of Dorothy Day, Jesuits Ignatius Loyola and Pedro Arrupe, Thomas More, and Martin Luther King, Jr. and their philosophies, the reader will be shown how the Christian faith enriches, perfects, and even surpasses the secular philosophies presented in the previous chapter.

SECTION HIGHLIGHTS

Unlike some more fundamentalist sects of Christianity, the Catholic Church recognizes that it is possible for non-religious people to achieve a certain level of virtue.

The Church believes in "Natural Law," the notion that every person has been granted a basic moral sense that allows him or her to discern what is right and wrong. Using reason alone, a person may often be doing God's will and not be aware of this fact.

The Church distinguishes between "natural" and "theological" virtues. Natural virtues perfect the purely human part of our nature. Theological virtues prepare and perfect the divine part of our nature; they prepare us for eternal life with God.

Faith, hope, and charity are the three main theological virtues. They are gifts from God that are infused into people, though people must freely accept these gifts, as well. They are not acquired through habit or human effort alone.

Faith is "the theological virtue by which we believe in God and believe all that he has said and revealed to us, and that the Holy Church proposes for our belief."[14] Hope is "the theological virtue by which we desire the kingdom of heaven and eternal life as our happiness, placing our trust in Christ's promises and relying not on our own strength, but on the help of the grace of the Holy Spirit."[15] Charity is "the theological virtue by which we love God above all things for his own sake, and our neighbor as ourselves for the love of God.[16]

The theological virtues perfect, unify, and harmonize the natural virtues.

QUESTIONS

To show that you understand the ideas presented in this section, answer the following questions in complete sentences on a separate sheet of paper.

1. The Catholic Church recognizes that it is possible for non-religious people to achieve a certain level of virtue. Why isn't this recognition a problem for or threat to Catholicism? Explain.

2. Explain in your own words what the point of the author's "caterpillar analogy" is. How does it illustrate the difference between natural and theological virtue?

3. What exactly does the Church mean by "charity"? How is it possible that our love for God could result in a love for our neighbor? Explain.

4. In this chapter, it was shown how faith, hope, and charity can influence and even perfect natural virtues; the examples of temperance, courage, and helping one's neighbor were used. Explain, using an example of your own, *another* way in which the theological virtues could perfect a different natural virtue.

5. Do you think that there might be a case in which one's obedience to the theological virtues—i.e., obedience to God—might require a person to do something that would not make any sense to Aristotle or someone who only recognized the natural, earthly virtues? Why or why not? Explain.

PART TWO:

LIVES ILLUSTRATING
THE DIFFERENCE CHRISTIAN BELIEF
MAKES TO ETHICS

This part of Chapter Three contains brief biological sketches of several notable Christians together with some of their writings and sayings. Your teacher may supplement these biographies with other research or he or she may choose to highlight entirely different Christians. In either case, the Christians chosen will serve to exemplify the difference that being a *Christian* makes to the ethical undertaking; in addition to a mastery of the natural virtues that Aristotle and others have described, these men and women will embody or write about the theological virtues that mark the life of a follower of Christ. We will see what difference Christianity made in their lives with respect to their overall worldview, with respect to the goals they set in their lives, and to the motivation they found for working courageously toward their goals even at the expense of enduring great personal suffering.

A.   ST. IGNATIUS LOYOLA

The founder of the "Society of Jesus," which is better known as "the Jesuit order," was a Basque nobleman born in the fifteenth century (1491 A.D.) to a family of the lower nobility of that region. Ignatius of Loyola, the thirteenth and youngest child of the Basque Onaz-Loyola clan, was born in his father's castle in the Basque Province of Guipuzcoa, located in the Pyrenees mountains between France and Spain. His baptismal name was "Inigo," a name that was Latinized to "Ignatius" by the officials at the University of Paris in 1534, and it is by this later name that he has come to be known.

At the age of 16, after both his parents had died, Ignatius was sent by his older brother to serve as a page (i.e., a youth in training to become a knight) to Juan Velazquez, the Treasurer of Castile, and after Velazquez' death, to the Duke of Najera, the Viceroy of the Province of Navarre. There he learned the art of war and the ideals of knightly service, and developed a very strong desire to please the ladies. Speaking in the third person about himself during this period, Ignatius wrote in his autobiography: "Up to his twenty-sixth year, he was a man given to worldly vanities, and having an overpowering desire to gain renown, he found delight in the exercise of arms."[17]

It was in service to the Duke of Najera in May 1521 that Ignatius' life took an unexpected turn. The French, with a large army, invaded the territory of Ignatius' master, the Duke, and sought to capture its principal city, Pamplona. A large segment of the Duke's much smaller army fled. But to Ignatius, flight appeared dishonorable. He chose to stay in the area, and not only that, he went to the city's fortress and persuaded the small garrison there to stand and fight. Before the battle, realizing that he would very likely die, Ignatius made his confession to one of his comrades. Shortly afterward, the battle and the bombardment began. On the third or fourth day, Ignatius, the mainstay of the resistance, was seriously wounded by a canon ball, which broke and crushed his right leg and also injured his left leg, though less seriously. With Ignatius down, the commander of the fortress surrendered.

After the manner of chivalry of those days, the French saw to it that Ignatius was carried back to his home. There, he nearly died from his wounds on June 29, 1521, but having confessed his sins and received communion, he began to rally. It would take him a long time to heal. As he began to get well with the help of local physicians, he saw that his knee bone was protruding and his right leg was shortened; thinking how ugly he would appear (to the ladies), he made the request that the protruding bone be sawed off (there was no such thing as anesthesia, in those days), and that the leg ligaments be stretched so that he could walk without a limp. This stretching would require that he be confined to bed for many months, but despite the protest and advice of his brother, Ignatius determined that he would undergo "the butchery" and prolonged confinement so that he would walk with grace and be able to charm the women he wished to charm.

Months in bed! Nothing to do! No T.V., no radio, no computer! So, as he lay recuperating, he asked to see the few books that were in the castle. (The printing press had just been invented. There were very few books in print at that time.) In the castle were only *The Life of Christ* by Ludolph and *Flos Sanctorum*, a book about saints. Ignatius began to read about Jesus and about the saints who followed Him, such as Dominic and Francis of Assisi. "I could do what they did," he seems to have thought. Ignatius, with his macho sense of competition, began to think about a different way of life than the one he had long envisioned for himself, i.e., the way of worldly knighthood. And suddenly, he had working inside of himself two opposing lines of imagination about his future: one of the chivalrous knight and lady's man; and the other, of a man who would dedicate himself to the service of God and Christ. He pursued both lines of imagining and noted how each affected him. His thoughts of knightly achievements and masculine conquests excited him, but in the end they left him feeling somehow empty. His thoughts of changing his life entirely, adopting a spirit of penance, and dedicating himself wholeheartedly to God and Jesus and their service, though initially repugnant to him, in the long run, left him with a feeling of peace. He pondered his choices and what course his life should follow. Then, finally, with the decisiveness and courage that had led him onto the ramparts of the fortress of Pamplona, he opted to change his way of life. He would go to Jerusalem as a penitent pilgrim and there place his life in the hands of God and Jesus.

In March 1522, Ignatius, now 31 years old, was sufficiently healed. Without telling his family of his decision, he set off for the port of Barcelona, Spain. The road there took him to the shrine of Mary on Montserrat. There he bought a pair of sandals, a pilgrim's staff, and a long tunic (outer garment) made of rough sack-cloth. On the eve of the Feast of the Annunciation, dressed now in his pilgrim's clothes, he gave away his fine clothes to a beggar and spent the night before the statue of Mary, kneeling and standing in prayer, in a knightly vigil of arms. At daybreak, leaving his sword and his dagger hanging on the wall in the chapel, he asked Mary to intercede for him with her Son. (He was "Our Lady's knight" now!) Ignatius resumed his journey to Barcelona.

Next, on the way to Barcelona, he stopped at the town of Manresa. There he found a cave where he prayed, intending to spend three days. However, he ended up spending ten months. It was at Manresa that his spiritual warfare and his spiritual education began in earnest. He would pray for seven hours a day, work several hours in a hospital, helping the sick, and then beg humbly for his food. There he had both wonderful and terrible visions, and many very difficult struggles. There he came, finally, to understand the deep mysteries of God, was convinced of God's great love for him and for all of humanity, and came to an understanding of how God works with people. Much of his understanding came because he learned, with God's help, how to read the movements of the spirits working inside him. Providentially, Ignatius recorded in a journal much of his experience and a number of his insights. This journal has come to be published as *The Spiritual Exercises of St. Ignatius*. It is a book meant to be, not so much a journal of truths, as a set of exercises that enable a person to have an encounter with the living God so that assisted by a "director," the person may read correctly his or her own spiritual experiences and discover the way that God wishes the person to walk. Ignatius' distinctive, holy, and lifelong desire to be a "helper of souls," i.e., to help others find God for themselves, originated at Manresa where many of the townspeople, recognizing the holiness of this "poor man," began to seek him out to help them find God's will for them.

In February 1523, Ignatius left the town of Manresa, traveled to Barcelona, sailed from there to Rome, then to Venice, then on to Jerusalem, which he reached on September 4. With much devotion, he visited many of the sites where Jesus had walked and taught and suffered. However, his stay in the Holy Land was much shorter than he wished. Because of the tensions between the Muslims and the Christians, he was not permitted to stay and was sent back to Europe by the Franciscan who was the superior of all the Christians in that region.

So he returned to Venice and then to Barcelona. By this time, he had determined that he would become a priest, so that he might better "help souls" discover God's love for themselves and realize how they could best serve the cause of Ignatius' new "Lord," Jesus Christ. For Ignatius, assisting a soul meant helping a person to rediscover the peace, sense of love, justice, and compassion that had been lost when people had been seduced by the spirit of evil into allegiance to a false philosophy of selfish desire—greed, lust, and cruel power—and drawn away from the true philosophy that Jesus had preached in God's name and had embodied in Himself—a philosophy of generosity, altruistic love, and humble service.

So, back in Barcelona, Ignatius began his studies for the priesthood by sitting in on classes with young boys so that he could learn the grammar he would need to study philosophy and theology. There is a much more to tell in his story, but suffice it to say that after he learned grammar, he went to other universities in Spain—Alcala and

Salamanca—to study philosophy and theology, and finally to the most famous university of that day, the University of Paris. It was in Paris that he met the men who would become the first Jesuits; Francis Xavier (an outstanding athlete as well as a very bright man) is the best known of these men. Each of these men recognized Ignatius' mastery of the spiritual life and his closeness to God; and to each, he was able to give the *Spiritual Exercises* that he had written down.

In 1534, these men together with Ignatius took vows of chastity and poverty, and decided to place themselves at the service of the Pope, who could direct them to go wherever they would be of the most help to others. On June 24, 1537, Ignatius and four of these friends were ordained priests. Some months later, after much prayer together, the group decided to form a religious order. They went to Pope Paul III with a written proposal, and this proposal was formally accepted on September 27, 1540. When asked how they would be called, they answered that they wished merely to be referred to as "Companions of Jesus." ("Jesuits" seems to be the diminutive form of Jesus—"little Jesuses"—and may have been coined derogatorily.)

Despite his own objections and his vote against himself, Ignatius Loyola was chosen to be head of this group by vote of his companions. He would write their rules of life, and he would work with the Pope to send them wherever there was need to "help souls." Ignatius sent his closest friend, Francis Xavier, to India and then to Japan, never to see him again, though they wrote to each other many times. This new group became a new entity in the Church, a religious order not bound to communal recitation of "the Office" (the well-developed formulas of prayer for morning, noon, evening, and nightfall recited each day in common by orders like the Benedictines). Rather they would focus their energy on a readiness to go anywhere in the world where there was special need of persons to "help souls." The new order was to be "a priestly order," though the group would include "brothers" who would not serve as priests but do work that would itself be "priestly" (give retreats or teach in schools) or would aid priests in their ministry.

Throughout the remainder of his life, Ignatius Loyola spent his time in Rome, writing most carefully the rules for the order he inspired and directing the many men who came to work for the goals of the order he founded. Each of these men would do the *Spiritual Exercises* that Ignatius had recorded; these would be the source of their vision and of their understanding of the ways of God, and often they would be the tools by which the men would help men and women to find God's will for their lives, the path by which they—lay and cleric, Catholic and non-Catholic—could best serve God and Christ with their personal talents. When Ignatius died in 1556 at the age of 65, he had a reputation for practical mysticism and was revered as a person close to God.

From his life and his *Spiritual Exercises*, we learn how Ignatius differs from Aristotle and the philosophers described in Chapter Two with respect to outlook on life and manner of making moral decisions. First of all, he is convinced that God is the creator of the world and that all of life is to be lived so that God can be glorified and His will done; earth is but a preparation for eternal life after death. As Ignatius wrote in one of his most important fundamental exercises:

> God freely created us so that we might know, love, and serve Him in this
> life and be happy with God forever. God's purpose in creating us is to draw
> forth from us a response of love and service here on earth, so that we might
> attain our goal of everlasting happiness in heaven. All things in this world,
> then, are gifts of God, created for us, to be the means by which we can
> come to know God better, love God more surely, and serve God more
> faithfully.[18]

Ignatius' view of human life then is very God-centered. And this viewpoint
relativizes many of the "goods" of human life; for he goes on to say:

> As a result, we ought to appreciate and use these gifts of God insofar as
> they help us toward our goal of loving service and union with God. But
> insofar as any created things hinder our progress toward our goal, we ought
> to let them go. In everyday life, then we should keep ourselves indifferent
> or undecided in the face of all created gifts when we have an option and
> we do not have the clarity of what would be the better choice. And in
> such situations, we ought not to be led on by our natural likes and dislikes,
> even in matters such as health or sickness, wealth or poverty, living in the
> east or in the west, becoming an accountant or a lawyer. Rather, our only
> desire and our choice in every life situation should always be that decision
> which will lead us to the goal for which God created us.[19]

So, in the view of Ignatius Loyola, God might want me to risk sickness or endure
death for the sake of some worthy cause, much as martyrs for the faith (e.g., Thomas
More) or for justice (e.g., Archbishop Oscar Romero, the religious sisters and Jesuits
killed in El Salvador, or Martin Luther King, Jr.) did. God might want me to give up
the chance to be an outstanding physician if I could do something greater as Fr. Pedro
Arrupe did, who became a missionary to Japan. He might want me to be willing to
suffer the unjust loss of my material possessions, as did many people who stood up to
injustice in Nazi Germany or to dictatorships in Latin America or Africa. In Ignatius'
view, someone who believed in God and in the justice of God would be willing to
undergo all these deprivations if he saw that by doing so, he could make the world a
better place, and thus honor God.

In Ignatius' view then, this world is a place in which sin occurs and mars the
good order God intended to have here. Therefore, God sent Jesus to help draw people
away from the evil spirit of selfishness. Jesus is Ignatius' hero, the Lord and King, to
whom he pledges his life. He sees Jesus leading us all to freedom in this life and
ultimately to the joy of eternal life with God and doing this in a very concrete way.
Jesus invites us to companionship with Him, to labor with Him, to take the same food
and the same risks and to suffer the same discomforts that He did, with the absolute

assurance of final victory for those who do not desert. This leader did not have to suffer, but He chose to do so out of love for us. Ignatius asks then, "Who would refuse to follow such a leader?"

Ignatius sees clearly that Jesus' strategy is quite the opposite of that of the Spirit of Evil. Evil teaches men and women to be selfish, first by ensnaring them to be seduced by riches (greed), then by the desire for honor ("Make me more important than others"), and finally by pride ("I am *better* than everyone else, even the so-called 'God'"). Jesus, however, motivates people to be willing to let go of the desire to be rich and motivates them to be willing to give up material goods so as to help others. He also draws people to be willing to suffer insults as He did for the sake of justice and peace and love (e.g., people who have stood up against public bigotry and injustice against minorities, as Jesus did). He draws people to be genuinely humble and to serve others, as He did. These are the strategies Ignatius sees Jesus proposing so as to make a better and happier world and to encourage people to live so that they may finally join in the eternal life of God.

It is very clear that the inspirational model for this ethical quest for Ignatius Loyola is Jesus, who is God come down to live and suffer with us. No king, no lord has given more for the cause he asks his friends to believe in than Jesus did. Other leaders can command their troops to be valiant; for Ignatius, his leader said, "Follow me; I won't ask you to suffer more than I will suffer in your place. But I need your help."

Ignatius Loyola is the first of several Christians we will study to see what Christianity adds to the ethical quest. Let us look now at what we can learn about the Christian "difference" from the lives of several other well-known Christian heroes.

B.   DOROTHY DAY

Dorothy Day has been called "the most significant, interesting, and influential person in the history of American Catholicism."[20] For many people, Day was an enigma; she just did not fit into any of the common categories. Though she endeared herself to communists by railing against the abuses of capitalism, she infuriated them with her singular devotion to Christ and her pacifism. Though she endeared herself to liberals by advocating the cause of the poor and the dispossessed, she alienated them by refusing to rely on the federal or state government for assistance in this endeavor. In some ways, her Catholicism could not have been more conservative; she strictly adhered to some traditional Catholic positions, such as the Medieval ban on "usury," i.e., the practice of charging interest on loans. But at the same time, she rejected some mainstream Catholic positions; for example, she unequivocally condemned the "just war" theory as being incompatible with the Gospels. Day once declared that her mission was "to comfort the afflicted and to afflict the comfortable," and she certainly followed through with her declaration. Always her own woman, Day was never far from controversy throughout the course of her life, and even today, the question as to whether or not she should be declared a saint is passionately debated within the Catholic Church.

However, there is no debate over the fact that Day devoted her life to the poor and forgotten members of American society and that her theological virtues of faith, hope, and charity were, at bottom, the ultimate moving force behind this devotion.

Day was born in Brooklyn on November 8, 1897 but grew up in Chicago, and from an early age she felt a deep need to identify and rectify the injustices in the world. As a child she was moved by such great works as Upton Sinclair's *The Jungle*, which recounted the horrible working conditions in the meatpacking plants in Chicago. In her autobiography, *The Long Loneliness*, Day recounts the way this book shaped her social conscience:

> [T]hough my only experience of the destitute was in books, the very fact that *The Jungle* was about Chicago where I lived, whose streets I walked, made me feel that from then on my life was to be linked to theirs, their interests were to be mine; I had received a call, a vocation, a direction to my life.[21]

Additionally, Day was attracted to the literature and lives of many socialist and communist writers and activists, such as Eugene V. Debs and Karl Marx, who called attention to the injustices suffered by the working class or "proletariat." Authors such as Marx highlighted evils such as child labor, the de-humanization of factory workers, the exploitation of women in the workplace, and the lack of economic and political power of the working class. While an undergraduate, Day joined the socialist party at the University of Illinois at Urbana, and after graduation, she began a career as a reporter in New York City, first for *The Call*, a socialist daily newspaper, and then for *The Masses*, a magazine run by a loose affiliation of socialists, anarchists, pacifists, and liberals of nearly every bent. Among these radical groups, Day found a natural outlet for her love of social justice.

But also from an early age, Day had a deep religious sense, which found a natural outlet in Christianity, especially Catholicism. In her autobiography, Day recalls being introduced to a life of a saint by the mother of her friend Mary Harrington and immediately being taken with this saint's singular devotion and heroic virtue:

> ... I do remember one particular occasion when [Mary's mother] talked to me about the life of some saint. I do not know what saint it was, and I cannot remember any of the incidents of the life; I only remember my feeling of lofty enthusiasm, and how my heart almost burst with desire to take part in such high endeavor.[22]

Day saw the life of the saint as a thrilling "spiritual adventure,"[23] as she put it, and this life would remain with her as an ideal for the rest of her life. Additionally, she enjoyed attending services with her family at the local Episcopal church, especially hearing the Psalms recited. Moreover, even as a child, Day was acutely aware of the presence of God in the natural world:

> If only I could sing, I thought, I would shout before the Lord, and call upon the world to shout with me, 'All ye works of the Lord, bless ye the Lord, praise Him and glorify Him forever.' My idea of heaven became one of fields and meadows, sweet with flowers and songs and melodies unutterable, in which even the laughing gull and the waves on the shore would play their part.[24]

And as would be expected in a budding journalist and avid reader, Day would often write of God in her diary and enjoy reading the Bible, as well as Russian authors such as Leo Tolstoy and Fyodor Dostoevsky who wrote about Christian themes.

However, until she reached her mid-30s, Day found herself torn between these two loves; in particular, she could not reconcile, what she believed to be, the otherworldly emphasis of Catholicism with the pressing worldly needs of the poor and marginalized. She simply did not see the Church as an advocate for the poor. Reflecting on her college years, Day wrote:

> I felt at the time that religion would impede my work. I wanted to have nothing to do with the religion of those whom I saw all about me. I felt that I must turn from it as from a drug. I felt it indeed to be an opiate of the people and not a very attractive one, so I hardened my heart. It was a conscious and deliberate process.[25]

Yet, try as she might to suppress her natural religious inclinations, Day was not able to sever her connection to God and the Catholic Church. For example, even though she had aligned herself with various Marxist and socialist movements—all avowedly atheist—she often would slip away to St. Joseph's Catholic Church after her long days of work at *The Call* or *The Masses* in New York City.

Indeed, more than anything else, it was Day's religious convictions that led her to end her common-law marriage to Forster Batterham, a biologist who was opposed to the institution of marriage and regarded religion as a destructive superstition. Day shared his love of the natural world and respected his intellect, but she could not deny her religious vocation. Prior to her common-law marriage to Batterham, Day had had a brief affair with a journalist when she was a nurse trainee in a Brooklyn hospital. She became pregnant, and fearing that the baby would ruin her budding relationship, she procured an abortion, an event that haunted her throughout the rest of her life. For a time, she worried that God would never again bless her with the grace of parenthood. Thus, when she conceived a daughter, Tamar, to Batterham, she expressed the deepest gratitude to God and vowed that her daughter would be baptized and raised in the Catholic Church. Shortly after this decision, she and Batterham went their separate ways.

Now resolutely embracing Catholicism, Day sought some way to wed her Catholicism with her passion for social justice. When she met Peter Maurin, a dynamic, former Christian Brother who embraced voluntary poverty, she finally found that way. Emphasizing the teachings of the Sermon on the Mount and Jesus' identification with the poor, Maurin showed Day that the Gospels could be revolutionary "dynamite" if properly understood. Maurin had a plan for a society "where it would be easier for men to be good."[26] He argued that every parish in America (and beyond) should have "Houses of Hospitality" that would feed, clothe, and house the destitute; that people needed to engage in more discussion about substantive issues such as war, poverty, and faith; that Americans should renounce capitalism, with its emphasis upon materialism and individualism, and embrace self-sufficient farming communes; and that, incidentally, Day should start a newspaper that deals with issues of social justice. Though initially hesitant to embrace Maurin's vision, Day eventually came on board, and the Catholic Worker movement was born.

Armed with little more than an old typewriter, Day set to work writing articles that addressed issues of urban poverty, industrialization, and the plight of the worker in general. Within a few short months, Day and Maurin's newspaper, *The Catholic Worker*, was being read by over 100,000 people. Word quickly spread about the Catholic Worker movement, and before Day and Maurin knew what had hit them, the poor were knocking on their office doors asking for food, clothing, and shelter. In this spontaneous fashion, the first House of Hospitality was born. Today, there are over 185 such houses throughout the United States and abroad.

Yet, Day did not want her readership merely to rely on parishes or charitable organizations to perform such corporal works of mercy as feeding the hungry and sheltering the homeless; she advocated a "personalist" approach to social justice, an approach that called upon every individual—as opposed to the federal or state government—to fulfill his Christian obligation to love his neighbor. For example, following Maurin, Day called upon her readers to set aside a "Christ Room" in their homes, a custom practiced by earlier generations of Christians. Day explains:

> In every house then, a room was kept ready for any stranger who might ask for shelter; it was even called "the stranger's room"; and this not because these people … could trace something of someone they loved in the stranger who used it, not because the man or woman to whom they gave shelter reminded them of Christ, but because—plain and simple and stupendous fact—he *was* Christ.[27]

When Jesus told his disciples, "[W]hatsoever you do to the least of people, that you do unto me" (Mt. 25:40), Day took him literally, and she enjoined her readers to do the same. To the world, the notion of setting aside a Christ Room in one's house is sheer folly. As one of Day's correspondents who was robbed when she took in a stranger could testify,[28] there is nothing sentimental, charming, or simple about instituting a Christ Room. Many men are dangerous, filthy, lewd, dishonest, lazy, inebriated, high, or armed. How could one see Christ in such people? To embrace such people seems foolish to the world, but armed with the theological virtues of faith, hope, and especially charity, Day was happy to be a fool for Christ.

Throughout her life, Day continued to be a fervent advocate for the poor and oppressed throughout the United States. From California, where she joined Cesar Chavez's United Farm Workers' Union (UFWU) in their fight to renew the contracts of immigrant farm workers, to Georgia, where she visited Koinonia—a racially integrated Christian agricultural community—she offered her love and support, often at great risk. At Koinonia, for example, Day found herself under attack from Ku Klux Klan members, who had burnt crosses on community grounds and fired machine-guns at community houses. While manning a sentry post at the community, Day came under fire, and had it not been for a steering column in front of her face, she would probably have been killed. Moreover, like such saints as Paul and Thomas More, Day was no stranger to prison. In California with the UFWU, Day spent nearly two weeks in prison for joining the mass protests against the growers. And in New York, Day went to prison three times between 1956 and 1959 for refusing to participate in the state's annual civil defense drill. During this time, New York state tried to prepare the citizenry for a possible nuclear war. When a siren was sounded, the citizens were required to go through with the drill; for example, students would curl up under their desks to protect themselves. Day objected to such rehearsals for war on the grounds that she would in no way contribute to the illusion that a nuclear war could be won, that a nuclear war could be just, or that financing a nuclear arsenal could be morally justified.

As one would imagine, Day, who prided herself on carrying out her mission to "afflict the comfortable," cared very little about receiving recognition for her acts of charity. "Too much praise makes you feel you must be doing something terribly wrong,"[29] she once noted. But nonetheless, toward the end of her life, she did receive a great deal of recognition for her life, works of mercy, and writings. Various publications, such as *Newsweek*, *Life*, and *America*, featured profiles on her, and the University of Notre Dame bestowed on her the Laetare Medal, the oldest and most prestigious award given to American Catholics. (Later winners of this medal included novelist Walker Percy, Cardinal Joseph Bernadin, and noted death penalty abolitionist Sister Helen Prejean, CSJ). Additionally, when she was too feeble to travel, Day was visited by Mother Teresa, founder of the Missionary Sisters of Charity; earlier in Day's life, Mother Teresa had made Day an honorary member of the order by pinning on her the order's cross.

Dorothy Day died November 29, 1980, and she remains a controversial figure inside Catholic circles; in particular, the debate rages as to whether or not she should be canonized. Some object to Day's canonization by noting that she had an abortion early in life, forgetting that St. Paul actively persecuted Christians prior to his conversion. Others object that she had a common-law marriage to Batterham for a number of years and brought a child into this sinful union, forgetting that St. Augustine lived under the same arrangement for a much longer period of time and fathered a child out of wedlock. As for Day herself, at times she shunned the notion of becoming a saint, fearing that such a title might make people regard her less seriously; to many, saints are quaint, beloved, and revered, but they are not usually seen as social revolutionaries. But at other times, Day openly declared, "We are all called to be saints ... and we might as well get over our bourgeois fear of it."[30] The actual process of canonization is complicated, involving thorough examination by Church officials who use a variety of criteria. But if we accept Lawrence S. Cunningham's description of a saint, then there is little doubt that, indeed, Day was one:

> A saint is a person so grasped by a religious vision that it becomes central to his or her life in a way that radically changes the person and leads others to glimpse the value of that vision.[31]

C.   MARTIN LUTHER KING, JR.

Few, if any, individuals have had as great and positive an impact on 20th century America as Dr. Martin Luther King, Jr. Though King himself was aware of the dangers of drawing attention to oneself—what he called "the drum major instinct"[32]—no honest person can deny the distinctive place that King occupies in American history. More so than any other person, King helped to elevate the economic, social, and psychological condition of African Americans, a group that has labored under prejudice and deprivation throughout their history in this country. As a tribute to this accomplishment, nearly every city in America now has a boulevard or avenue named after King, and the nation as a whole now celebrates his birthday every January. But more importantly for our purposes here, there are few men in recent history whose lives, works, and writings illustrate the way that theological virtues should inform, motivate, and perfect the natural ones the way that King's life, works, and writings do.

Born the son of a Baptist preacher on January 15, 1929, King, named after the Protestant reformer Martin Luther, had religious impulses right from the start. Indeed, even before graduating from Morehouse College, King received a license to preach and became an assistant to his father at Ebenezer Baptist Church, arguably the most prominent African-American church in Atlanta, Georgia at that time. But because his father protected him so well from the outrages of Southern racism and chose not to discuss racism at length, Martin did not immediately seek concrete steps to achieve racial justice in America. Of course, as a youth, he was deeply conscious of the horrors of segregation, having experienced them firsthand. But, as King recounts in his intellectual biography, "Pilgrimage to Nonviolence," "Not until I entered theological seminary ... did I begin a serious intellectual quest for a method to eliminate social evil."[33]

At Crozer Theological Seminary in Chester, Pennsylvania, King encountered the writings of various theologians and religious leaders who emphasized the social responsibility that is entailed by being a Christian. One particularly powerful influence on King was a work by Walter Rauschenbusch, a Baptist minister who worked with the poor and was a voice for industrial workers in New York City. King described the central insight he took from Rauschenbusch's *Christianity and the Social Crisis* in the following way:

> The gospel at its best deals with the whole man, not only his soul but his body, not only his spiritual well-being, but his material well-being. Any religion that professes to be concerned with the souls of men and is not concerned about the slums that damn them, the economic conditions that strangle them and the social conditions that cripple them is a spiritually moribund religion awaiting burial.[34]

Works such as Rauschenbusch's and those of other theologians such as Reinhold Niebuhr and Paul Tillich helped King to realize that, in order for Christianity to be a truly living religion, it must actively seek to bring about the Kingdom of God *here on earth*. But now the question for King was *how* to bring about this Kingdom in segregated America.

As is well known, the answer to King's question came from Jesus of Nazareth himself and Mahatma Gandhi, the Indian philosopher, spiritual leader, and revolutionary whose campaign of nonviolent resistance eventually led to the peaceful withdrawal of the British from India. As King notes, "Christ furnished the spirit and motivation while Gandhi provided the method."[35]

Behind all of King's successful campaigns of nonviolent resistance lay the Christian notion of *agape*—"God's love" or what St. Thomas Aquinas would call the theological virtue of charity. In an article entitled "An Experiment in Love," King describes this divine kind of love:

> [*Agape*] is the love of God operating in the human heart ... *Agape* is disinterested love. It is a love in which the individual seeks not his own good, but the good of his neighbor (1 Cor. 10:24). *Agape* does not begin by discriminating between worthy and unworthy people, or any qualities people possess. It begins by loving others *for their sakes*. It is an entirely "neighbor-regarding concern for others," which discovers the neighbor in every man it meets. Therefore, *agape* makes no distinction between friends and enemies; it is directed toward both.[36]

In this passage, one sees quite clearly the concrete way in which the theological virtue of charity motivated King's ethical quest for racial justice. Because King saw all of his fellow men and women as having the same Father in heaven and, thus, saw all men and women as being brothers and sisters, he was motivated to seek what was best for *everyone*, both the oppressed African Americans *and their white oppressors*. Just as Jesus made no distinction between friends and enemies when he preached, "But I say to you, Love your enemies and pray for those who persecute you, so that you may be sons of your Father who is in heaven" (Mt. 6:44), King made no distinction either, for he was motivated by Christian charity. Armed with this fundamental Christian way of seeing and loving one's neighbor and with the tactics of nonviolent resistance that he learned from Gandhi, King was ready to transform the fallen world he saw before him.

After graduating from Crozer, King became pastor of Dexter Baptist church in Montgomery, Alabama, and soon after, he was able to begin his nonviolent campaign against segregation. On December 1, 1955, Rosa Parks refused to move to the back of a Montgomery bus when a white bus driver ordered her to give way to a white customer who had just boarded. "It was a matter of dignity;" Parks later recalled, "I could not have faced myself and my people if I had moved."[37]

Parks was arrested and released on bond, but had determined to stand and fight against the Alabama bus segregation law. E.D. Nixon, the informal leader of the Montgomery African-American community, decided to back her with a bus boycott and phoned King, asking for his endorsement from the pulpit and asking if Dexter Baptist could be used as a launching site for the boycott. Meeting at Dexter, the group chose King to be the spokesperson for the protest committee.

From this point, King's life took a course that would lead him to glory and, eventually, martyrdom. On December 5, 1955, the boycott officially began. As King anticipated, though, the forces of segregation and the status quo were not about to give up so easily. At every stage of the boycott, King and his fellow protesters faced adversity. For example, on January 26, 1956, as he picked up protestors who were walking to their jobs, King was arrested and imprisoned in Montgomery City Jail on the frivolous charge of "speeding thirty miles in a twenty-five mile an hour zone." Four days later, a bomb was thrown onto his front porch. Providentially, no one was injured, but this incident led King's father to try to persuade him to withdraw from his political endeavors for the sake of his own life and the lives of his family members. And the violence and threats of violence continued. But King would not yield. Surrounded by all of this turmoil, King prayed deeply and experienced a real awareness of an "inner voice" empowering him to meet whatever challenge lay ahead. Because of his *faith* that, in matters of good and evil, God is not neutral and because of his *hope* that God would rescue his poor and oppressed people—as He had throughout history—King was able to persevere. "And so here in Montgomery," King summarized, "after more than eleven long months, we can walk and never get weary, because we know there is a great camp meeting in the promised land of freedom and justice."[38]

The boycott continued, and things continued to look bleak. Using a 1921 statue, a grand jury was preparing a criminal indictment against the leaders of the committee for promoting a boycott "without just cause or legal excuse." King was booked again but immediately released until his trial. As the boycott continued, Montgomery city officials petitioned a state court for an injunction banning the car pool system as "an unlicensed municipal system of transportation." The request was granted. All looked lost, but then came the unexpected! On November 13, 1956, the Supreme Court of the United States affirmed the decision of a three-judge panel that Alabama's segregation laws were unconstitutional. The case against bus segregation was won, and for King, this was a victory for everyone, both the victims of segregation as well as their oppressors. Reconciliation of the human family was always his ultimate earthly objective.

This account of the Montgomery boycott is but one episode in the struggle for civil rights, for justice and reconciliation, which would occupy Martin Luther King, Jr., until his death. There would be many other tragic and difficult episodes—the Freedom Rides, the killing and maiming of children and innocent people standing up for their right to vote and to have fair public accommodations and fair opportunities for education, the scheming of prominent national politicians seeking their own advantage at the expense of justice, the machinations of J. Edgar Hoover and the FBI against King and other civil rights leaders. But there also would be the high moments and the great achievements such as the integration of schooling in the South, the March on Washington, and his great "I Have a Dream" speech which sketched a vision of a new and better world. Through it all, King suffered enormous strain, lived with the constant threat of violence, and sometimes fell into sinful personal indulgences, but overall he carried on bravely and would not give in to those from the white or the black community who preached hate and division; his dream and his strategy was the way of non-violence, of peace and brotherhood. It was the way, he believed, that Jesus had preached.

Did King have a premonition of his own death? He had been told of a bomb threat as he flew to Memphis to speak at a rally of the union of African-American city sanitary workers who were striking because of unfair treatment by that city's government. His last public words spoken at the Memphis rally seem prophetic:

> Well, I don't know what will happen now. We've got some difficult days ahead. But it doesn't matter with me now, because I've been to the mountaintop. And I don't mind. Like anybody, I would like to live a long life. Longevity has its place. But I'm not concerned about that now. I just want to do God's will. And He's allowed me to go up to the mountain, and I've looked over, and I've seen the Promised Land. I may not get there with you. But I want you to know tonight, that we, as a people, will get to the Promised Land. And so I'm happy tonight. I'm not worried about anything. I'm not fearing any man. Mine eyes have seen the glory of the coming of the Lord![39]

The next morning, April 4, 1968, Martin Luther King, Jr., was shot dead on the balcony of his Memphis motel room as he stepped out to welcome the morning sun.

In the epilogue[40] to his massive tome on Martin Luther King, Jr., and the Southern Christian Leadership Conference, David J. Garrow cites these two evaluative statements about the significance of Martin Luther King, Jr.: The first comes from Charles Willie, one of King's Morehouse classmates and now an educator: "By idolizing those whom we honor, we do a disservice both to them and to ourselves. By exalting the accomplishments of Martin Luther King, Jr., into a legendary tale annually told, we fail to recognize his humanity—his personal and public struggles—that are similar to yours and mine." The second comment comes from Christine Farris, King's sister, who said of Martin: "My brother was no saint, but an ordinary man." The truth of Mrs. Farris declaration lies in the realization that King struggled with real weaknesses. In reading about his life, one is struck by the blend of real weakness and true greatness in this man. His flights of rhetoric, his courageous personal witness to justice and to nonviolence, his capacity to excite in others a vision of a better world were traits and gifts that touched the hearts of many in his generation and in the generations that have followed. Yet, he personally struggled with his own lusts, his infidelities to his beloved wife; he knew himself to be a sinful and guilty man, much in need of God's forgiveness. As he once told his congregation at Ebenezer, "You don't need to go out this morning saying that Martin Luther King is a saint. I want you to know that I am a sinner like all of God's children, and I want to hear a voice saying to me one day, 'I take you in and bless you because you tried. It was well that it was within your heart.'"[41] King voiced his hope for himself in these words: "God does not judge us by the separate incidents or the separate mistakes that we make, but by the total bent of our lives." By such a standard, Martin Luther King, Jr., stands as a great man, one who "fought the good fight."

D.   ST. THOMAS MORE[42]

"A man for all seasons" is the description of Thomas More penned first by his friend, the great Dutch humanist Erasmus. Thomas More was one of the great figures of sixteenth century England, perhaps the greatest!

Born in London in 1477, the son of the lawyer and later knight, John More, Thomas More was educated in London's best school of the time, St. Anthony's, and then in the household of John Morton, archbishop of Canterbury and Chancellor of England, then at Oxford, and finally at Lincoln's Inn. Morton quickly saw the greatness of his protégé, whom he described admiringly as "this marvelous man." More was so bright and so hard-working that during his study of law, he also was able to find time to pursue readings in Holy Scripture, the Church Fathers, and in the classics, all in their original languages. Determined to do God's will, whatever that was for him, he tested out a possible calling to the priesthood by living for four years with the Carthusian monks next door while studying law at Lincoln's Inn. Although attracted to the Franciscan order, More decided that he would best serve God and his fellow men as a lay Christian.

In 1501, More became a full-fledged lawyer. In 1504, he married and began a family. He would have four children. But his first wife whom he loved dearly died in 1511, probably during childbirth. He immediately remarried a widow named Alice Middleton and assumed responsibility for her two children.

In his legal career, More quickly gained a reputation for absolute honesty, excellent judgment, hilarious wit, and incredible industry. His household was revered for its atmosphere of genuine piety and learning; the great humanists of the day would come to visit there. More loved and knew music, and was himself a published historian (a life of Richard III) and well-known essayist (*Utopia*).

Thomas' work in the courtroom soon gained him the attention of Cardinal Wolsey, the new Chancellor of England, and then of King Henry VIII. More was made "undersheriff" of London (in this capacity, he would adjudicate cases), was enlisted by Henry VIII to respond to the written attacks on the Catholic faith made by Luther and his followers in England, and then was made high steward of the universities of Oxford and of Cambridge, respectively.

Throughout his entire adult life, More never abandoned the habits he had begun to practice when he lived with the Carthusian monks: of early rising, prolonged prayer, frequent fasting, and wearing the hair shirt. God remained the center of his life. Yet, as historian Germain P. Marc'hadour has noted:

> [H]e shrank from nothing that imparted an innocent pleasure, even of a bodily kind; he had a speaker's voice and a memory that served him well and for extempore rejoinders. 'Born for friendship,' he could extract delight from the dullest people or things. ... His family affections were warm yet not obtrusive. ... [And] amid his intense professional activity, he found hours for prayer and for supervising [a] domestic school.[43]

King Henry VIII became more and more reliant on Thomas' counsel and in 1529 asked him to replace Wolsey as Chancellor of England, i.e., as chief operating officer of the country. More was not eager to assume the second highest office in the land. For, indeed, he saw the great cloud on the horizon. King Henry was displeased with the fact that the King's marriage to Catherine of Aragon had yielded no heir to the throne. He had already sought More's approval for his desire to divorce Catherine, on the grounds of incest. (She had already been married to his late brother, Henry VII.) More had told the King that he could not in conscience support such a view.

The King continued to pressure the Pope of the time to declare his marriage void, but to no avail. Then, on May 16, 1532, the chapter of the Diocese of Canterbury declared the King's authority over the Church. The next day, More resigned as Chancellor, and quietly retired to his modest home.

In 1533, Henry married Anne Boleyn, who was crowned queen on June 1 of that year. More, remarking to one of his family, "I will be devoured but not deflowered," refused to attend the coronation. Thereby, he became a marked man! Historian R.J. Schoeck writes:

> Given his reputation throughout Europe and his position as the most respected layman in the land, it was impossible for Henry to proceed without his submission. [So] on April 12, 1534, More was cited to appear before the commission at Lambeth to swear to the Act of Succession and to take the Oath of Supremacy [of the King over the Church]. More was willing to accept the succession [Anne Boleyn was, de facto, the Queen] but refused the Oath of Supremacy, which denied the Papacy.[44]

On April 17, he was sent to the prison of the Tower of London.

After many unsuccessful attempts to find grounds on which to declare More "a traitor," on July 1, 1534, Thomas Cromwell—upon the perjurous testimony of his own henchman, Richard Rich, that More had in Rich's presence, publicly denied that the King was the head of the Church in England (More had neither affirmed nor denied that publicly)—passed a "guilty" sentence on More for treason. He was sentenced to be hanged and eviscerated. At the direction of the King, this sentence was "commuted" to "beheading."

More appears indeed to have foreseen his impending death for several years, for during that time, he wrote a *Treatise on the Lord's Passion.* In the Tower, he suffered his confinement cheerfully, saying that the close quarters suited him just fine, but he was saddened at his family's sorrow and grief, and the hardship they had to endure. For their part, they asked him to capitulate to the King's wish, but his conscience would not permit such a move.

Therefore, on July 6, at 9 a.m., he was taken to the scaffold where he was to be beheaded. Prison had enfeebled him, so he asked humorously of the hangman that he assist him up the steps: "See me safe up, but for my coming down, let me shift for myself." Before he was executed, More made his final declaration: "I die the King's good servant, but God's first!"

The author of the *Encyclopedia Britannica* account writes: "The news of More's death shocked Europe. Erasmus mourned the man he had so often praised, 'whose soul was more pure than any snow, whose genius was such that England never had and never again will have its like.' The official image of More as traitor did not gain credence even in Protestant lands."[45] More's head was displayed publicly on the London Bridge. Then, it was later preserved by his daughter Margaret and now lies in the Roper (More's son-in-law) vault at St. Dunstan's in Canterbury. Thomas More was declared a saint by the Roman Catholic Church, on February 10, 1935.

E.   PEDRO ARRUPE, SJ[46]

"Persons [Men and Women] for Others!" This phrase, popular in Catholic circles these days, seems to have originated with Fr. Pedro Arrupe, SJ, the twenty-eighth Superior General of the Jesuit order, in a talk he delivered to the International Congress of Alumni of Jesuit Schools. In this talk, he criticized the consumerism, permissiveness, and selfishness so characteristic of modern society, and asked the alumni present to help to create a new and more just society by embracing a greater simplicity of life, a commitment to change every unjust social structure, and a willingness to put themselves at the service of others, especially the poor.

This was an invitation that came from a man who himself had grown up in a modest, secure middle-class family in Bilboa, the Basque area of northern Spain. Pedro Arrupe was born in 1907, the sixth child and only son in a very happy and loving family. His father was an architect; his mother, the daughter of a doctor. Pedro, the lone boy and youngest family member, was the true joy of his sisters, who found him absolutely charming and delightful.

The tranquility of the Arrupe household suffered a terrible blow, however, when in 1916, its matriarch Senora Dolores died. Pedro's father tried to console 8-year-old Pedro by pointing to a statute of Mary, the Mother of Jesus, and saying, "From now on, she will be your mother too."

Pedro Arrupe first studied in his native city of Bilboa. There he completed his baccalaureate in 1922. He then applied to the University of Madrid, was admitted, and took up residence with a number of other Catholic students from Bilbao who were studying at the University. Pedro was an extremely successful medical student; he won the First Prize for Anatomical Studies in his first year, the Physiology Prize in his second year, and then the Prize for Therapeutics. But study was not all he did. Together with his friend Enrique Chacon, he took time to join the St. Vincent de Paul Society, and thus through his visits to the direly poor in Madrid, a whole new and awful world was opened up to him. He saw two women and six cold and starving children in a dark and dank room, with terrible sanitation and only one bed. This exposure would mark his life with a real compassion and sensitivity to the marginalized, the poor.

At the end of his medical studies in 1926, Arrupe was at the head of his class. The runner-up to him, Dr. Severo Ochoa, would gain the Nobel Prize in Medicine in 1946 for his synthesis of RNA. Pedro Arrupe himself had a brilliant career in medicine ahead of him, and no one realized this more clearly than the Dean of the Medical School, Dr. Negris. However, by means of a tragedy, God would turn Arrupe's life in an unexpected direction. Just as he was graduating, his beloved father, Don Marcelino, died.

Heartbroken, Pedro, together with his sisters, sought some reprieve from their grief. They decided that before he resumed his medical studies in graduate school, they would go to Lourdes in France, the famous shrine to the Blessed Mother, known for the claim that it was the scene of many miracles. They traveled through the beautiful Pyrenees Mountains. As George Bishop explains, when the train arrived at Lourdes, "Pedro went to the Medical Verification Bureau, to offer his services in the examination of cases and to verify any so-called miraculous cures, which were reported on some occasions. So often he had heard his professors ... scoff at the 'superstition' surrounding Lourdes and the so-called 'miracle cures.'"[47] Well, now he would see for himself!

The next day, the family went to the Shrine's huge Basilica. A bishop came in holding high the Blessed Sacrament in a monstrance, making the sign of the cross over the crowd. A nun paralyzed from Potts' disease (tuberculosis of the spine) suddenly rose from her stretcher and shouted, "I'm cured." Prior to the service, x-rays showed pus eating away her vertebrae. Arrupe, as an authorized doctor of the Verification Bureau, was able to examine the nun and the x-ray photograph of her condition. He was convinced that he had witnessed a miracle.

On the next day, an elderly woman in advanced stages of cancer of the stomach was completely cured. According to Bishop, "Arrupe was there when the verifying doctors, many of whom were unbelievers or agnostics, x-rayed her stomach. There was no trace of the cancer that had been plainly visible before."[48]

Several days later, he witnessed a third miracle. A lad about twenty years old, whose body was completely deformed by polio, was being wheeled around by a nurse and followed by his mother. Arrupe's sister remarked to Pedro, "Look at that poor boy." Again, as the Blessed Sacrament was carried in front of the young man, he got up from his chair and shouted that he was cured. Bishop relates, "And, again, with his medical permit, Arrupe was able to investigate the young man's case at close hand and to certify that there could be no possible explanation for what happened."[49]

Pedro Arrupe returned to Madrid ostensibly to begin his post-graduate studies in medicine, but another thought had entered his mind and eventually it captured his heart. He would leave medicine and become a "doctor of souls" as a Jesuit. When he announced his decision, the Dean of the Medical School, who would later become the Prime Minister of the Socialist Republic and was an avowed atheist, was beside himself. He begged Pedro's sisters to dissuade him, and he even went in person to the Jesuit novitiate in northern Spain to visit Arrupe and to ask him personally to reconsider. But Pedro believed that he heard God calling him to a different life, and in this belief, it would appear he was not mistaken.

In the Jesuit Novitiate, Arrupe proved to be a wonderful companion. A great mimic and tease, a gifted musician, a deeply spiritual and very intelligent person, a delightful companion and a very generous man, Pedro Arrupe was much liked and admired by his companions.

In 1932, however, civil war broke out in Spain, and the Jesuits were expelled. For further studies, Arrupe was sent to Belgium and then to Holland, where the Jesuit community was very poor. He completed most of his study of theology and was ordained a priest in 1936, then sent to United States for a final year of theological study in Kansas and then one more year of ascetical training in Cleveland. On June 6, 1938, he received a letter from the leader of the Jesuits to whom he had written a petition, telling him that his request to go to Japan as a missionary had been approved. He set sail for Japan and arrived there on October 15, 1938. The morning of the day he arrived was only the third time in his life that he cried as a man; the first, when his father died; the second time, when he said farewell to maximum security prisoners in New York where he had spent some time working during 1937. But this time, he cried for joy.

Arrupe's work in Japan involved, of course, learning the language and the culture, then serving as a pastor in Yamaguchi. Then, in March, 1942, he was given the very important responsibility of training the Japanese Jesuit novices, and sent to the Novitiate in Hiroshima, a duty he was discharging on August 6, 1945, when the atomic bomb was dropped on that city. The Jesuit Novitiate was outside the range of the terrible blast, though widows in that building were blown out, but the horror of the aftermath visited them within an hour as survivors made their way from the epicenter to seek God-knows-what help and as the Jesuit novices and priests on the novitiate staff rushed into the city to help those who were badly injured. One hundred thousand persons had died instantly with the blast. Fifty thousand more would die of their wounds, many horribly. Thirty thousand were severely wounded. It was people from this last group who began to appear at or were brought to the Novitiate to be cared for. As a doctor, Arrupe rendered what valuable help he could, but he had little access to medicine; nonetheless, all but one of the people who came to the Novitiate survived. Years later, while Arrupe was attending some meeting, a film on Hiroshima was shown; Arrupe had to leave the theatre; it evoked in him such terrible memories of the awful human suffering and pain he had witnessed.

Arrupe so distinguished himself in his work in Japan and in his love of that land and its people that he was chosen to be the leader of the Jesuits there, and then in 1965, he was elected to lead the whole Jesuit order. He held this position (usually life-long) until a severe stroke incapacitated him on August 6, 1981, the 35th anniversary of that terrible day at Hiroshima. With that stroke, Arrupe—a man who had spoken six languages fluently, whose beautiful smile had lit every room he entered and had touched the hearts of so many of the Jesuits he led, whose workdays would see him up early in the morning after about five hours of sleep to pray for two hours and not to stop work until late into the night, this wonderful, charismatic leader—was severely incapacitated. He would hang upon this cross for ten years, with his beautiful and warming smile still in occasional evidence, until God saw fit to take him home on February 5, 1991. In his last condition, he was so like the poor to whom he had urged his Jesuit brothers to reach out in the name of Jesus: able to offer little more than his humble, silent presence. His final official message to his Jesuit brethren was given as his resignation was formally announced, and his successor chosen:

> More than ever, I now find myself in the hands of God. This is what I have wanted all my life, from my youth. And this is still the one thing I want. But now there is a difference: the initiative is entirely with God. It is indeed a profound spiritual experience to know and feel myself so totally in His hands.

> At the end of eighteen years as General of the Society, I want to first of all, and above all, give thanks to the Lord. His generosity toward me has been boundless. For my part, I have tried to respond, well knowing that all his gifts were for the Society, to be shared with each and every Jesuit. This has been my persistent effort.

> In the eighteen years, my one ideal was to serve the Lord and His Church— with all my heart—from the beginning to the end.[50]

F.   CONCLUSION

This chapter has afforded the reader an opportunity to reflect on whether God and Christianity make a difference in the way ethical decision-making is done by presenting an exposition on the significance of the theological virtues in human endeavors and by offering five case-studies of Christian leaders admired not only for their human virtues but also for their Christian virtues of faith, hope, and love. Certainly, with regard to the case-studies, there are other women and men who deserve examination: e.g., Mother Teresa of Calcutta; St. Catherine of Sienna; the male and female, religious and lay martyrs of modern El Salvador; Archbishop Oscar Romero; Caesar Chavez; Pierre Toussaint; Bishop Desmond Tutu; St. Maximilian Kolbe; St. Theresa of Lisieux; etc. The list could go on and on. But the purpose of the chapter will have been achieved if, using whatever study of whatever lives the instructor chooses, the reader can now answer the questions that follow in an informed way.

QUESTIONS

Answer the following questions in paragraph form. Write your answers on a separate sheet of paper.

1.   Does belief in God and Christ make any difference to the way that humans make ethical decisions? Why or why not? Explain carefully and at length, using examples from the lives presented in this text or by your instructor.

2.   Were any of the lives presented of special interest to you? If not, why didn't you like them? If so, say which spoke to your own personal experience and personal questions.

3.   Were you puzzled or bothered by the motivations of any of the persons whose lives were presented here? Explain.

4.   Do you have any questions or points of dispute or inquiry that you would like to raise concerning Ignatius Loyola's view of the world or concerning his philosophy for making a choice? Name one point in his philosophy that you found challenging or one that you found enlightening.

CHAPTER FOUR:
KEY CONCEPTS FOR UNDERSTANDING CHRISTIAN ETHICS

From your study and discussion of Chapter Three and of other connected materials presented by your instructor, you hopefully have gained some insight into the difference in ethical outlook that belief in God and in Jesus can make to the virtuous person.

What follows, in the final three chapters of this textbook, is a careful examination of the Christian approach to ethical decision-making. This chapter (Four) will look at four pivotal concepts that form the ethical perspective of a Christian. The next chapter (Five) will examine how Catholics use the Christian scriptures, the teachings of their Church, and principles of natural law to arrive at responsible ethical decisions. (Non-Catholic Christians and others will also find this study helpful to the development of their own ethical approach.) The final chapter (Six) will acquaint you with several sets of guidelines which St. Ignatius Loyola articulated to help people figure out God's will for them and present two practical daily aids to help people keep on track as they journey through life.

PART ONE:
FREEDOM

If there is one slogan or phrase that could summarize the Christian view of what it means to be a human being, it would probably be the phrase "man (i.e., the human person) is made in the image and likeness of God." This biblical description of the human—clearly set out in the book of Genesis, continually present throughout Church history, and universally accepted by Christians—has been interpreted to mean a great many things. As the book of Genesis makes clear, this phrase is used to show that, as God has dominion or rule over all of creation, human beings have dominion or rule over creation, as well: "Then God said, 'Let us make man in our image, after our likeness; and let him have dominion over the fish of the sea, and over the birds of the air, and over the cattle, and over all the earth, and over every creeping thing that creeps upon the earth'" (Gen. 1:26). Additionally, as we briefly saw in the section on Aristotle and happiness, St. Thomas Aquinas, as well as other Church Fathers and saints, concluded that a human being's *rational capacity* is what distinguishes him from the rest of the animal kingdom; only human beings have the ability to know God and eventually be unified with Him in the beatific vision.

But the phrase "man is made in the image and likeness of God" also has at least one additional meaning that is central to the Christian vision of the human; as God is free, so is the human person, made in God's likeness, free. As St. Irenaeus succinctly states, "Man is rational and therefore like God; he is created with *free* will and is master over his acts."[1] It is this notion, that humans are *free*, which will occupy us in the following section of Chapter Four.

We are responsible for humanity and earth

A.   DIFFERENT SENSES OF "FREEDOM"

Though people—especially musicians, activists, and politicians—regularly speak of freedom, they do not usually use the word the way philosophers or theologians do. When Paul McCartney praises America for her love of liberty in his song "Freedom" and President George W. Bush argues that terrorists hate America because of its freedom, they understand "freedom" as *the state of having little or no legal or physical restraints upon one's actions.* In this sense, Americans have "freedom of speech," i.e., almost no legal restrictions on expression, and many citizens of Islamic countries do not have "freedom of speech," i.e., legal restrictions prevent them from voicing their ideas.

When philosophers and theologians speak of "freedom," however, they mean it in a way that is related to the popular understanding of the term but is more basic or fundamental. Sections 1731 and 1732 of the *Catechism of the Catholic Church* adequately define freedom in this more specialized sense:

> Freedom is the power, rooted in reason and will, to act or not to act, to do this or that, and so to perform deliberate actions on one's own responsibility.
>
> As long as freedom has not bound itself definitively to its ultimate good which is God, there is the possibility of *choosing between good and evil,* and thus of growing in perfection or of failing and sinning. This freedom characterizes properly human acts. It is the basis of praise or blame, merit or reproach.

From the perspective of the *Catechism,* then, freedom is a capacity to choose— "to act or not act, to do this or that"—that is particular to a human being. Chairs cannot choose whether or not to be sat upon, so we do not praise or blame chairs. Even dogs and cats, though certainly capable of being trained, do not have this capacity; they have no choice but to run to or flee from the most appealing or frightening object, for they are wholly ruled by appetite. On the other hand, humans have a power to choose that can rise above appetite, a power that no law or jail cell can take away. Having this capacity to choose is, in part, what the Church means when it states "God made man (i.e., the human person) in His own image and likeness."

B.   PHILOSOPHIES THAT OPPOSE THE NOTION OF FREEDOM

But there are voices aplenty today in academia saying that there is no such thing as freedom; these voices assert that, instead of freely choosing between good or evil, human beings are *determined* or *conditioned* to act in a certain way. This great philosophical and theological debate—"the *freedom vs. determinism* debate"—has been raging between scholars for centuries. But what exactly do these people mean when they say human beings are "determined" or "conditioned," and not free?

B1. Determinism

Determinism is a philosophical position that began to take root shortly after the advent of modern science, particularly after the work of one of science's greatest minds, Sir Isaac Newton. As will hopefully be remembered from your science class, Sir Isaac Newton discovered and articulated three laws of motion that all natural bodies must obey. When he coupled these laws with his law of gravitation and a few other corollary observations, he was able to describe and predict the motions of certain heavenly bodies, i.e., planets, the moon, and comets, as well as some earthly bodies. Armed with Newton's laws and observations (sometimes called "Newtonian mechanics"), modern science was able to predict and manipulate the forces of nature in a way that was previously unimaginable.

Though Newton originally set out to show God was behind these laws—that "this most beautiful system of the sun, planets, and comets, could only proceed from the counsel and dominion of an intelligent and powerful Being"[2]—one of the results of his findings was that the natural world, in fact, became much less mysterious and wonderful for many people. For them, it seemed that the causes of motion of most things could be known simply by applying the laws of mechanics. The world became likened to an enormous machine, and the role of God in this machine was minimal, if not entirely absent. The motion of most things seemed to be *determined* by the laws of nature. Most things were not free; they were merely pushed or pulled from place to place.

Now, it was only a matter of time before some scientists and philosophers took the next logical step. Though Newton himself was unsure whether his laws would apply to plants or animals, some thinkers asserted that there was no reason to believe that Newton's laws did not apply to human behavior as well as that of planets and rocks. Perhaps, human beings were determined as well. Perhaps, these philosophers hypothesized, if we could know enough about the inner workings of a human body and the exterior influences on that body, we could predict how a human will act in the same way we can predict where a rock from a catapult will land or where a billiard ball will end up when it is hit. Hence, determinism, *the idea that human actions are dictated by and can be predicted from the laws of nature*, arose.

During this period of thought, known as the Enlightenment, philosophers began to speak of man (and nature) as a machine whose actions and behavior were programmed. And though this position has been refined and amended, it is still believed and advocated by some philosophers and psychologists today. When a philosopher assumes this viewpoint, he regards humans as devoid of free will and therefore no longer responsible for their actions; praising and blaming human actions becomes as silly as praising or blaming a chair or an automobile. As Bertrand Russell, a determinist and great enemy of Christianity asserted, "When a man acts in ways that annoy us we wish to think him wicked, and we refuse to face the fact that his annoying behavior is a result of antecedent causes which, if you follow them long enough, will take you beyond the moment of his birth and therefore to events for which he cannot be held responsible by any stretch of imagination."[3]

[handwritten margin note: The laws of nature are not contradictory to the laws of God]

B2. Conditioning

Additionally, there are voices from the psychological community who also question the reality of human freedom. The idea that human beings might not be free to respond to situations in many different ways but, rather, might be *conditioned* to respond in a certain manner began to take shape shortly after the work of a Russian Nobel-Prize-winning psychologist, Ivan Pavlov. During his investigations into the digestive systems of dogs, Pavlov noticed that the salivary glands of a dog would often secrete saliva even when there was no food present. Pavlov had a hunch why this was happening and conducted an experiment to test his hypothesis. He performed a minor surgical procedure on a dog, hooking up a tube to the dog's cheek, to measure the amount of saliva secreted at any given time. When a light flashed in the dog's face, the dog would not salivate, for obviously, salivating is not a natural response to seeing a light flash. When meat powder was placed in the dog's dish, the dog would salivate, a natural response to the presentation of food. But Pavlov decided to pair the presentation of the meat powder with the light flash over a period of time; a light would flash every time the dog was presented his dinner. Eventually, the mere presence of the light flashing was enough to cause the dog to salivate. The dog, in Pavlov's words, had been "conditioned" to respond to a stimulus in a certain fashion.

Since Pavlov's time, many similar experiments have been conducted on all sorts of animals, including people. For example, psychologists have demonstrated that certain natural reactions (or involuntary responses) can be conditioned in people, as well. When a person gets cold, the small blood vessels close to the body surface normally constrict or shrink—a response that keeps the body warm; this bodily reaction is known as "vasoconstriction." Now, biologists have found that vasoconstriction will occur in the veins of a person's hand if it is immersed in ice water. As part of an experiment, some psychologists decided to activate a buzzer at the same time a person's hand was being immersed in the ice water. Eventually, the mere activation of the buzzer was sufficient to cause vasoconstriction in the person's hand. (Likewise, experiments have even been conducted on babies who became conditioned to blink at the mere sound of a certain tone.) This kind of conditioning—the kind illustrated by Pavlov's dog and the hand in the ice water, in which a natural reaction in a person or animal is elicited by an unnatural stimulus, i.e., something that does not normally elicit that reaction—is known as *classical conditioning*.

"But," one may ask, "what in the world does this have to do with human freedom? When people speak of free actions they do not mention salivating or blood vessels constricting; freedom deals with the area of intentional or voluntary activity, the area in which humans operate in and on the world." Well, it was only a matter of time before someone attempted to expand Pavlov's notion of conditioning into other areas of life; this someone was Harvard psychologist B.F. Skinner. Skinner wanted to demonstrate that conditioning not only applied to involuntary reactions like salivating and vasoconstriction but also to other areas that were normally considered more voluntary. To test his hypothesis, Skinner and his colleagues constructed a box, which came to be known as a "Skinner box," with nothing in it but a small lever and a food receptacle below the lever. The experimenters placed a rat in the box and observed the rat to see how many times it would push the lever. At first, the rat rather randomly explored his new environment, attending to the lever about as frequently as he did anything else in the box. Eventually, the experimenters hooked up the lever to a mechanism that would release a food pellet into the receptacle. Over time, the rat learned to associate the pulling of the lever with the foot pellet; by *reinforcing* certain behavior with a reward, Skinner and his associates were able to increase the frequency with which the rat pulled the lever. This type of conditioning, in which what were thought to be *voluntary* actions of an animal are manipulated or dictated by a system of rewards (or punishments), is known as *operant conditioning*, for it conditions the way animals (and people) *operate* on and in the world. Overall, this general way of understanding human actions is known as "behaviorism."

Now, instead of being content with the idea that animal behavior and probably human behavior is *highly influenced by* the effects of environmental conditions, Skinner went so far as *to deny human freedom altogether*. In order to further his theory, he even constructed an enormous Skinner box like the one constructed for the rat; only this time, he placed his own daughter in it! (Evidently, Skinner himself had not been conditioned well.) Skinner had concluded that freedom is an illusion, and people are merely "the sum total of their past experiences." There is neither moral good nor evil in the world nor is there reason for praise or blame. Humans do not commit evil because they have chosen to do so; they do evil because they were conditioned to do so as children.

C.   A CHRISTIAN RESPONSE TO THESE PHILOSOPHIES?

How, then, is a Christian or any defender of human freedom to reply to the ideas that human beings are either determined or conditioned? The first thing that should probably be admitted is that there is a great deal of truth in both determinism and conditioning. Human biology and environmental factors play an enormous role in the behavior of human beings. Human beings are biological creatures by nature, and as science continues to understand the human body in all of its complexity, it becomes clearer and clearer that even such things as a person's moods and how one learns—things that were originally thought to be entirely within one's control—have a large biological or chemical component. Likewise, in regard to conditioning, the *Catechism* itself acknowledges that a person's "responsibility for an action can be diminished or even nullified by ... habit, inordinate attachments, and other psychological and social factors."[4] How one is raised is of prime importance; as the master Aristotle states, "It makes no small difference, then, whether we form habits of one kind or another from our very youth; it makes a very great difference, or rather *all* the difference."[5] Nonetheless, Christians still maintain the reality of freedom, even if it is bounded by biology and environment. On what grounds do they affirm this reality in the face of such opposition?

Admittedly, there does not seem to be any "official" Catholic or Christian argument against the positions of determinism and conditioning, and additionally, it must be conceded that it will be truly difficult, if not impossible, to refute these positions definitively. For, to nearly every argument that could be put forward in favor of freedom, the determinist or defender of conditioning can reply in the same manner. If, for example, a defender of freedom were to state that human behavior is free and, therefore, unable to be predicted, the determinist would respond, "Well, at this point in the development of science, we are admittedly not able to forecast human behavior, but this state of things only arises from a lack of information. If we knew more about human biology, we would be able to predict human actions." Likewise, if a defender of freedom were to put forward the argument that certain actions, as, for example, throwing oneself on a hand grenade during wartime, could never have been conditioned because there has never been any situation comparable in one's past, the defender of conditioning could merely respond, "Well, at this point in the development of psychology, we are admittedly not able to forecast all human behavior, but this state of things only arises from a lack of information. If we knew more about the way people become conditioned and all of the subtle influences that, together, make up a person's life, we could surely predict human behavior." Indeed, this reply that "we currently do not have enough information" seems to be a convenient way for a determinist or believer in conditioning to weasel out of any argument. But there is one argument or observation that the enemies of human freedom must concede: undoubtedly, every human being lives his life believing he is free.

D. AN ARISTOTELIAN RESPONSE: A "PRACTICAL REFUTATION"

In one of his greatest philosophical works, the *Metaphysics*, Aristotle writes about an argument he has with a man who denies what is called the "principle of contradiction." This principle, which Aristotle was defending, states that no thing can, at the same time, be both X and not-X in the same way. For example, it is not possible for a chair to be three feet tall and not three feet tall at the same time; it is not possible for a ball to be, at the same time, red all over and not red all over; it is not possible for a book to be, at the same time, on my desk and not on my desk. This principle seemed to Aristotle to be irrefutable, but the man with whom he was arguing refused to budge. Aristotle could not convince him, but he knew that, once the man left the room and stopped arguing, he would lead his life *as if* he believed the principle. Regardless of what he *said* he believed, his *actions* would show that he did not truly believe the position for which he was arguing. To put the matter in philosophical jargon, Aristotle offered a "practical refutation" of an argument, i.e., he showed his opponent's position to be false because in practice it is impossible to carry out.

And the defenders of determinism and conditioning are stuck with this very dilemma; ironically, *they have no choice* but to live their lives believing they are free. Every morning they will get up and make a decision about what to eat for breakfast, believing they could have eaten Cheerios instead of the last pop-tart; they will order a Coke for lunch, believing they could have ordered a Sprite; they will buy an American car, believing they could have bought the luxurious and fashionable Toyota Corolla; they will praise their neighbors for their generosity and chastise their friends if they catch them in a lie. They will do all of these things and many more, knowing all the while that their very lives are being lived in complete contradiction to their philosophical position. The only thing they can possibly say in their defense is that we are all, themselves included, deluded.

Indeed, the reality of freedom is so basic to our understanding of what it means to be a human being that no one outside of a philosophy or psychology classroom really takes these positions seriously. If you were to go to court pleading, "I am not to blame for my actions; my behavior has been determined by the chemicals in my brain and the activity of my central nervous system," the judge would throw the book at you (and, perhaps, have you severely beaten for good measure). We praise and blame people as well as counsel them because we know that, ultimately, they are responsible for their lives, before God and their neighbors. As the *Catechism* states, "God willed that man should be 'left in the hand of his own counsel,' so that he might of his own accord seek his Creator and freely attain his full and blessed perfection by cleaving to him."[6]

Freedom is truly the crowning glory of the human being, but unfortunately, freedom is not the end of the story. For with the reality of choice comes the possibility of sin.

SECTION HIGHLIGHTS

Christians attribute freedom to humans because they think that the human person is made in the image of God, Who is free.

According to Christians, this is the essence of human freedom: it is the power, rooted in reason and will, to choose between good and evil.

According to Christians, no other earthly creature has been given the gift of free will.

Determinism is a philosophy that maintains that humans are not free and that human actions are dictated by and can be predicted from the laws of nature.

Behaviorism is a psychological form of determinism that claims that humans are not free but are conditioned by agents outside themselves to act in the way that they do.

One counter-argument to determinism is Aristotle's "practical refutation": despite all claims to the contrary, no determinist lives his or her life as if he or she has no capacity to make choices.

QUESTIONS

To show that you understand the concepts presented in this section, answer the following questions on a separate piece of paper. Use complete sentences.

1. According to Christian tradition, what *three* attributes does God share with humans?

2. How did Newton's genius in physics contribute to the development of the philosophy of determinism?

3. What is the difference between "operant conditioning" and "classical conditioning"?

4. A "practical refutation" of determinism depends in some measure upon the concreteness of the examples given to show that all humans must live their lives as if they were free. Mention three concrete examples to show that, despite their protestations to the contrary, behaviorist and determinist philosophers live their lives believing they are free.

PART TWO:
SIN

The next key concept in the Christian moral framework is "sin."

A.   WHY BOTHER WITH "SIN"?

These days "sin" is not the most popular of terms. Indeed, many people try to avoid using moral language at all, or if they must, they wish to use it as little as possible for fear of being "judgmental" or "righteous." And even fewer people want to be seen throwing around words like "sin" that not only refer to morality but also, heaven forbid, to God. "It is bad enough that a person would try to impose *his* or *her* morality on others," so the sentiment goes, "but imagine the audacity someone must have to believe that he or she is a spokesperson for *God's* view of morality!" If we speak of "sin," we immediately seem to be characterized as either small children, who still have a quaint attachment to simple, old-fashioned notions, or as hysterical religious fanatics, who are either off their rockers or interested in making money at the expense of others.

Additionally, the Catholic Church in particular has, at times, had quite a bad track record when it comes to talking about sin. Catholics are infamous for having the guiltiest consciences of perhaps any religious group of people. Many of your parents or grandparents can probably remember the upbringing they received in Catholic schools, and those memories are not always pleasant ones. At times, some religion teachers seem to have enjoyed hitting children with rulers and talking about the fires of hell more than they did showing compassion and talking about the love and grace of Jesus. For example, author Frank McCourt, whose book *Angela's Ashes* won the Pulitzer Prize, said on a talk show that he could forgive everybody who had ever wronged him—even his alcoholic father whose bouts with the bottle left his family impoverished and emotionally neglected—except the priests who had taught him in school. Evidently, the Church's teachings on sin have not always been the highlight of everybody's religious education.

Indeed, one might ask, "Why do we even have to bother talking about sin at all? What good does it do to fill people's heads and hearts with guilt or scare the devil out of them with discussions of sin and the fires of hell? Why don't we just concentrate on all of the positive messages of Scripture, in general, and Jesus' message, in particular, and leave out any reference to sin?"

B.   WHY SIN IS A NECESSARY CONCEPT

One of the most obvious reasons why we must follow up our discussion of freedom with one of sin is that *it is real.* Avoiding a discussion of unpleasant things may, indeed, be more pleasant, but what is pleasant is not always the same as what is real or true. As one rather cynical author put it, "Sin is one of the few religious doctrines for which we have empirical evidence." Unlike the doctrines of the Trinity or transubstantiation that cannot be verified through observation, the reality of sin is so prevalent it is difficult *not* to observe it nearly every hour of every day. "Sin" is not an abstract or esoteric concept; it is concrete and painful. From the father who refuses to pay child-support to feed and clothe his offspring to the rich and comfortable who do nothing to better the lives of the uneducated, starving poor in Third World countries, sin confronts us every day of our lives.

But there is another reason, besides mere intellectual honesty, why Christians need to have an understanding of sin: Jesus' life and message make no sense except in the context of this concept. In the Gospel of Matthew (1:21), for example, an angel of the Lord appears to Joseph and says, "[Your wife Mary] will bear you a son, and you shall call his name Jesus, for he will save his people from their sins." So, according to the Gospels, even Jesus' name indicates why He has been sent here: to save His people from their sins. In effect, Jesus came to rescue us from the perils of sin, and His rescue mission would make little sense if we were not really in the grip of this malady.

Indeed, it is helpful to understand sin as a malady or sickness, for doing so puts the importance of discussing this concept in its proper perspective. Humanity is suffering from a sickness, and Jesus is going to help cure us. But Christians believe they must participate in their own recuperation; they must participate in their own salvation. And just as a doctor cannot begin to prescribe the proper remedy for a disease *until she knows what that disease is*, we cannot hope to cure ourselves until we have a proper diagnosis of exactly what ails us. Understanding what sin is and how it afflicts us is the first step in our spiritual recovery.

Unfortunately, however, because the term "sin" is regarded suspiciously in American culture, a great many people have no idea of their spiritual condition. "Sin" as a concept has been replaced by "bad parenting" or "chemical imbalances." Of course, there are bad parents and chemical imbalances, and it is important for us to acknowledge the role these play in human life. But the condition of sin that underlies all of our earthly difficulties is rarely acknowledged. In short, people need to be made aware, if they are not so already, that they are suffering from a spiritual sickness. As Pope John Paul II puts it, "Conversion requires convincing of sin"[7]; people are not going to seek help unless they realize they need it.

Regrettably, in the past, the need to alert people of their condition often ended up in the hands of people who were, at best, overly enthusiastic or, at worst, disturbed or maniacal. Needless to say, it *is* possible to have a discussion and analysis of sin without putting everybody in a psychiatric ward, and hopefully, our discussion and analysis will be successful in this regard.

C.   TYPES OF SIN

"Sin," like the word "bad," is meant in many senses. If a small child were to ask the question "What does the word 'bad' mean?" it would be difficult to give a general answer, for a "bad shortstop" is quite a different thing from a "bad cut" or a "bad man" in general. In a similar way, an answer to the question "What does the word 'sin' mean?" would be difficult to provide, for "original sin" is a different thing from "personal sin" which is a different thing from "social sin." Of course, the senses of "bad" and "sin" are intimately interrelated, but it is best if we start with a description of each type of sin rather than give a general definition that, because it is so general, would be rather useless.

C1. Original Sin

Once upon a time, so the story goes, a number of friends were gathered together to frighten each other with ghost stories. Before beginning his tale, one man asked the question whether anyone present *really* believed in ghosts, to which one very clever but now anonymous person responded, "No, but I am still afraid of them."

This famous one-liner is, in many ways, similar to the feelings that people have about original sin. On the one hand, no one in the 21st century *really* wants to believe that a man named Adam, on the advice of his wife/girlfriend, ate an apple from a forbidden tree and, consequently, threw the world into absolute turmoil. Even the language—"Adam" meaning "earth" and "Eve" meaning "beginning"—betrays the fact that this story is meant to be taken, at least in part, figuratively. When was the last time that anyone saw "a tree of the knowledge of good and evil" in her backyard or out in a field? Like the existence of ghosts, the story of original sin is hard to swallow. On the other hand, however, an individual would have to be blind if she is unable to see that something is severely out of whack with nature, in general, and human nature, in particular. When discussing the story of Adam and Eve (or the reality of ghosts) over a cappuccino at our local artsy café, we laugh at how silly people must be to believe in such nonsense. But when we step out of the café into the street (or we walk home through a cemetery at the wee hours of the night) and see a homeless family sleeping over a grate (or a hazy figure in the distance), the notion of original sin (or ghosts) does not seem so silly anymore.

"I sought whence evil comes and there was no solution,"[8] says St. Augustine in his autobiography *The Confessions*, and in regard to original sin, the *Catechism of the Catholic Church* writes, "[It] is a mystery that we cannot fully understand."[9] How the wrongdoings of two primeval people could result in the downfall of the entire human race is as complete a mystery as how the death of one man, Jesus Christ, could result in the redemption of the entire human race.[10] These doctrines are matters of faith, and as Christians, we occasionally have to accept things that go beyond the comprehension of human reason.

Why there is original sin in the world is a complete mystery, but *that* there is original sin is the most obvious thing in the world. From the wars that rage between nations in the human kingdom to those that rage between species (and members of one species) in the rest of the animal kingdom, the sense that there is something terribly wrong with this planet pervades our experience.

Though "sin" is predominantly used to describe an action or the product of an action—e.g., Roy "sinned" (or "committed a sin") against Marie by spreading false rumors about her—"original sin" is not something we *do* to one another. Roy cannot "original sin" against Marie, or anyone for that matter. Though original sin is said to have been transmitted to the whole of mankind because of what one human being did, original sin is not just an action; it is also a state or condition in which we find ourselves.

St. Paul described this condition very aptly in his Letter to the Romans (7:19-20): "For I do not do the good I want, but the evil I do not want is what I do. Now if I do what I do not want, it is no longer I that do it, but sin which dwells in me." "Original sin," then, is a force or drive like gravity within human beings that pulls them toward evil desires and actions, sometimes against their explicit wishes to do the good. All too often, doing the right thing is like running up a very steep hill; as we progress, we feel gravity's pull ever stronger. Would it not just be easier to turn around and go back down the hill?

A vending machine has been knocked over and broken, and before we know what happened, we have looted a handful of candy bars, even though we really had no desire for them in the first place. We know that we should devote time and money to helping the poor, and yet even with this knowledge, we hoard our resources and waste hours of our lives watching "reality" shows or playing video games. Like St. Augustine before his conversion, we ask God to please help us avoid immoral sexual behavior … tomorrow. And is there not something deep inside us that is pleased when we see that our neighbor has failed a test, even though we know that everyone is called to love his neighbor? All of these misdeeds and disordered desires are a result of original sin. At times, it is almost as if our lives were not our own, as if we were possessed by some kind of an evil spirit. Despite our most desperate efforts, we cannot seem to overcome this permanent barrier in our lives. As Protestant theologian Paul Tillich puts it, sin is like a state of "separation": separation between people, separation within a person between who he should be and who he is, and separation of human beings from God.[11]

C2. Personal Sin

"Original sin" manifests itself most clearly in the sins of individual people, and as everyone is painfully aware, there are many different ways that humankind can and has gone astray. Though it might seem like a morbid preoccupation—like collecting animal corpses or memorizing the names of famous Nazis—cataloguing the various kinds of sin is an important endeavor. Why? Because if we understand the types of sin, we will understand in what way we have gone astray, and hopefully, we will know how not to go astray the next time. Knowledge of why a sin is a sin and what makes one sin more serious than another is like the knowledge of the different types and degrees of illness; only with a proper diagnosis is (physical or moral) health possible.

Possible Ways of Categorizing Personal Sins[12]

Sins can be classified in any number of ways, all of which highlight a different aspect or dimension of the sin in question. For example, if we analyze the sin of adultery—the sin a married person commits when he or she engages in sexual actions with someone besides his or her spouse—we can understand better why it is a sin or what type of sin it is if we classify it in the following ways:

C2a. According to the virtues or goods the sin opposes

One way of understanding why adultery is a sin is by understanding that it is opposed to certain virtues or goods. Adultery is opposed to the virtues of temperance—the virtue in regard to food and sex—and it breaks a lifelong vow that a man or woman has made before God, friends, and relatives. It dissolves the bonds of trust, as well, and it can undermine the stability of the family, the most important institution in any society.

C2b. According to the Commandments they violate

Adultery is also clearly forbidden by the Ten Commandments. In the book of Exodus, the sixth commandment that God revealed to Moses reads "You shall not commit adultery." Thus, a sin can be understood as a sin *because* it violates a commandment.

C2c. According to whom they offend or concern

Once adultery is understood to be a sin, we can go about refining our understanding of what kind of a sin it is by asking who is hurt by this offense. Adultery is primarily an offense against one's spouse, but it also involves many more people than simply a wife or husband. A man who is unfaithful to his wife is also jeopardizing the emotional well-being of his children; whether he acknowledges it or not, his children are profoundly affected by the type of relationship that exists between him and his wife. Even if he is the best actor in town, the relationship with his wife will be strained, and the children will feel the stress. And this is assuming that the wife never finds out. If she does, they may get divorced, and even the enlightened men and women of America are beginning to acknowledge the profound negative effects that children suffer when their parents divorce.

But adultery often also involves the further sin of *scandal*. Everyone in America who pays attention to politicians has heard the word "scandal," but for most of us, the word simply means that people in power have been caught doing something bad. Though scandal of course has this meaning, people today are not truly aware why, so to speak, scandals are scanda*lous*. The sin of scandal is especially grave because people in authority are entrusted with setting the standards by which a community or nation lives. When people in positions of authority—parents, teachers, politicians, and priests—commit grave sins, their acts are "scandalous" because they chisel away at the very foundations of society and lead young people astray. If teachers, parents, politicians, and priests go astray, who will teach young people? And an adulterous parent is both setting a bad standard for his children as well as weakening the institution of marriage as a whole, an institution on which everybody depends.

And adultery is, of course, a sin against God. It involves an intentional violation of one of His commandments, and it creates an obstacle that stands in the way of our relationship with Him. God is always willing to forgive us our trespasses, but that does not mean that we can take God and His mercy for granted. Like any friendship would be, our friendship with Him is strained by sin.

C2d. According to whether they are sins in thought, word, deed, or omission

The nature of adultery can also be further clarified as a sinful "deed," or action, for adultery is fundamentally something that someone *does*; a married man or woman has sex with someone besides his or her spouse. But a person does not have to perform a disordered deed in order to commit a sin. A person can also be guilty of harboring and fostering sinful thoughts; for example, a teenage boy may fantasize about girls in a lustful way or a disgruntled employee may take delight in daydreaming about ways to kill his boss. Additionally, somebody can harm someone else with words; the famous children's saying "Sticks and stones may break my bones, but names will never hurt me" is only true if "hurt" is understood as bodily harm. Words in the form of false rumors and hateful personal attacks on someone's character can damage people emotionally. And, as the story of the Good Samaritan demonstrates, people can also sin by *not* doing something, by *omitting* to do something. These sins are called "sins of omission," and we are often more guilty for what we have failed to do than we are for what we have actually done. Most of us are not murderers, chronic liars, or bank robbers, but all too often, we are guilty of apathy, laziness, or wasting away our lives pursuing new ways to amuse ourselves.

C2e. According to their gravity: mortal and venial sin

But for Catholics, perhaps the most important way of categorizing sins has to do with their gravity or severity. "Just how bad is this sin I have committed?" we may wonder as we reflect on our failings as human beings.

Drawing on Scripture and tradition, the Catholic Church has always distinguished between "mortal" and "venial" sins. Even though the early Christians did not use the terms "mortal" and "venial," the Bible shows that they were aware of different degrees of sin. The author of 1 John 5:16-17 speaks of sins that are "deadly" or "unto death," on the one hand, and sins that are "not deadly" and "not unto death," on the other. Indeed, this is why the term "mortal" came to be used, for "mors" or "mortis" is Latin for "death."

Mortal sins are those that are so grave or serious that their very commission seriously jeopardizes our relationship with God; they are actions that directly damage our friendship with God or reject His love. In order to repair the damage done to this relationship, we must, according to the Church, receive God's mercy through the sacrament of reconciliation.

Venial sins, by contrast, are those that are still sinful but not to such a degree that, by themselves, they jeopardize our friendship with God.

The author of 1 John did not, however, spell out which sins could be mortal, and it was not until a second and third century African theologian named Tertullian came along that a list of "deadly sins" was attempted. Tertullian listed idolatry, blasphemy, murder, adultery, fornication, false witness, fraud, and lying as "deadly sins," and later St. John Cassian and St. Gregory the Great listed the "seven deadly sins": pride, avarice, envy, wrath, lust, gluttony, and sloth. The modern Church also teaches that a number of the rules specified in the Ten Commandments deal with grave matters, and the violation of one of those rules could result in a mortal sin.

However, the Catholic Church has traditionally recognized that, in order for a sin to be considered "mortal," it must meet the following three conditions: *It must be a) a grave matter which is b) committed with full knowledge and c) deliberate consent.*

What exactly is to be considered a "grave" matter is difficult to say, and different theologians have different interpretations. But it is clear by the nature of the offenses that acts such as homicide, adultery, blasphemy, and perjury are grave matters and that stealing a pack of gum, giggling when someone trips, or making fun of someone's haircut are not so serious.

But even if a person does commit an act that is sufficiently grave, she may not be guilty of a "mortal sin"; a person must be fully aware that what she is doing is seriously wrong, and she must perform this act with the full consent of her will. For instance, if a man who has been diagnosed as a paranoid schizophrenic commits suicide in order to rid himself of the living nightmare that his life has become, it would be wrong to conclude that he was guilty of a mortal sin, for even though suicide is a grave matter, a mentally ill person can hardly be said either to have full knowledge or to be able to give the full consent of his will. Nor, perhaps, would a woman who commits perjury be guilty of a "mortal sin" if she or her family were being threatened by mobsters, even though perjury is a grave matter and this person has full knowledge[13] that it is a grave matter, it is difficult to say that she has given her full consent to this action.

When one of the three conditions outlined above is not fully present, the sin in question is called a "venial sin."[14] But merely because a sin is "venial" does not mean that it is of no consequence. "Venial sins" are still sins, and as such, they need to be recognized and duly punished. St. Augustine warns of the importance of paying close attention to "venial sins" in the following colorful way:

> But do not despise these sins which we call "light" [i.e., "venial"]: if you take them for light when you weigh them, tremble when you count them. A number of light objects makes a great mass; a number of drops fills a river; a number of grains makes a heap.[15]

Indeed, how else could people commit mortal sins, if not through the repeated practice of committing venial sins? Do people suddenly wake up one day and say, "What a great day to kill somebody!" or "Today, I feel like becoming a heroin addict!"? Just as almost all heroin addicts probably began their drug careers with less harmful drugs such as alcohol and, later, require ever increasing levels of this drug or new drugs to satisfy their hunger, people who recklessly commit many little sins will soon find that the more serious sins are much easier to commit. It is not a coincidence that serial killer Jeffrey Dahmer began his life of ignominy torturing bugs and small animals or, in general, that hardened criminals usually have a record, extending back to their adolescent years, that details a series of lesser crimes.

C3. Social Sin

On a Friday night, after defeating their archenemies in football, the students of Yahoo High decide that it is time for a party. As always, somebody's parents are out of town, and as a consequence, the beer is flowing like water. The corner market never checks ID's, and why should they when Reggie, though only seventeen, practically has a full-grown beard? Billy, of course, had to show up for the party because he intercepted two passes during the game, and though he wanted to join in the celebration, he did not want to drink. When he walked into the party, he immediately felt the pressure to drink. It was not like those cheesy 80's movies in which someone comes up to a nerd and says, "Hey you sissy, why aren't you drinking like the rest of us?" But nonetheless, he could feel it in the air; there was an expectation that he should drink, even though no person in particular confronted him.

Just as many venial sins can build up in each person a disposition to perform ever more serious mortal sins, the sins of many individual people can build up in society to form powerful institutions or structures of evil that theologians call "social sin." "Social sins" are the product of individual sins, but they are not simply the individual sins of people. It is almost as if each person's sins leave behind a residue or deposit which continues to live long after the person's actions have been completed.

Though teenage drinking is not the most grievous crime humanity has ever known, the foregoing example does illustrate some of the characteristics of this type of sin. In the example above, a number of teenagers have broken the law, but their conduct does not simply affect them; it creates an atmosphere in which underage drinking is expected and breaking the law becomes something commonplace.

With time and the repetition of personal sins, sinful practices become institutionalized: underage drinking and "experimentation" with sex become expected; people who are overweight, uneducated, or uncoordinated are invariably ridiculed; corporate executives lay off hundreds of employees while giving themselves multi-million-dollar raises because "that's just the way capitalism is"; the inhabitants of Third World countries starve to death or migrant workers from Mexico work for slave-wages in California and Texas, but little attention is paid to these things because "there's nothing anyone can do about those people." "You can't change these sinful institutions," says the conventional wisdom, "and if you try to change these institutions, you will end up going mad or you will be crushed like a bug in the process." If anybody dares to question these unholy traditions, she is immediately ostracized, made to be a pariah in one way or another.

Indeed, it takes maturity to face the social sin that is at work in the world. It takes courage and faith to decide to dedicate your energies to opposing and defeating these institutions, but these institutions will not take any of your efforts lying down. Just ask Martin Luther King, Jr., who lost his life trying to bring an end to the tyranny of racism, a social sin that has been a plague to American society since its inception. Just ask Jesus, who was put to death in large part because He exposed the institutional hypocrisy of the Jewish leaders, the Pharisees. Or just try *for one week* not to give in to the temptations to tease overweight people, to tell racist or ethnic jokes, to join in the crowd and smoke or drink. You will probably find that there are very strong forces both inside and outside of you that are going against your efforts. "Social sin" is real.

SECTION HIGHLIGHTS

Though the subject is often unpleasant, it is necessary to study, analyze, and categorize sin for at least the following reasons: a) Sin is real and cannot be overlooked; b) Jesus' message and life as redeemer make little sense unless it is understood that we are in need of redemption; and c) By diagnosing the kinds and degrees of sin, we will be in a much better position to cure ourselves or let Christ cure us.

Sin can be understood in many ways. The labels or divisions of sin that have been most frequently used are: original sin, personal sin, and social sin.

Original sin is a force or drive like gravity within a human being that pulls him toward evil desires and actions, sometimes against his explicit wishes to do the good. It is not a type of action or something one person does to another; it is a condition in which people find themselves.

Personal sins are committed when people fall short of their obligations or fail to fulfill what genuine love requires. The Catechism of the Catholic Church classifies personal sins in the following ways: according to the virtues or goods they oppose; according to the commandments they violate; according to whom they concern; according to whether they concern God, neighbor, or oneself; according to whether they are sins in thought, word, deed, or omission; and according to their gravity.

The most grave (or serious) sins are called "mortal sins" or sins "unto death," for they put the soul in a condition to be excluded from Christ's kingdom. The Catholic Church maintains that such sins remove a person from a state of grace and that a person who has committed such a sin must receive the sacrament of reconciliation in order to prepare him or her to receive God's forgiveness.

In order for a sin to be considered mortal, it must meet three conditions: a) it must be involve a grave matter; b) it must be carried out in full knowledge that the action in question is seriously disordered; and c) it must be carried out with the full consent of the will. A venial sin is any sin that has less than the full presence of these three conditions.

The repetition of personal sins in society can result in "social sins," evil institutions or practices that become entrenched in a society and whose influence seems to go beyond that of any group of individuals.

QUESTIONS

To show that you understand the concepts presented in this section, answer the following questions in complete sentences on a separate sheet of paper.

1.   In this Section of Chapter Four, the author noted that the notion of original sin engendered mixed feelings in most Christians; he compared people's feelings about this type of sin to their feelings regarding the existence of ghosts. What do you believe about the notion of original sin as expounded above? Is it a reality? How is a modern, scientifically-minded person to understand the story of Adam and Eve?

2.   Among the seven deadly sins are listed both pride and lust. Are pride and lust *really* bad things? Explain your answer and use an illustration or two to prove your point.

3.   A number of years ago at one high school, some students cleverly found a way to break into the school's records and change a number of their grades. Analyze this action in terms of the guidelines or distinctions outlined in the fourth paragraph from Section Highlights on the preceding page, and then explain why you believe that such an action could or could not be grave enough to be regarded as a *mortal sin*.

4.   Describe a social sin, besides underage drinking, that you believe pervades American society in general or your school in particular. How does this sin meet the definition of a social sin given in this chapter?

PART THREE:
CONSCIENCE

With a careful examination of the Catholic concept of sin, we have begun study of what the Catholic Christian tradition says about the way that human persons come to know what is right and wrong. The next part of our study will focus on the topic of conscience. It will focus on a clarification of what is meant by the word conscience, how conscience differs from "superego," and what are the three related ways that our conscience functions so as to lead us to judgment about right and wrong.

Write out two paragraphs that treat this statement: *"There is both a good and a bad way to understand the saying, 'Let your conscience be your guide.'"* In these paragraphs, you may either explain the good and the bad ways, or say why you disagree with the statement.

A. WHAT IS CONSCIENCE?

We are examining the Catholic Christian tradition's outlook on how members of that faith and, to some extent, of other Christian denominations can arrive at a correct judgment about what is right and wrong and about what should and should not be done, if one wishes to be an ethical person. As we said in the opening pages, about non-religious ethical systems, one's ethical framework will be determined in large measure by how one views human nature.

People of the Christian faith like Martin Luther King believe that a portion of the process of reaching a true judgment about what is right and what is wrong in- volves *not only reasoning* but recourse to a range of values derived from an experience which they call *"faith."* In their view, *God has spoken* to the human family *through the teachings of Jesus* about how to attain happiness. So faith leads Christians to take very seriously the values proposed by Jesus of Nazareth, the values recorded in the writings of the New Testament.

Catholic Christians include in their ethical choices another faith tradition that complements the tradition recorded in the Bible. They attend to the accumulated wisdom of the Christian community that draws upon centuries of reflection about how to apply Jesus' teachings to the new problems of successive generations; this wisdom is recorded in Church teaching. The Catholic Christian community believes that this twofold experience of faith—from the Bible and from Church tradition— helps a member of its denomination to reach a judgment of conscience about what is right and what is wrong.

In a number of pages that follow, we will explore very specifically how Catholic Christianity sees a person forming her conscience responsibly. It will be helpful for persons of other Christian denominations to study that process and to make judg- ments about how they should go about making responsible judgments of conscience.

The process followed by the Catholic Christian community and by the non-Catholic Christian communities will have many points in common.

The focus of this particular section is quite modest. It aims to clarify what is meant by the word conscience as that concept appears in the expressions, "He is a 'conscientious' person," and "Let your conscience be your guide."

First it should be said that quite obviously, people understand by conscience that internal voice in each human that says to a person, "This is right! That is wrong! You should not do this!"

B.   CONSCIENCE vs. SUPEREGO

While it is quite simple to know of this reality since we all have experienced it already in our lives, we have also experienced that we sometimes hear *several conflicting voices* inside our heads and we are sometimes unsure which of those is the true voice of conscience. Which of these voices is "the true voice," the voice, which believers say, is the voice of God within us?

This section aims to clarify what exactly is meant by *the word* conscience and to say how its true voice can be distinguished from other voices in our heads.

The first consideration to be made in this regard is the difference between conscience and what the renowned psychiatrist Sigmund Freud dubbed the superego. While we may not agree with Freud's views about religion, we Christians have been helped by what he has told us about superego. Freud noted that in making decisions people are often influenced by the teachings of their elders and the teaching of their society. These teachings help to moderate the person's instinctual drives, which are often dominated by the pleasure principle. To be crude, how do people learn to be continent ("potty trained"), not to reach for the potatoes with their pinky, or to eat with moderation? Their parents *tell* them what they should and should not do, and they reward them for good behavior and sometimes punish them for bad behavior. This process of instruction operates on the full range of instinctual drives, and helps a person to learn what it is to be "civilized." Freud himself recognized and concurred with the need for restraint of instinctual drives if a person is going to be properly socialized so as to become a positive contributor to human society.

But Freud also encountered people who were inhibited in their behavior by an overdeveloped, tyrannical superego, i.e., by a whole set of instructions from the major authorities in their lives that did not allow them sufficient freedom and opportunity to learn how to act responsibly. A tyrannical superego does not give a person sufficient autonomy to enable him to make judgments about what is right and wrong independently of the authorities in his life, and it fills him with false shame for actions that are not truly wrong.

The consequence of being dominated by their superego for these people, as Freud and others have observed, is that these people are emotionally crippled by scruples and by neuroses. (Some people wash their hands twenty to thirty times a day because they feel a false sense of guilt and unworthiness.) Some people, while not crippled with guilt, are susceptible to being overpowered by authority figures who direct them to obey commands to do evil. Such were the German soldiers during World War II who justified slaughtering Jewish women and children because their commandant had told them to do it; "we obeyed as good soldiers." Such were the U.S. Marines at My Lai who slaughtered helpless Vietnamese women and children, under the orders of their Captain (Medina) and Sergeant (Calley).

Not all of the directives of our superegos are wrong or crippling, like the ones mentioned in the paragraph above. In fact, many of the directives that our superegos provide are helpful to right behavior and to our becoming healthy human beings. One of the tasks of growing up is to decide more and more whether the voice we hear from our superego is giving us healthy guidance or not, and to make a judgment about that issue. This process is often a painful one. But it is a process which leads us to become truly mature, free, responsible human beings who can assume responsibility for our own futures and who are capable of becoming *leaders* in the world, leaders who can move the world toward good and toward sanity. The result of such a process is *the maturation* of a healthy conscience.

C.   THREE WAYS OUR CONSCIENCES FUNCTION

Now that we understand the difference between conscience and superego, let's take a look at three ways in which our consciences function.

First of all, the conscience in each of us moves us to seek both to know and to do what is good, and conversely to avoid what is evil. *This instinct within us* is rightly called conscience.

There is then a second phase of conscience. When we are confronted with complicated ethical questions, for example, the question of whether to withdraw life-support systems for a relative who has been seriously injured in a car crash and is "brain dead," we have to seek information about what is the morally right decision for our family in this situation. Such situations require us to seek reliable sources of guidance if we are to make the decision that will help the human community and honor God's will for us. This process of seeking to see truly and to think honestly is a second function of conscience.

A third function of conscience is the upshot of this process. We reach a decision that says: "This is what God wants *me* to do." The characteristic of this facet of conscience is that it is a decision about what God wants from me, and therefore, what is right for me to do. In some cases, this personalized decision is absolutely unique to the individual, as in the case of someone who may be called to join a religious order. In some cases, this personalized decision may also apply to others as well, as in the case of some student seeing that it is wrong and not Christ-like to make fun of a classmate who is easily classified as "nerd." But in both cases, one's conscience has persuaded him that "this is what I must do to be an honorable person."

Some pointers offered by theologian Richard Gula, SS, about conscience are worth mentioning here. Gula writes:

" [A] criterion of a mature moral conscience is the ability to make up one's mind for oneself about what ought to be done. Note: this criterion says *for* oneself, not *by* oneself. The mature conscience is formed and exercised in community in dialogue with other sources of moral wisdom. The criterion also implies that if a person spends his or her whole life doing what he or she is told to do by some authority simply because the authority says so, or because it is expected by the group, then that person never really makes moral decisions which are his or her *own*. For moral maturity one must be one's own person. It is not enough merely to follow what one has been told. The morally mature person must be able to perceive, choose, and identify the self with what one does. On the moral level, we perceive every choice as a choice between being an authentic or an inauthentic person. ... *As long as we do not direct our own activity, we are not yet free, morally mature persons.*"[16]

D. FORMATION OF CONSCIENCE

How does a person develop a mature conscience? Historical study of how Catholic Christian educators approach the formation of conscience in recent years reveals that this effort has been focused very much on teaching a person how to answer the questions: *"What ought I to do?"* Formation of conscience became "a matter of acquiring the necessary skills for making right judgments."[17] The necessary skills were these: how to know and to assess morally relevant factors, the ability to consider all sides of an issue, the ability to maintain a steadfast will, etc.

Catholic ethicist Richard Gula recognizes the importance of mastering these skills; so he devotes a number of chapters in one of his books to helping with that process. But he goes on to point out that there is another important dimension of forming one's conscience. One must address another moral question: *"What sort of person ought I to become?"* As Gula emphasizes, "Attention to *character* has been a sorely neglected side of the formation of conscience."[18]

E. CHARACTER FORMATION

Immediately, we all understand, to a degree, what is meant by the word "character." It is, in Gula's words, "the pattern of actions which reflect [our] attitudes [and] dispositions, and [our] readiness to look [at] things and to make choices in certain ways. Character predisposes us to choose in certain ways, even though it does not predetermine every choice."[19] Gula recognizes that Christians aim to imitate the loving, heroic character of Jesus.

Gula indicates the practical impact the failure to recognize the role of character has had on the formation of character. What educators failed to attend to sufficiently in the formation of conscience over the past years was the impact which images, stories, and the community-tone in a person's world has upon the formation of her character, and ultimately upon the way she comes to make a decision.

Who are held up in our communities as heroes? What kind of images do we feed on in watching television or reading magazines or the newspapers, or in attending school, or in conversing with our peers? Our society's heroes and favorite images will shape the way we look at the world, and the way we look at the world shapes the way we arrive at decisions about right and wrong.

Think for a moment of the worlds you personally live in: your ethnic community, school, sports, family, church, politics, advertising, mass media, entertainment, circle of peers. What are the major images and influences in each of those worlds? How do they shape your outlook on success, sex, use of weapons, wealth's importance, euthanasia, etc.? What impact do they have on the formation of your ideals and, therefore, on your character? All of these factors shape our vision and help to mold our character.

So it is necessary for us to be aware of how we are subtly and sometimes subconsciously influenced by our environment. As Gula says, we need to ask ourselves, "What sort of person do I want to become?" Am I being wise in the choice of images I am allowing myself to be nourished by each day?

After Gula has called attention to the issue of *character*, he turns to consideration of a general method of moral choice—how to respond to the question, *"What ought I to do?"* Gula writes, "Asking the right questions to analyze [a] situation is the way to move toward seeing reality rightly. The reality-revealing question of 'situational analysis' can help us to test our vision, character, and conscience."[20] Gula enumerates seven questions for moral analysis of a situation.

F. MORAL ANALYSIS AND CONSCIENCE FORMATION

Gula suggests that we ask ourselves the following questions. (The examples provided are taken from his *Reason Informed by Faith*.)

WHAT? *What* is really the case? "Whether war is justified, for example, depends on *what* war is, *what* nuclear weapons do. In medical matters, we need to know *what* chemotherapy does, *what* death is, *what* abortions do. In sexual matters, we need to know *what* masturbation does, *what* contraceptive pills do, *what* sexual intercourse is."

Next is WHO? "Whether I am a conscientious objector or a coward alters the reality of my draft registration. Whether I am a diabetic affects the morality of my eating habits."

WHEN and WHERE? "Driving 55 m.p.h. has different moral meaning when it is done in a school zone at three o'clock than when it is done on Interstate 80."

WHY and HOW? "*Why* illumines the crucial matter of motivation: For example, do I care for my ailing parents as an expression of love for them or to guarantee a cut in their inheritance? *How* is also a crucial matter and can change the morality of an otherwise good action: For example, today we hear some assert that though the *why* of saving many American lives in World War II was a good one, the *how* of atomic bombing Nagasaki and Hiroshima did not justify the killing and maiming of thousands of Japanese citizens."

Finally, the WHAT IF and WHAT ELSE? *"What if* can teach us to look at the long term results of an action: For instance, euthanasia relieves the suffering of a dying patient in the short run, but what will result from the practice of euthanasia in the long run and from a social point of view? It threatens the trust upon which the physician-patient relation depends, and it can devalue human-life as well as the quality and attitude of mercy among health care providers."

"What else?" "What else can be done?" "What alternatives do we have to abortion ... to driving alone to work ... to television as our primary source of family entertainment?"[21]

SECTION HIGHLIGHTS

Conscience is the internal voice that tells a person which actions are morally right and which are morally wrong.

Catholic Christians look not only to the work of reasoning but also to the teachings of the Bible and to the Catholic tradition, i.e., to the accumulated wisdom of the Christian community codified in official Catholic teachings, for guidance about correct moral behavior.

"Superego" refers to the internal voice within us that originates from the teachings and the directives of the authorities in our lives—e.g., the teachings and directives of our parents, of our society's laws and customs, of our society's officials.

The teachings and directives of our superego can give good moral guidance or bad moral guidance. In the first case, our superego will help us to do what it is right; in the second case, it will impede morally good and healthy behavior.

Conscience helps us: a) by urging us to move toward the good and the true; b) by motivating us to gather the information we need to find the correct answers to complex moral problems; c) by enabling us to reach a personal decision that "this is what God wants me to do."

Formation of conscience entails not only learning a method for determining "what I ought to do" but also contemplating "what sort of person I should become"—i.e., thinking about "my character."

"Character" is shaped by the images and the heroes one chooses to cultivate. Therefore, it is important to attend to what one reads, looks at, and chooses to talk about, as well as to attend to the images and ideas that one's society is "feeding us."

Judging what one should do requires careful analysis of the particular moral situation one is facing. Such analysis is accomplished by asking: WHAT?; WHO?; WHEN & WHERE?; WHY & HOW?; WHAT IF & WHAT ELSE?

QUESTIONS

Write your answers to the following questions on a separate piece of paper. Write in complete sentences.

1.   What is the difference between the way a non-religious ethical system and a religious ethical system will tackle a moral problem?

2.   Give an example of when a person's superego helps and an example of when it hinders right moral decision-making.

3.   T-F: A person who makes a moral decision about a complex issue without trying to gather good information about the issue has a healthy conscience.

4.   What are the dominant images in your culture? Do they help or do they impede the development of a good character? How? Why?

PART FOUR:
THE PARTS OF A MORAL (OR IMMORAL) ACT: "OBJECT," "INTENTION," AND "CIRCUMSTANCE"[22]

"I know that you're not supposed to steal, but I wanted to give my mother something nice for her birthday."

"Ladies and gentlemen of the jury, it is one thing for a woman, in a fit of anger, to shoot her husband after catching him in the act of adultery. But it is quite another for her, as a form of revenge, to slowly poison him to death over the course of a few months!"

"True, he did cheat on his exam, but he is only seventeen years old! Wouldn't you do the same if your parents were never satisfied with your report card? And, to tell you the truth, he wouldn't have gotten into Georgetown if he hadn't cheated."

If we truly wish to be virtuous people and if we wish to counsel our friends in their pursuit of the good, then we must learn how to evaluate morally significant human actions. But evaluating or analyzing human actions is a tricky business. Sure, the Ten Commandments prohibit stealing, but what if someone steals out of love for his mother? Does that love make the stealing acceptable? If so, why? If not, how does that love affect the action? What difference does it make whether a woman shoots her husband in cold blood or poisons him over the course of a few weeks? Is one less severe than the other? Or, a little closer to home, can pressure from parents or the prospect of getting accepted into the school of your choice ever make cheating acceptable? What relation do these issues have to your decision to cheat?

After centuries of reflection on these matters, the Catholic Church, largely following the wisdom of Jesus and Christians such as St. Paul and St. Thomas Aquinas, has come to understand that human actions can be broken down into three basic components: *object, intention,* and *circumstance.* Though it may be difficult to draw the line as to where exactly the "object" starts and the "circumstances" begin (or, for example, where exactly the "intention" stops and the "object" starts), most actions can be analyzed fairly neatly into these compartments. Once an action is analyzed in this way, its character becomes much clearer. This way of viewing actions, then, can be a great benefit to our own moral development or that of our neighbors.

The *object* of an action is *what* you have chosen to do; it is the concrete, physical action you have taken. In the first example above, the object of the son's act is "stealing a Michael Bolton CD (or whatever he stole for his mother)"; in example two, the object of the woman's action is either "shooting her husband" or "poisoning her husband." In the third example, "cheating on the exam" would be the object of the action.

The *intention* of an action is *why* exactly you have chosen to do the object in question. The will has chosen some object—stealing, poisoning, or cheating—*for some particular reason or reasons.* The son obviously stole the Michael Bolton CD *in order to express his affection for his mother.* The wife killed her husband, in whatever gruesome manner, *in order to exact revenge on him, free herself up for another partner, collect life insurance money, or for some other reason.* Notice that, as the case of the jilted wife illustrates, it is possible to have more than one intention or motive; isn't it handy to be able to exact revenge and collect life insurance money at the same time! Likewise, on the brighter side, it is possible to have one ultimate intention or end for all of one's actions and then to have additional intentions for each object chosen. For example, a woman who has committed her life to loving and serving Christ may give a large sum of her income to the poor, not only to express her love and devotion to God and His Commandments but also to help better the earthly condition of people in need.

Together, the object and the intention make up the core of a human action; they are the primary elements of a human action. But surrounding that core are a number of secondary elements known as *circumstances.* The circumstances of an action can be a number of different things that affect either *a) the person who is performing the action or b) the content of the action itself.* For example, the situation or surroundings of a person, such as his or her age, economic status, psychological state, etc., fall into the category of "circumstances." The boy who decides to steal a CD may come from a poverty-stricken home and lack the money to buy the CD, or the student who decides to cheat on his exam may be receiving daily reminders from his parents of how well his *brother* did at Georgetown. Likewise, the circumstances surrounding the wife who shoots her husband—viz., the fact that she was overwhelmed with anger at the sight of her philandering spouse—are different from those surrounding the wife who poisons her husband—she is not overwhelmed with anger but is, rather, calm, cool, and calculating. The circumstances surrounding the object of an action itself can change. For example, the boy who stole the CD might have decided to steal a television—a much more expensive item—or the student who cheated may have only cheated on a reading quiz, as opposed to an exam. Or, perhaps, the woman who shot her husband also robbed three children of a father and left many other people without this friend or relative, whereas the woman who poisoned her husband may have only left his friends and relatives to grieve his death.

Given an understanding of these three parts of human actions, we are now much better equipped to evaluate our conduct. According to the *Catechism of the Catholic Church, both the object and the intention of an action must be good in order for the action as a whole to be morally praiseworthy.* Unlike Immanuel Kant, who believed that the motive is the only important part of a human action, both St. Paul and St. Thomas Aquinas among others explicitly state that an evil action cannot be justified by a good intention. Hence, even though the boy stole the CD out of love for his mother, stealing a CD is immoral, and his action as a whole is not praiseworthy. Conversely, an object of an action that is good in itself, such as helping an old lady cross a street, can be corrupted if the intention is bad, such as hoping that one's boss will witness this "kind" act (which just happens to take place under her office window) and give the person a promotion.

The circumstances surrounding a person or her actions are only secondary elements of the action as a whole, but they do greatly affect its moral status. In general, the circumstances affect both a) the level of responsibility of a person and b) the level of moral goodness or evil of an action. For example, a teenage girl from a poor family who procures a first trimester abortion, i.e., one within the first three months of pregnancy, does so under very different circumstances than a successful and wealthy woman in her late twenties who procures a third trimester abortion, i.e., one within the last three months. First, though the object of both actions is morally disordered—one should never intentionally take innocent life—the girl is poor and young, two circumstances which lessen her level of responsibility. However, the wealthy woman has both the means and the emotional maturity to raise a child, but she chooses an abortion anyway, making her level of responsibility much greater.

One final important point: No matter how grave or outlandish they may become, the circumstances surrounding an object can never change an inherently immoral object into a good one. Even if a girl is young and poor and people close to her are pressuring her to have an abortion, the intentional taking of life is always in itself wrong. This view runs counter to utilitarianism, the philosophy which states that "the end justifies the means." The consequences of an action, which fall into the category of "circumstances," cannot make an evil object good.

However, there are rare occasions when the intention and object of an action can be good, but the circumstances might be such as to make that action as a whole inappropriate. For example, there is nothing wrong with two parents discussing the problems they are having raising their boy, but this conversation would be inappropriate if the boy's younger sister were in the room. Likewise, a married couple may wish to make love to show each other affection, but one of the partners may have a medical condition that makes lovemaking hazardous at this particular time.[23] There is certainly nothing disordered about a married man and his wife making love, but if the husband has been diagnosed with hepatitis or the wife is still recovering from childbirth, then sexual intercourse, under these circumstances, would be imprudent.

These distinctions between the object, intention, and circumstances of a human action are not overly sophisticated distinctions made by theologians and philosophers who live in ivory towers. People make these distinctions everyday; theologians and philosophers have simply organized these insights and clarified them a bit. In court, for example, judges must make distinctions between first and second degree murder. First degree murder is done with the full consent of the will and with full knowledge of the gravity of the crime; the woman above who poisoned her husband committed first degree murder. Second degree murder is missing some component of first degree murder, either full consent or full knowledge; the woman mentioned above who was overcome with rage—whose will was overpowered by anger—committed second degree murder. Both actions are judged to be crimes, but the court takes *circumstances*, such as the mental state of the person, into account when passing judgment.

Likewise, in the Gospels (Luke 21:1-4 and Mark 12:41-44), we are told that one day Jesus was watching people giving alms in the Temple. Luke tells us that Jesus saw "rich people dropping their gifts in the Temple treasury, and he saw a very poor widow dropping in two little copper coins. He said, 'I tell you that this poor widow put in more than all the others. For the others offered their gifts from what they had to spare of their riches; but she, poor as she is, gave all she had to live on." Jesus does not condemn the rich; he recognizes that the object of giving alms is good in itself, but the circumstances surrounding the woman, viz., that she was extremely poor, enriched the moral goodness of her action.

SECTION HIGHLIGHTS

The Church (and others) divides human actions into three components: object, intention, and circumstance.

The object of an action is what exactly you have chosen to do; it is the concrete physical action you have taken.

The intention of an action is why exactly you have chosen to do the object in question. There can be many intentions or levels of intentions for any one action.

The circumstances of an action are secondary elements that affect either the person who is performing the action or the content of the action itself. As such, they can affect both the level of responsibility of a person and/or the level of moral goodness or evil of an action.

A morally good action will have a good object, will be done with the right intention(s), and will be performed under the proper circumstances.

EXERCISES

Using a separate piece of paper, complete each of the following tasks (in writing) for each of the two scenarios below:

1. Identify the object, intention(s), and circumstances of the action of the main character.

2. Evaluate the action and the main character. Is it a morally good or morally evil action? *How* good or evil? What level of responsibility does the agent have? Explain.

3. Change one of the circumstances and show how this change affects the level of responsibility of the agent and/or the level of goodness or evil of the action.

A.   *Malachi never was very good with the ladies. He was always just a bit too thin and a bit too awkward for his own liking. Even though he was a junior in high school —almost 17 years old—he had only had one girlfriend, and she moved away freshman year. And his friends were really coming down hard on him these days. Was he really a "dork" or a "weirdo" like some people were saying?*

Well, one night at a party after having a few drinks, Malachi was told by his friends that a new freshman girl thought he was really "artistic" and that she wanted to meet him. Eventually, after a few more drinks, Malachi got up the nerve to talk to Thelma. She really seemed to like him, but she really just did not interest him. She giggled all the time and played with her gum. When she excused herself to go to the bathroom, Malachi's friends returned and told him this was his big chance! In fact, by now nearly everyone had their eye on him and this girl. When she returned, everyone left them in the room together, but before leaving, his buddy Felix told him he wanted to know "all the details" later on. When Thelma tried to kiss him, he did not resist, and they ended up making out. "Well, at least I can give Felix a good report," he thought to himself.

B.   *Sitting next to Vinnie in physics was not a pleasant experience for Paul. Not only was Vinnie big and mean, he was a really poor student. Why should he bother with school when his hockey abilities would get him into any college of his choice? On the other hand, Paul, who was kind and disciplined, routinely earned A's on his report card; he had no sports career on which to rely.*

Test time was always an anxious time for Paul; not only was there the pressure of exams to deal with but Vinnie always wanted to cheat off of him. And even though Paul had never given in before, everyone who followed the hockey team, as he did, knew that the Eagles were hopeless in their championship game without their star goalie—who just happened to be Vinnie. And a failure on this test would mean academic probation for the hockey star; he had let everyone, especially Paul, know this unfortunate fact.

When the tests were handed out, Vinnie immediately began to ask for help. Despite the pressure, Paul ignored him throughout the test. Needless to say, Vinnie failed, the hockey team lost, and Vinnie was not exactly happy.

CHAPTER FIVE:
SCRIPTURE AND TRADITION: SOURCES FOR THE FORMATION OF CONSCIENCE

PART ONE:
USE OF SCRIPTURE–
A CATHOLIC VIEW

Now we begin to look at the resources used in the Catholic ethical system: recourse to Christian Scripture, to the Church, and to the Church's tradition of wisdom and holiness. In this section of the chapter, we will look at Scripture and how it is employed in ethical decisions made by Christians.

One way to understand why Scripture plays such an important role in the Catholic ethical system is to view Scripture as a set of books inspired by the author of Christianity that tell folks how to live a good life. Christians believe that just as Aristotle explained his system for finding happiness to his followers in the *Nicomachean Ethics*, God has presented the main theoretical blueprint for the human race to achieve happiness in the Bible. The Bible reveals what God has done, is doing, and will do for humankind, as well as what He expects humans to do to make His efforts on their behalf fruitful.

But the Bible is not like every other book. One of the wonderful paradoxes about the Bible is that, in one sense, virtually everyone knows how to read it yet, in another, virtually no one can agree on how it is to be read. Though the Scriptures might be a bit more difficult to read than *Green Eggs and Ham*, they are certainly no more difficult to read than *The Phantom Tollbooth* or *The Red Pony*, books that everyone tackled (or could have tackled) in elementary school. However, as the ever-growing number of different Christian denominations indicates, there is little consensus as to *how* the Bible is to be read. Indeed, if the Bible is not the most problematic book ever written—which it may very well be—it is unquestionably the most controversial.

So, before diving headfirst into the central question of this chapter—how to use Scripture in Catholic Ethics—it will be necessary to wade into some of the more fundamental issues confronting anyone who wishes to read Scripture *for any purpose*.

A.   DIFFICULTIES OF INTERPRETATION AND SOME BRIEF RESPONSES

A1.   Divine Inspiration

Though some avid readers of popular fiction might idolize the authors of those works, few would be willing to claim that God Himself helped write them. Stephen King might be good, but he is not God. However, Christians not only believe that the Bible is a human testament of God's loving relationship with the Jews and, eventually, all His peoples; they also believe that, in some sense, God had a hand in writing these sacred books. The Bible itself attests to this belief: "All Scripture is inspired by God and profitable for teaching, for reproof, for correction, and for training in righteousness …" (2 Tim. 3:16).

Needless to say, this central Christian belief, that the Bible is "divinely inspired," in a way no other collection of books is said to be, has been a center of controversy for believers for as long as the Bible has been in existence. To what degree or in what way is the Bible a *divine* document and to what degree or in what way is it a *human* one?

The extreme conservative position on this issue is represented by the *fundamentalists*, who, for the most part, are members of Protestant denominations. They believe that God's relationship to the human authors of the Bible was like that of a puppeteer to his puppet or, as a second-century Christian writer put it, a flute-player to his flute.[1] The human role in the whole process becomes that of a mere instrument or tool of divine activity, and thus for this group of believers, the Scriptures are the first, last, and final say on any matter whatsoever. Indeed, this view has something of its own support in Scripture itself: "First of all you must understand this, that no prophecy ever came by the impulse of man, but men moved by the Holy Spirit spoke for God" (2 Peter 1:20-21).

The extreme liberal position is constituted by Catholics and Protestants who, though believing that Scripture is divinely inspired, maintain that this inspiration is not any different than the inspiration that led St. Augustine to write his *Confessions* or the inspiration that led Mother Theresa to help feed and comfort the lepers of Calcutta. Such liberal thinkers emphasize the truly human aspect of the Scripture. Historians and theologians have shown throughout the 19th and 20th centuries that the books of the Bible have historical inaccuracies; they are inevitably shaped by the specific cultures from which they originated; and their authors were limited in knowledge about a great many scientific matters. Emphasizing these limitations, such thinkers downplay the divine role in the formation of Scripture.

As with most things in life, as Aristotle observed, the middle course is usually the most advisable, and in regard to this centuries-old debate about the nature of "divine inspiration," a middle path that acknowledges the truth in both extremes, while avoiding their excesses, is probably the closest to the truth.

One helpful way of finding a middle ground in this relationship between the human and the divine in the Bible is to try to understand them in the light of the mystery of the Incarnation. Today, all Christians affirm that Jesus of Nazareth was God Himself, even though He was fully a human being as well, but in the early days of the Church, there was not nearly as much consensus. In an effort to make this incomprehensible mystery more intelligible, some early Christians tried to de-emphasize either the divine or human element of Jesus. Those guilty of what came to be called *"Docetism"* denied the truly human aspect of Jesus; He only *appeared* to die on the Cross, and as the all-knowing God, He only *appeared* to "increase in wisdom and in stature, and in favor with God and man" (Lk. 2:52) as He matured. Those guilty of what came to be called *"Ebionitism"* and later *"Arianism"* denied the truly divine aspect of Jesus; He was perhaps the greatest of all religious leaders, the most astute observer of human nature, the most exalted of prophets and ethical teachers, but He was not God Himself.

As with the theology of the Incarnation, so too, any approach to the Scriptures should avoid the extremes that devalue either the *human* or *divine* nature of Holy Scripture. This middle approach must acknowledge both the divine authority of the Scriptures as well as the limitations of any human author living in a certain time in a certain part of the world. As the *Catechism* states, "Indeed the words of God, expressed in the words of men, are in every way like human language, just as the Word of the eternal Father, when he took on himself the flesh of human weakness, became like men."[2] The fundamentalists are guilty of a "Docetic" approach to Scripture; they fail to recognize the human limitations and historical circumstances of the Bible. Similarly, the liberal Protestants and Catholics are guilty of an "Ebionite" approach to Scripture; they fail to recognize the fully divine nature of the Scriptures, especially its infallibility in spiritual and moral matters.

A2. Infallibility and the Meaning of Truth

If, as all Christians maintain, God is, in some sense, the author of the various books of the Bible, then these books must be infallible, containing nothing but the truth. If the divine Word is not trustworthy, then whose word is? However, just as the meaning of "divinely inspired" has shown itself to be variously interpreted and much disputed throughout history and across Christian denominations, the meaning of "infallible" has shown itself to be equally controversial and elusive. In a fashion parallel to (because it is dependent upon) the controversy concerning divine inspiration, Christian denominations have run the gamut from the extremely conservative to the extremely liberal.

The most famous modern representatives of the former position are, again, the fundamentalists. Their creed could be embodied in the catchphrase "the literal truth, the whole truth, and nothing but the truth *because* of God." In their estimation, the divine origin of this text guarantees that *all* of its claims—historical and scientific, as well as theological—are strictly and literally true.

For example, some fundamentalist Protestants have tried to calculate the exact moment of creation by working backward from the genealogies in the book of Genesis, which list how old each patriarch was when his oldest son was born. In the 1930's, one vice-chancellor of a British university thought that he could narrow down the date of creation to 4004 BC at 9 a.m. on October 23rd![3] Though this conclusion and ones similar to it fly in the face of everything that science has to say about the age of the earth, fundamentalists often take solace in Proverbs 30:5-6: "Every word of God proves true; he is a shield to those who take refuge in him. Do not add to his words, lest he rebuke you, and you be found a liar." Additionally, fundamentalists also make reference to a Protestant doctrine known as "total depravity," the idea that every fiber of man is infected with original sin. In its more extreme interpretations, this doctrine would lead one to question his own reason before God's Sacred Scriptures. "If my reason or the reason of other people tells me something contrary to God's infallible teachings," such a believer might argue, "then my reason must be much more corrupted than I ever imagined."

Needless to say, one does not have to be a fundamentalist to believe in the infallibility of Scripture; Martin Luther, John Calvin, and all of the Protestant reformers believed in this doctrine, but none aligned himself with the school of fundamentalist thought just described. John Calvin, for instance, warned that the account of creation in Genesis 1 is not intended as an instruction manual for the natural sciences, especially not astronomy.[4] Likewise, Catholics maintain that "the books of Scripture firmly, faithfully, and without error teach that truth which God, *for the sake of our salvation*, wished to see confided to the Sacred Scriptures."[5] And this belief does not deter Catholic high schools throughout the nation from teaching Darwin's views about the evolution of species or the views of cosmologists about the age of the universe. Even Pope John Paul II has recently given his blessing to the biological truths of evolution.

But the question still remains: How can the Bible be "infallible" if there are obviously "false" statements in these books?

First, it should be noted that no answer to this question could ever (or should ever expect to) remove the element of *mystery and faith* from the Holy Scriptures; neither Christianity, in general, nor the Scriptures, in particular, can be reduced to or translated into a number of statements that can be rationally or scientifically verified. At the heart of the Christian message is the mystery that God became human in the person of Jesus Christ, a mystery taken on faith that will never be proven or refuted by scientists or rationally confirmed or rejected by philosophers.

Second, the Bible itself attests to the fact that divine messages contained within its covers do not simply pour out onto anyone who happens to open it. Catholics and Protestants alike have consistently maintained that the spiritual truths and mysteries of the Scriptures require the intervention and illumination of the Holy Spirit if they are to be understood and taken to heart by man. As St. Paul observed in his First Letter to the Corinthians (2:13), "[W]e impart [our understanding of the gifts bestowed upon us by God] in words not taught by human wisdom but taught by the Spirit, interpreting spiritual truths to those who possess the Spirit." Paul cautions that, according to "the unspiritual man" who lives by worldly standards, the central meaning of Christ's death and resurrection will always seem to be foolish or absurd.

However, keeping these limitations in mind, some useful hints or observations for understanding this problem can be put forward. One of the wisest and most carefully crafted statements about the infallibility of the Bible comes from a Protestant theologian, Donald G. Bloesch:

> The Bible contains a fallible element in the sense that it reflects the cultural limitations of the writers. But it is not mistaken in what it purports to teach, namely, God's will and purpose for the world. There are no errors or contradictions in its substance and heart. It bears the imprint of human frailty, but it also carries the truth and power of divine infallibility. *It is entirely trustworthy in every area in which it claims to be trustworthy.*[6]

If one is looking for a scientific account of the beginning of the universe or an understanding of medicine, astronomy, or even history,[7] the Bible is not the right collection of books to consult. *As a fully human text, the books of the Bible could not help but reflect the limitations and specific character of the culture from which they originated.* The authors of the Gospel could no more have known about the theory of relativity than the authors of Genesis could have known about continental drift or electromagnetic fields. But did the Bible ever really advertise itself as a geology or medical textbook? Scripture testifies to the experience of the living God in the lives of the Jews and the Gentiles, and it advertises God's promise of everlasting life, as well as God's commandments for living a life in accordance with His will. In these *spiritual and moral matters*, Christians believe the Bible to be infallible.

Additionally, the fact that "the Bible" is usually referred to as merely one book often deceives us into thinking that this one book could be approached in one way, and in a classroom setting, that one way is almost always understood to be the same way other books in other subjects are to be approached: literally. However, the phrase "the Bible" is actually a translation of the Greek "ta Biblia" which means "the books." For Catholics, the Old Testament contains 46 books and the New Testament 27. The Bible contains laws, history, philosophical reflection, letters to communities, love ballads for weddings, commandments, parables, allegories, and prophecies, to name a few of the different kinds of writings. Needless to say, these different books were written by different authors, in different styles, in different times and different circumstances, for different audiences, and for different purposes; in other words, each book is different. Given this understanding of "the Bible," it should be obvious that the thought of imposing a uniform criterion of truth on all the books of Sacred Scripture is preposterous.[8]

To illustrate this point, let us take a famous story outside of Scripture, Aesop's fable of the fox and the grapes:

> A famished fox saw some clusters of ripe black grapes hanging from a trel-lised vine. She resorted to all her tricks to get at them, but wearied herself in vain, for she could not reach them. At last she turned away, hiding her disappointment and saying, "The grapes are sour, and not ripe as I thought."

Is this fable "true"? If asked this question, an astute person would respond, "Well, in what sense do you mean 'true'?" If the *historical* or *scientific* accuracy of this tale is at issue, then surely it is false; there never were, nor is it physically possible that there ever will be, a talking fox. However, as anyone who has ever been turned down for a date is aware, this fable is clearly "true" in another sense: When people are unable to secure some good thing they desire, they are likely to feel rejected and, consequently, to find fault with the good thing they could not acquire. "Oh, she really wasn't that good looking after all," a young man might tell his friends to maintain his self-esteem. In a similar fashion, a great deal of the Bible's writing is often true in a non-literal sense, somewhat like a fable, as a brief survey of the books of the Bible should reveal.

Finally, it is important to note one more danger of the overemphasis on historical and scientific accuracy in the Holy Scriptures. In history or science class, there is usually only one exact answer, as every student by now is painfully aware. As a result, young people in particular tend to ask such questions as, "What is the exact meaning of this passage? Is that the true interpretation?" Just as we wish to know when exactly Abraham Lincoln was shot or the exact chemical formula for Iron Sulfide, we have a tendency to want to know all of the *facts* about the Bible. In part, this tendency is a good one, for one of the vital tasks for the proper understanding of a particular passage is to know the facts: who wrote the book, when, to what audience, what would that audience have understood by the word "Messiah," etc. To these questions there may be a single "true" answer or a very limited range of "true" answers, but after the facts have been gathered, many people may take different "truths" from a certain passage. As St. Augustine wrote in one of his prayerful outpourings to God in his *Confessions*:

> [W]hat harm comes to me, if various meanings may be found in these words, all of which are true? ... Therefore, while every man tries to understand in Holy Scripture what the author understood therein, what wrong is there if anyone understand what you, O light of all truthful minds, reveal to *him* as true, even if the author he reads did not understand this ... ?[9]

Many passages may have a richness or depth to them, and it is not relativistic to acknowledge the validity of many different applications of a given passage to a contemporary problem.

For example, in the Gospel of Luke (20:19-25), there is a description of an event involving "spies" who have been instructed by the scribes and the chief priests to lay a trap for Jesus. After offering some flattering remarks in order to soften him up, the spies try to goad Jesus into incriminating himself by speaking out against the government. They ask him, "Is it lawful for us to give tribute (i.e., pay taxes) to Caesar, or not?" Understanding their true motives, Jesus asked them whose likeness was inscribed on their money. After hearing that it was Caesar's, Jesus replied, "Then render to Caesar the things that are Caesar's, and to God the things that are God's." Now, what exactly is the "truth" of the latter statement? Would it be true to state that Jesus would have seen taxation as lawful, as long as the taxpayers did not give their spirit, but only their money, to their leader? Would it be true to state that this passage supports the idea that Jesus believed the religious life should be divorced from government involvement, for a divine vocation should not embroil itself too much in worldly affairs? Would it be true for a young German who, during the 1940's, read this passage and believed that it was telling him that his fanatical devotion to his country was misplaced, and that only God is worthy of complete and undying faith and love? Though certainly there *are* invalid interpretations, all of the interpretations just mentioned seem to be perfectly legitimate and true interpretations of this rather cryptic saying.

A3. The Place of Scripture in Matters of Faith and Morality

Though many Protestants and Catholics would probably be able to reach consensus on the meaning of "divine inspiration" and "infallibility" as these relate to Scripture, they tend to part ways when it comes to the relationship between Scripture and other sources of theological and ethical wisdom.

Following Martin Luther, John Calvin, and the other Reformers, Protestants today generally subscribe to a doctrine called "*sola Scriptura*," the belief that the Bible *alone* is sufficient to meet all of man's theological and ethical needs. Not surprisingly (and as the only logical possibility), this view is based on Scripture itself: Proverbs 30:5-6 warns, "Every word of God proves true. ... Do not add to his words, lest he rebuke you, and you be found a liar," and Mark 7:13 describes Jesus condemning the Pharisees for "making void the word of God through [their] tradition which [they] hand on." Sacred Scripture is the only true source of Revelation for many traditional Protestants; indeed, consistent believers in *sola Scriptura* must and do maintain that Scripture itself contains guidelines for its own interpretation.

Though Catholics agree with their Protestant brothers and sisters that there is, indeed, only one source of divine inspiration—namely God Himself, in the person of the Holy Spirit—they maintain that this Source has revealed itself in two different ways: orally (Sacred Tradition) and in writing (Sacred Scripture).[10] This view, they believe, is confirmed in Scripture, as well. According to the Acts of the Apostles, Jesus appeared before his apostles after his resurrection and told them of their upcoming mission. "[Y]ou shall receive power when the Holy Spirit has come upon you; and you shall be my witnesses in Jerusalem and in all Judea and Samaria and to the end of the earth" (1:8). Catholics believe that this empowerment of the apostles by the Holy Spirit was the beginning of the Catholic Church as a formal institution. Before any of the books of the New Testament were even composed, the apostles were busy healing the sick, converting unbelievers, performing many signs and wonders, and teaching as a testimony to the power of Jesus. These events marked the beginning of the oral tradition of the Church, a tradition that Catholics believe is continued to this day through the bishops. *Within* this community of believers, certain men of particular talent and insight were chosen by the Church and inspired by the Holy Spirit to put down into writing the various narratives, prophecies, and letters that make up the New Testament. Thus, the written works of the New Testament arose after "the Way" or the Christian Church came into being and Catholics believe that "Scripture is ultimately subject to the judgment of the Church which exercises the divinely conferred commission and ministry of watching over and interpreting the Word of God."[11] In the straightforward language of St. Augustine, "But I would not believe in the Gospel, had not the authority of the Catholic Church already moved me."[12]

Needless to say and without further argumentation, the Catholic approach to Scripture will be the one proposed in this text. In its deliberations about theological and moral matters, the Church uses other sources in addition to Scripture, most notably "natural law," that are part of her tradition. However, Catholics should not only recognize the vast similarities that exist between their faith and that of the Protestants; they should also thank them for their helpful criticism and guidance. As Protestants rightfully note, Catholics are often alarmingly ignorant of Scripture, and the Catholic Church itself has recognized the need for the study of ethics, in particular, to be "more thoroughly nourished by scriptural teaching."[13]

For instance, before the Second Vatican Council, which brought about many reforms in the Catholic Church in the 1960's, there was an unfortunate tendency in Catholic ethical thinking to use Scripture as merely a "*proof-text*" for natural law arguments. In other words, a moral theologian would first develop a position for or against a certain ethical issue *using natural law or tradition alone* and then afterwards, as an afterthought, tack on a Biblical passage or two to bolster his or her natural law argument. Such an approach only pays lip service to Scripture, and as a frequent consequence, the Biblical passages that were cited in this manner were often used inappropriately.

For instance, one Catholic moral theologian in the 1950's used proof-texting in his treatment of the issue of contraception or birth control.[14] Only after putting forth an extensive argument against contraception based on natural law and the teachings of various popes did this thinker make reference to the Bible, and when he did, he only cited the Onan story of Genesis 38:8-10. However, it is improbable that this Biblical story specifically relates to the issue of contraceptives:

> And Judah took a wife for Er his first-born, and her name was Tamar. But Er, Judah's first born, was wicked in the sight of the Lord; and the Lord slew him. Then Judah said to Onan (Er's brother), "Go in to your brother's wife, and perform the duty of a brother-in-law to her, and raise up offspring for your brother." But Onan knew that the offspring would not be his; so when he went in to his brother's wife he spilled the semen on the ground, lest he should give offspring to his brother. And what he did was displeasing in the sight of the Lord, and he slew him also (Gen. 38:6-10).

Though it is true that a man (or couple) who uses contraceptives is preventing conception—just as Onan's action had prevented conception—Onan's crime seems to have been his willful failure to fulfill his duty under Jewish law. As Deuteronomy 25:5-10 makes clear, a man whose brother died was obligated "to perpetuate his brother's name"; in other words, according to Jewish law, the first born son of this new union would be considered the offspring of the deceased so that his "his name [would] not be blotted out of Israel." Any man who was unwilling to fulfill his duty as a brother-in-law was publicly shamed by having his sandals removed and his face spat on by his brother's widow. Onan would probably have been slain by God even if he abstained from sex with Tamar altogether or used the Church's approved method of family planning by only having sex during the infertile periods of her cycle.

Needless to say, this story does not provide sufficient reasons for prohibiting contraceptive use, for it is an isolated passage taken out of context. To be understood properly and to be instructive, the Onan story needs to be understood in its original context and combined with a much larger analysis of the Biblical view of sexuality in general. As frequently happens with proof-texting, this Biblical passage has been extracted from its context and uncritically annexed to a natural law or traditional argument.

A4. Inconsistencies between the Old Testament and the New

One of the first generalizations that people who study Scripture learn is that the Old Testament preaches a vengeful and angry God whereas the New Testament teaches a God of love, forgiveness, and mercy. Without a doubt, this generalization is, at best, an exaggeration of the differences between the two testaments and, at worst, a gross distortion of the truth. The supposedly vengeful and angry Old Testament teaches the following:

✛ "You shall not take vengeance or bear any grudge against the sons of your own people, but you shall love your neighbor as yourself" (Lev. 19:18).

✛ "If you meet your enemy's ox or his ass going astray, you shall bring it back to him. If you see the ass of one who hates you lying under its burden, you shall refrain from leaving him with it, you shall help him to lift it up" (Ex. 23:4-5).

✛ "If your enemy is hungry, give him bread to eat; and if he is thirsty, give him water to drink" (Proverbs 25:21).[15]

Likewise, Jesus understood his mission on earth as being compatible with the teachings of the Old Testament. "Think not that I have come to abolish the law and the prophets," Jesus told the crowds in his Sermon on the Mount. "I have come not to abolish them but to fulfill them"(Mt. 5:17). Nor was Jesus a flower child of Woodstock and the 1960's mentality, preaching nothing but peace, love, and understanding. "Do not think that I have come to bring peace on earth," Jesus declared. "I have not come to bring peace, but a sword"(Mt. 10:34). Additionally, at the final judgment, Jesus says that the Son of Man "will say to [the wicked], 'Depart from me, you cursed, into the eternal fire prepared for the devil and his angels'"(Mt. 25:41).

However, this generalization of the Old and New Testaments is not without its element of truth; the Old Testament does contain passages that contrast starkly with the message and life of Jesus, as they are presented in the New Testament. For instance, in 1 Samuel 15:3, the Lord is said to have commanded King Saul to "go and smite the Amalek, and utterly destroy all that they have; do not spare them, but kill both man and woman, infant and suckling, ox and sheep, camel and ass." Indeed, when Saul does not follow through with this command because he "spared ... all that was good" about the Amalekites, the Lord is said to express regret that he has made Saul king! Passages such as these immediately prompt Christians to ask the question: How is one to reconcile the teachings of Jesus, such as "Love your enemies, do good to those who hate you" (Lk. 6:27), with barbaric commandments such as this?

Though, as mentioned above, Catholics *do* believe that all of Sacred Scrip-

ture—both the Old and the New Testaments—is divinely inspired and that it contains "that truth which God, for the sake of our salvation, wished to see confided to
the Sacred Scriptures,"[16] that belief is not the same as the belief that all the Scriptures
carry equal weight. The terrain of Scripture is not flat; the Gospel accounts of Jesus'
words and deeds are the pinnacle from which all other Sacred Scripture is to be viewed.
Christ should be the lens through which the whole of the Bible is viewed and understood, and
as a consequence, Old Testament teachings that are wholly irreconcilable with Jesus'
message must be regarded as "imperfect" or "provisional" teachings of God. When
the Church states that certain teachings are "imperfect" or "provisional," they mean
that they are only applicable to a certain period in Jewish history; they were estab-
lished before Jesus' coming and, therefore, only show a partial understanding of God's
divine ways. As a result, they are no longer binding for Christians. Hence, whatever
the spiritual purpose of 1 Samuel 15:3 may be—whether it is to illustrate God's authority over life and death or to test Saul's faith, as God had earlier tested Abraham's
faith, or to show us, who have been taught by Jesus, how privileged we are and how
weak human insight into God's ways is without God's help—its literal meaning must
be rejected as incompatible with the Christian teaching that innocent blood can
never be shed intentionally.

In support of this view, in various passages throughout the New Testament, it is
clear that Jesus himself and the early Christians regarded some of the ethical and
theological teachings of the Old Testament to be merely provisional. For example, in
His famous Sermon on the Mount, Jesus modifies, purifies, or intensifies a number of
ethical teachings that His audience would have immediately recognized as traditional
Jewish laws. Jesus preached, "[Y]ou have heard that it was said to the men of old, 'You
shall not swear falsely, but shall perform to the Lord what you have sworn.' But I say
to you, do not swear at all …"(Mt. 6:33-34). The first teaching that his audience is
presumed to have heard is a precept of the Jewish law (see Lev. 19:2, Num. 30:2, and
Dt. 23:21), but Jesus teaches the contrary, that a simple "yes" or "no" is the appropriate response to any questioning. Indeed, Jesus uses this format—beginning with an
Old Testament teaching ("You have heard it said …") and raising it to a higher level
("But I say to you …")—to modify traditional Jewish teachings on various issues such
as divorce, revenge, and love (Cf. Mt. 5:31-32; 38-48).

B.   GUIDELINES FOR THE USE OF SCRIPTURE IN ETHICAL
THINKING

Having addressed some general difficulties facing anyone who chooses to read
Scripture for any purpose and having laid down some general guidelines for that same
general reader, it is now time to offer some specific guidelines for the use of Scripture
in the realm of ethics. In an effort to avoid the Protestant excess of "fundamentalism," on the one hand, and the Catholic excess of "proof-texting," on the other, Fr.
Kenneth Himes, OFM, has identified a number of interrelated "tasks" or principles
that should be carried out or followed when using Scripture as a guide in ethical

decision-making.[17] These tasks will be the subject of the section to follow.

Scripture is not an ethical cookbook that can be opened and followed like a recipe, as the fundamentalists would have it, nor is Scripture merely a collection of good quotes meant to serve natural law or philosophical arguments, as proof-texting Catholics would have it. Scripture is one of the great pillars of Catholic ethics, and as such, it needs to be examined with a critical eye and used wisely.

B1. The Exegetical Task

One of the most important and obvious tasks that confronts the reader of Scripture is *to determine the original meaning of a particular text.* This task is called "exegesis," and needless to say, it is no simple matter. In addition to the difficulties addressed above, the books of the Old Testament were written *over two thousand years ago,* translated into Greek, and then translated into Latin or English from that translation. Moreover, the distance that separates ancient Jewish culture and 21st century American society is not merely time and language. Everything from their idioms and literary styles to their "scientific" worldview and their political system must have been vastly different from our own. Indeed, this task is a highly complex one:

> To know what the text meant in its historical time and for its particular audience, then, we must understand the historical circumstances surrounding the text, the presuppositions of the author and the audience, the socioeconomic and intellectual environment, the language, literary structure and context of the text, and so on.[18]

Thus, moral theologians or anyone interested in forming a Christian ethic must often rely on the scholarly work of historians, linguists, and archaeologists, whose work would be instrumental in determining the meaning of a given passage.

In order to appreciate just how difficult this task must be, perform the following experiment: Ask *your* parents what the word "phat" means. Unless your mom and dad have spent a great deal of time with you and your friends—a prospect both you and your parents might find horrifying—they probably think you have misspelled the word "fat." Likewise, ask yourself if you know what it would mean to call a fly ball in a baseball game a "can of corn" or what a "fondue" hairstyle would look like. And if the distance between your parents' generation and yours is that great, imagine how much difference 2000 years and an entirely different culture makes!

Nor should this task of retrieving the original meaning of a passage be minimized or downplayed. The importance of this task comes to light when we look at Luke 12: 25-6:

> Great crowds were travelling with him, and he turned and addressed them, "If anyone comes to me without hating his father and mother, wife and children, brothers and sisters, and even his own life, he cannot be my disciple."

A modern reader who had no knowledge of ancient Greek would probably be horrified—and appropriately so—at Jesus' apparent command to "hate" one's family members. To understand what Jesus meant in this passage, one must have an understanding of ancient Greek and the culture in which this Gospel appeared. Noted New Testament scholar, Joseph Fitzmyer, SJ, throws light on the meaning of the word "hate" in this passage:

> From [my commentary on Luke] 16:13, one learns that *misein*, '*hate*' is the opposite of *agapan*, '*love*.' Misein has already been used in [Luke] 6:22, 27 to describe the attitude of outsiders toward Christian disciples; now it is used by the Lucan Jesus as a figure to express the character of allegiance to himself demanded of the disciple. One is called to such 'hatred' [of one's kin] to the extent [only] that such persons would be opposed to Jesus; the choice that the disciple has to make is between natural affection for kin and allegiance to Jesus.[19]

Fitzmyer then continues, quoting another scholar A. Plummer:

> In most cases these two [love for one's kin and allegiance to Jesus] are not incompatible; and to hate one's parents as such would be monstrous. … But Christ's followers must be ready, if necessary, to act toward what is dearest to them as if it were an object of hatred. … Jesus, as often, states a principle in a startling way, and leaves His hearers to find out the qualifications.[20]

We see then from the commentators' explanation how language was being used by Jesus in the original context—in a way that would be more obvious to His original hearers than to us: the "hate" Jesus prescribes is not a "monstrous" hatred of one's family but a predilection for Jesus. What Jesus is stating is that people must make their relationship with Him of paramount importance in their lives. If—and only if—people find their relationship with their mother, father, or any other family member becoming a serious obstacle to their relationship with Him, then—and only then—should they be willing to sever these unhealthy family ties.

Indeed, careful exegesis can sometimes put an ethical passage from the New Testament into an entirely new light. For instance, suppose one were to read the following passage from chapter 7 of 1 Corinthians, in which St. Paul gives advice to his congregation in Corinth about choosing a state in life:

> There is something I want to add for the sake of widows and those who are not married; it is a good thing for them to stay as they are, like me, but if they cannot control the sexual urges, they should get married, since it is better to be married than to be tortured. (vv. 7-8)

> Let everyone stay as he was at the time of his call. If, when you were called, you were a slave, do not let this bother you; but if you have the chance of being free, accept it. (vv. 20-21)

Each one of you, my brothers, should stay as he was before God at the time of his call. About remaining celibate I have no directions from the Lord but give my own opinion as one who, by the Lord's mercy, has stayed faithful. Well then, I believe that in these present times of stress this is right; that it is good for man to stay as he is. If you are tied to a wife, do not look for freedom; if you are free of a wife, then do not look for one. But if you marry, it is no sin, and it is not a sin for a young girl to get married. They will have their troubles, though, in their married life, and I should like to spare you that. (vv. 23-28)

As noted above, understanding the context of a passage—both the historical circumstances in which it was written as well as the rest of the text itself—can help us retrieve the true intentions of the author. Later in 1 Corinthians, Paul tells his readers "a mystery," that "[w]e shall not all sleep, but we shall all be changed, in a moment, in the twinkling of an eye, at the last trumpet" (1 Cor. 15:51). In other words, there is evidence that he believed that the end of the world was imminent; not everyone to whom he was writing would see death—i.e., "sleep"—before Jesus returned and transformed our mortal natures into immortal ones (1 Cor. 15:53). Because he almost certainly believed at the time that he wrote this letter that the world was coming to an end, he did not wish anyone to be unduly distracted by earthly affairs. Jesus was believed to be on the way, and consequently, people should not let their choice of a state of life draw them away from preparation for the impending apocalypse. In this spirit, Paul likewise instructed the community at Corinth to abstain from marriage, a distracting earthly occupation, if at all possible.

When evaluating Paul's ideas about the attitude one should have toward a choice of vocation or toward the institution of slavery, we would have to agree with New Testament scholar Pheme Perkins who states that some of Paul's recommendations "are so clearly tied to the conviction that the end is right around the corner, that they would need reevaluation in other contexts."[21] Though it might be advisable, *if the Second Coming were looming near*, to regard marriage as a distraction more than a sacred calling and therefore to abstain from marriage if at all possible, and though it might be advisable for the same reason not to struggle to abolish the institution of slavery, these end-game scenarios should clearly not be the standard by which Catholics today live their lives. Marriage is regarded as a sacred calling (vocation) and not a distraction. Celibacy is chosen because it is judged to be a calling in which people can do greater good for the Kingdom of God than they could if they were single. Slavery is regarded as an evil institution to be abolished so that God's Kingdom will come to this earth. (Cf. the Lord's prayer.) Paul's counsels in 1 Corinthians may, indeed, have other inspirational value for the devout reader; however, the insights revealed by the exegetical task would prevent the Church from wholly embracing his recommendations. Because of Paul's outlook on the return of the Lord, his directives in 1 Corinthians should be regarded as somewhat "provisional," i.e., as more suited to a particular time and to particular circumstances.

We have clearer insight today into issues of vocational choice and issues of social change.

B2. The Methodological Task

Though, strictly speaking, the methodological task is really just a part of the exegetical task described above, it is so important to the proper use of Scripture in the field of ethics that it deserves separate consideration. In order to illustrate its importance, we shall take a detour from academics into the courtroom of everybody's favorite television lawyer, Matlock.[22]

In one memorable episode, the wily defense lawyer has to persuade the jury that there are "reasonable doubts" that his client is guilty of murder. Matlock tells the jury that they should not convict his client because, until this point in time, the prosecutors have not recovered the body of the allegedly murdered man. "Has the prosecution even shown you that a murder has taken place?" he asks. Then, after a dramatic pause, he informs the jury that, after he counts to 10, the "murdered" man will actually walk right through the back doors of the courtroom. "1… 2… 3… ," he counts, holding up a finger for each number called. Finally, at the count of "10," the entire courtroom, including the jury and the prosecutors, turn to the back of the room. No one enters. Knowing that the courtroom is wondering what he is doing, Matlock explains, "Every one of you turned toward the back of this courtroom because you knew it was possible that the missing man could have walked through those doors. You had a *reasonable doubt* that the missing man was even murdered in the first place. So, you must return a 'not guilty' verdict and set my client free." Needless to say, Matlock won the case.

But, one may reasonably ask, "What in the world does this Matlock episode have to do with ethics and the Bible?" The point that the Matlock episode illustrates is that *there are many different and very effective ways to make a single point.* In order to get his point across to the jury, Matlock simply could have ended his summation with the statement "The prosecution has yet to demonstrate that a murder has even taken place." But simple statements are often not enough to drive home a point; though the statement alone might have sunk into the jurors' skulls, the drama that followed made the jury really *feel* its truth in their guts.

In a similar fashion, there are many different and effective ways to develop moral character and shape behavior. Because of our legalistic culture, we tend to think that ethics is merely a subject about the *rules* of good and bad behavior. Though rules are crucial to the subject of ethics, almost no one (except, perhaps, Immanuel Kant) is *moved or inspired* by rules alone. When a priest gives his homily, he might list a moral rule or two, but if he is a powerful and persuasive speaker, he will tell stories, uses metaphors, exaggerate, throw in a good joke or two, and in general use a whole arsenal of rhetorical weapons to motivate his audience to act on those rules. People need to have more than their intellects engaged in order to develop a sound moral character; they need everything from carrots and sticks (i.e., rewards and punishments) to role models and inspirational stories.

And no book recognizes this facet of moral development more than the Holy Scriptures. For instance, 2 Samuel 11-12 tells the story of King David, Uriah the Hittite and his wife Bathsheba, and David's friend Nathan. To make a long story short, King David abused his authority, as politicians often do, and summoned the beautiful Bathsheba to his house to have sex with him. In an effort to cover up his affair, David eventually has Bathsheba's husband Uriah sent to the front lines where he is killed. "But the thing that David had done displeased the Lord,"(2 Sam. 11:27) and so, the Lord sent Nathan to chastise the king. Nathan simply could have scolded David and told him that the Lord had condemned his actions. However, he told him the following story before condemning him:

> There were two men in a certain city, the one rich and the other poor. The rich man had very many flocks and herds; but the poor man had nothing but one little ewe lamb, which he had bought. And he brought it up, and it grew up with him and with his children; it used to eat of his morsel, and drink from his cup, and lie in his bosom, and it was like a daughter to him. Now there came a traveler to the rich man, and he was unwilling to take one of his own flock or herd to prepare for the wayfarer who had come to him, but he took the poor man's lamb, and prepared it for the man who had come to him (2 Sam. 12:1-4).

Upon hearing of this dastardly deed, David became enraged and demanded the death of this scoundrel. Of course, as Nathan informed him, he was this scoundrel. More than any tongue-lashing or verbal rebuke, this parable brought home to David the egregious nature of his crime. For a moment at least, David could take a much more objective look at the crime he had committed and, perhaps, feel some of the outrage that the Lord must feel toward him. Nathan, then, rebuked him directly, and the Lord punished him severely, though He did spare David's life.

Because there are necessarily a variety of ways that moral character and behavior are developed, the astute reader must be able to discern the different kinds of approaches taken in Scripture. Indeed, one of the dangers of fundamentalism is that it tends to ignore the different literary styles used by the authors and the different purposes behind these styles. Insisting on a strictly literal interpretation hides the depth of the Bible from the reader and makes it appear absurd. *The methodological task, then, is to determine if a particular passage is to be taken literally, as an explicit moral rule, or in some other way, such as hyperbole intended to motivate an audience.*

Clearly, the Ten Commandments issued in Exodus 20 are to be taken as strict moral rules; they appear in a legalistic form—"You shall not ..."—and they are followed by numerous other laws in Exodus 21-23. In Mark 10:43, however, Jesus offers the following advice, which hopefully no one will take literally: "[I]f your hand causes you to sin, cut if off; it is better for you to enter this life maimed than with two hands to go to hell, to the unquenchable fire." Are all Christians required to cut off their hands if they feel the temptation to steal or to strike an innocent person? In the verses that follow this "command," Jesus substitutes "foot" and "eye" for "hand" in the foregoing formula. Are all Christians bound to go through life without hands, feet, or eyes? Or is it more probable that Jesus, who frequently taught in parables, is using exaggeration and a dramatic presentation to put forward a principle similar to St. Ignatius Loyola's idea of "indifference," i.e., that we should be ready to give up earthly goods and that obedience to God's will should be the only standard we use to judge the value of these goods?

Using context, the insights of Biblical scholars, reason, and (hopefully) divine enlightenment, the reverent reader of Scripture will be able to discover how any given passage should be approached.

B3. The Christocentric Principle

Though much has already been stated about the proper way to relate the Old Testament to the New, the "Christocentric" principle outlined above should be added to our list of guidelines for the proper use of Scripture in ethics. After the exegetical task has been performed and the original meaning of the text has been retrieved as fully as possible, the thoughtful scholar or layperson should view a given passage in light of Christ's life and teachings, for *Christ should be the lens through which the whole of the Bible is viewed and understood.* Obviously, this principle does not apply to passages that directly deal with Jesus' life or teachings, but it does put the rest of Scripture into its proper light.

For instance, returning to the issue of divorce, we find that the Old Testament has laid out very specific rules for writing a "bill of divorce":

> When a man takes a wife and marries her, if then she finds no favor in his eyes because he has found some indecency in her, and he writes her a bill of divorce and puts it in her hand and sends her out of his house, and if she goes and becomes another man's wife, and the latter husband dislikes her and writes her a bill of divorce and puts it in her hand and sends her out of his house, or if the latter husband dies, who took her to be is wife, then her former husband, who sent her away, may not take her again to be his wife, after she has been defiled (Dt. 24: 1-4).

Mosaic Law, then, *did* permit a husband to divorce his wife, though a woman—as a man's property—was not permitted to initiate a divorce with her husband. Additionally, this passage implies that remarriage was an acceptable practice for the Jews, for the woman in the passage is not condemned for taking a second husband. However, she was not permitted to remarry her first husband, should her second husband die or divorce her. It is clear from its legalistic tone as well as its setting within the book of Deuteronomy that the Jews would have considered this passage to be a *strict moral rule*, not an exaggeration or hyperbole to motivate an audience. Should, then, Christians permit divorce and one remarriage but forbid "re-remarriages"?

Applying the Christocentric principle, however, we see that Jesus Himself addressed this issue of divorce, and thus, His understanding of the matter should be taken as authoritative. In the Gospel of Mark (10:1-12), when the Pharisees approached Him, they attempted to goad Him into contradicting the Mosaic Law:

> They asked, "Is it against the Law for a man to divorce his wife?" [Jesus] answered them, "What did Moses command you?" "Moses allowed us, they said, "to draw up a writ of dismissal and so to divorce." Then Jesus said to them, "It was because you were so unteachable that he wrote this commandment for you. But from the creation *God made them male and female. This is why a man must leave father and mother, and the two become one body.* They are no longer two, therefore, but one body. So what God has united, man must not divide." Back in the house, the disciples questioned him again about this, and he said to them, "The man who divorces his wife and marries another is guilty of adultery against her. And if a woman divorces her husband and marries another, she is guilty of adultery too."

So, Jesus' teaching about the nature of marriage-commitment supersedes the laxer understanding of marriage-commitment adopted during the time of the Mosaic Law.[23]

B4. The Hermeneutical Task

For the most part, the three previous tasks were devoted to retrieving the *original* meaning and intention of the Sacred Scriptures. However, Christians do not read the Bible solely out of archeological or historical curiosity. As a living faith, Christianity is not only about what God *did* in history but also about what He is currently *doing*. *Relating this belief to Scripture and ethics, then, it will be necessary to determine what a given text has to say about contemporary ethical issues; this task is called "hermeneutics."* In order to prevent the abuse of proof-texting, it is necessary to perform the exegetical and methodological tasks described above so that Scripture passages are not distorted or manipulated to suit someone's private agenda. However, once the original meaning is more or less recovered, it is the job of every Christian—and most especially of the official teachers of the Church—to bring this original message into the present.

For instance, thanks to Charlton Heston and Cecil B. DeMille, virtually everyone one is familiar with Exodus 20:1-17, the Ten Commandments. And for the most part, carrying out the hermeneutical task on this passage requires little effort. "Honor your father and mother" and "You shall not steal" are as easy to apply to the 21st century after Christ as they must have been to the 10th century before Christ. However, we might wonder how the First Commandment could possibly relate to the present:

> You shall have no other gods before me. You shall not make any graven image, or any likeness of anything that is in heaven above, or that is in earth beneath, or that is in the water under the earth; you shall not bow down to them or serve them.

Of course, Biblical scholars have a mountain of information concerning the various gods that were worshipped during the time of the Jewish exodus from Egypt, especially those worshipped by the Egyptians themselves. But what relevance could "graven images" have for a modern Christian, one who already believes in "no other gods" than the God of Abraham, Isaac, and Jacob?

Though there are "false gods" loose in America, as devil worshippers or members of bizarre cults like the Branch Davidians demonstrate, the relevance of the first two Commandments has largely changed. However, understood in a new light, these moral/theological rules are still central to Christian worship and morality. Most of us do not worship Pharaoh or Voodoo fertility gods, but we might still have to ask ourselves whether we have set "other gods"—understood in a much broader sense—before God. Have we devoted our lives to Him or do we spend all of our time seeking the "gods" of popularity, money, or physical pleasure? If a false "god" is understood as any earthly thing that we "bow down to" or "serve," then Americans are guilty of "idolatry" in a very real sense, and accordingly, their lives need to be refocused.

In general, then, all Christians—both the religious and lay people alike—are continually performing the hermeneutical task; they are trying to bring the ancient wisdom and revelations of the Scriptures to life in the 21st century. When Mother Teresa read Jesus' command to Peter, "Feed my sheep" (Jn. 21:17), she understood that Jesus had called *her* to feed the poor and comfort the afflicted in Calcutta. When the Jesuits read this same line in the 1980's, they understood it as a call *to them* to help liberate the people who were suffering under the tyranny of the Nicaraguan government. Of course, not every attempt to bring Scripture into the present is a valid one. For example, the Pope declared that one Jesuit priest in Nicaragua was getting too intimately involved in politics; in other words, he was not following Jesus' *other* directive, viz., the one to "render to Caesar the things that are Caesar's, and to God the things that are God's" (Lk. 20:25). Of course, there will always be the possibility of honestly misreading God's will in a particular situation, but nonetheless, all Christians are called to do their best to hear what the Bible, the living word of God, is saying to them *today*.

B5. The Theological Task

The "theological task," the last task facing the conscientious Christian who seeks to relate Scripture to ethics, brings us back to our previous discussion about the place of the Bible in matters of faith and morality. Unlike some of the more conservative Protestants who follow the method of *sola Scriptura* in regard to matters of faith and morality, Catholics have always maintained that wisdom and guidance in these matters could be found in other sources. *The theological task, then, is to combine the Biblical message with other sources of moral wisdom.* In addition to the Bible, the Church recognizes a whole host of other sources that can provide insights into moral matters: prayer; the guidance and example of virtuous neighbors, parents, teachers, and friends; the natural law; the lives of the martyrs and saints; and most especially, the Church herself, especially through the teachings of the magisterium.

Together with Sacred Scripture, the Sacred Tradition of the Catholic Church can help complete the moral picture, especially in matters about which the Bible is relatively silent. Though the themes of the Bible, such as hospitality, love of one's neighbor, fidelity, and truthfulness, will always be relevant to any moral issue, each age faces its own particular dilemmas, and Catholics believe that the Holy Spirit continues to inspire the Church so that it can discern God's will in regard to these issues. In regard to moral matters, the Church largely relies on the teachings of the natural law which support and bolster the wisdom of the Bible.

In the section to follow, we will discuss the Church's role in Christian decision-making, as well as what exactly natural law is and what contribution it can make to this decision-making process.

SECTION HIGHLIGHTS

As Aristotle explained his system for finding happiness to his followers in his classic work, the Nicomachean Ethics, *so God has given His basic blueprint for finding happiness in the Bible, especially in the* New Testament.

Christians believe that God has a hand in the writing of all the sacred books of the Bible.

Fundamentalist Christians see the Bible as the work of God and therefore regard every statement in the Bible as literally true and unassailable.

Liberal Christians tend to downplay the reliability of the Bible because it contains some historically or scientifically inaccurate statements.

The Catholic Church maintains that "the books of Scripture firmly, faithfully, and without error, teach that truth which God, for the sake of our salvation, wished to see confided to the Sacred Scripture."[24]

Each book of the Bible is to be understood according to norms for understanding the genre of literature intended by its author and not according to the norms for understanding a different genre. For example, poetic myth should not be understood as if it is pure history; love poetry should not be understood as if it was meant to be a treatise on science.

Some Bible passages have different levels of meaning, all of them true.

The Catholic community, while venerating the Bible as a source of moral values, holds that from the beginning of Christianity, oral tradition—in the form of the teaching of official Church leaders—has provided an absolutely necessary complement to the Bible as a joint source of moral values.

Catholics can learn from Protestants' deep devotion to the Bible, and Protestants can learn from the Catholic understanding of the need for philosophical reasoning and the teaching of Church tradition to complement the Bible's teaching.

The generalization that the God of the Old Testament is vengeful and angry while the God of the New Testament is merciful and loving is an oversimplification. Nonetheless, it is clear that Jesus regarded some of the teachings found in the Old Testament as imperfect and provisional.

To discover the ethical teaching God wanted to communicate through the Bible, one must tackle three tasks: a) the exegetical task, determining the original meaning of a particular text; b) the methodological task, determining if a particular text is to be taken literally, as an explicit moral rule, or rather in some other way, such as hyperbole, offered to motivate an audience; c) the task of Christocentric evaluation, evaluating Old Testament ethical directives in light of Jesus' teachings, for often, Jesus' teachings will supersede these more imperfect and provisional directives.

Christians reading sections of the Bible that treat of ethical principles must try to see how these principles can inform behavior in their own times. This is the hermeneutical task.

QUESTIONS

Write your answers to these questions on a separate piece of paper. Use complete sentences.

1.   What does it mean to claim that all Scripture is "inspired by God"?

   a.   Your explanation should treat the issue of the reliability of every passage of Scripture;

   b.   It should also explain what "inspiration" has to do with the writer of a book of the Bible; how is he "inspired"? It should also explain what "inspiration" had to do with the authorities who decided that a particular book is divinely "inspired."

2.   T-F: The Book of Jonah is an example of an historical narrative. Explain your answer.

3.   Using principles from the pages above in Part One of Chapter Five, explain clearly and to the best of your ability the ethical teaching in each of the following biblical passages:

   a.   1 Samuel 15:3

   b.   Matthew 18:8-9

   c.   Matthew 5:38-39

   d.   Galatians 3:27-28

   e.   1 Corinthians 7:20-21

4.   What could Protestants and Catholics learn from each other's moral tradition as they try to develop a sound code of Christian ethics by which to live?

PART TWO:

THE ROLE OF THE CHURCH IN THE FORMATION OF A CHRISTIAN CONSCIENCE—A CATHOLIC UNDERSTANDING

A. THE ROLE OF TRADITION AND COMMUNITY IN OUR EDUCATION

If we stop to think about it, we see that we all depend a great deal upon our parents, teachers, and the preceding generations in our society for the knowledge and skills we acquire and for the wisdom we need to live life well.

Who taught us how to read or to drive? Who organized our Little League baseball teams? Who persuaded us of the values of being honest and kind? Who gave us a sense of world geography: taught us the difference between Austria and Australia, Boston and Bosnia, New York and New Guinea? It is amazing just how much we do stand on the shoulders of our ancestors, how much we rely on them to position us so that we can live our lives with style and finesse.

The way in which modern Christians appropriate the values and the "style" of Jesus is no different from the way in which they learn geography, honesty, or good manners. The community of Christians who went before us, generation upon generation of Christians, passed down Jesus' values. Jesus' companions told people about Jesus and about His teachings. Then our forebears chose to institutionalize Jesus' life story and His values in written documents about Him, which they called "the New Testament." When questions arose about the interpretation of those written documents, the Christian community's official leaders interpreted their meaning so that the true tradition of Jesus would be passed down intact.[25] Later the community, under the guidance of its leaders, pondered how the values and the principles Jesus taught could be lived out faithfully in situations that Jesus never experienced—e.g., in an age of nuclear energy and nuclear weapons, in an era of global economy and Internet communication, etc. And so the insights and wisdom that have been gathered up by the Christian community over the ages are passed on to each successive generation in both oral and written instruction. The transmission goes on within the settings of home, school, and church.

A person who believes that Jesus is God who has come to earth both to teach and show humans the pathway to God's home will study Jesus' teachings carefully and try to live by the values He taught and embodied. The Christian believer also will ponder seriously the traditional wisdom of the Christian community, which is preserved in its official instructions and handed on through its teachers and its leaders and which attempts to apply Jesus' values to the resolution of contemporary ethical questions.

B. THE ORIGIN OF THE MORAL TEACHING AUTHORITY OF THE CHURCH

The Catholic Church maintains that its official leadership has authority to teach in Jesus' name and to apply His values to contemporary ethical issues.[26] Some Christians question the right of any Church or any Church's leadership to give any moral direction to anyone. "By what right can a 'human' institution speak in the name of God about the duties of its members?" they ask. Especially is that question urged in view of the history of Church corruption—e.g., the moral degradation found in the medieval papacy—and in view of obvious mistakes by Vatican congregations—e.g., the Vatican's condemnation of the teaching of Galileo.[27] "Rather than pay attention to the teaching of the Church, shouldn't we simply look to Jesus' recorded Biblical teachings alone, and in honest solitude use them to work out our duties to God?"

Yes, there is a partial truth (a half-truth) in the notion that ultimately we all have to work out our life-choices in the depth of our own individual consciences. No one else can ultimately make up our minds for us. We are each responsible for ourselves. But to maintain that we can understand Jesus' values by ourselves, without help from another, seems to fly in the face of common sense, not to mention the teachings of the Person we say was God-come-to-earth, whose values we say we endorse. Here is why.

Where did our personal knowledge of Jesus' teachings originate? It came to us through a religious community—the teachings heard by us or by our parents in Church, the words of Jesus recorded in the New Testament section of the Bible, which is a book put together and authorized by the early Christian community. It was that community that decided which teachings were and were not the authentic teachings of Jesus. That community rejected some books written about Jesus as inauthentic or misleading.[28]

And if one attends carefully to the written Gospels, one sees that Jesus, besides offering a moral vision by His teachings found in the four Gospels, made it very clear that He wanted the leaders He designated to have authority to teach in His name and to adjudicate debates about moral issues that would arise after He was gone.

The following passages offer evidence of this commission from Jesus to the leadership of His community:

Matthew 10: (4) "These twelve, Jesus sent out, instructing them as follows: ... (6) [P]roclaim that the kingdom of heaven is close at hand. ... (14-16) And if anyone does not welcome you or listen to what you have to say, as you walk out of the house or town, shake the dust from your feet. I tell you solemnly, on the day of Judgment, it will not go as hard with the land of Sodom and Gomorrah as with that town."

Matthew 16:16-20 "Then Simon Peter spoke up, 'You are the Christ,' he said, 'the Son of the living God.' Jesus replied, 'Simon, son of Jonah, you are a happy man! Because it was not flesh and blood that revealed this to you but my Father in heaven. So I now say to you: You are Peter [a name which means 'Rocky'] and on this rock I will build my Church. And the gates of the underworld can never hold out against it. I will give you the keys of the kingdom of heaven: whatever you bind on earth shall be considered bound in heaven; whatever you loose on earth shall be considered loosed in heaven.'" [The terms "bind" and "loose" in rabbinical circles meant the power a) to exclude from or to admit to the community, and b) to declare a teaching or a particular duty binding or non-binding.]

Matthew 18:18 [Jesus extends some share in the power he has given to Peter in Matthew, chapter 16 to the other twelve apostles; see the parallel passages in Mk. 9:33-36 and Lk. 9:46-47, which indicate that the disciples in question are "the Twelve" apostles.] "I tell you solemnly, whatever you bind on earth shall be considered bound in heaven; whatever you loose on earth shall be considered loosed in heaven."

Matthew 28: (16) "Meanwhile the eleven disciples set out for Galilee where Jesus had arranged to meet them. (18-20) ... He said, 'All authority in heaven and on earth has been given to me. Go, therefore, make disciples of all the nations; baptize them in the name of the Father and of the Son and of the Holy Spirit, and teach them to observe all the commands I gave you. And know that I am with you always; yes, to the end of time.'"

John 20:19-25 "In the evening of that same day, the first day of the week, the doors were closed in the room where the disciples were, for fear of the Jews. Jesus came and stood among them. He said to them, 'Peace be with you,' and showed them his hands and his side. The disciples were filled with joy when they saw the Lord, and he said to them again, 'Peace be with you. As the Father sent me, so I am sending you.' After saying this He breathed on them and said: 'Receive the Holy Spirit. For those whose sins you forgive, they are forgiven; for those whose sins you retain, they are retained.'"[29]

These are just some of the New Testament passages which show that Jesus gave authority to teach His values to leaders in the community of the Church and that He also gave them power to adjudicate moral issues that would arise after His earthly departure.

C.   THE CHURCH: HOW "HUMAN," HOW "DIVINE"?

Jesus, then, clearly indicated that those who were given authority by Him (as well as their successors) would be assured of divine assistance in carrying out their mission of preaching His values and that they would be aided in the task of explaining how that message should be lived out in situations that differ from those of His time.

However, if this is true, what are we to make of the markedly embarrassing developments within the Church—the corruption in the medieval papacy, the sinful errors in the Inquisition, and the wrongful mistakes in matters like the Galileo affair? Are we to assert that Jesus was mistaken or misguided in His assurances? Are we to conclude that the Church cannot be counted on for reliable divine guidance? Or are we to judge with some of the saints who lived through such periods that God and Jesus still work through the authority-structure of the Church?[30]

Close study of Jesus' teachings shows that He anticipated scandal in the Church and possible misbehavior by those in authority:

> "Scandals indeed there must be, but alas for the man who provides them" (Mt. 18:7).

> "'But know this: if the owner of the house had known at what hour the thief was coming, he would not have let his house be broken into. You also must be ready, for the Son of Man is coming at an unexpected hour. Peter said, 'Lord, are you telling this parable for us or for everyone?' And the Lord said, 'Who then is the faithful and prudent manager whom his master will put in charge of his slaves, to give them their allowance of food at the proper time? Blessed is that slave whom his master will find at work when he arrives. Truly I tell you, he will put that one in charge of all his possessions. But if that slave says to himself, "My master is delayed in coming," and if he begins to beat the other slaves, men and women, and to eat and drink and get drunk, the master of that slave will come on a day when he does not expect him, and will cut him in pieces, and put him with the unfaithful. That slave who knew what his master wanted, but did not prepare himself or do what was wanted, will receive a severe beating. But the one who did not know and did what deserved a beating will receive a light beating'" (Lk. 12:39-48).

> "Then addressing the people and his disciples, Jesus said, 'The scribes and the Pharisees occupy the chair of Moses. You must therefore do what they tell you and listen to what they say, but do not be guided by what they do; since they do not practice what they preach'" (Mt. 23:1-3).

Jesus' position seems to have been that He will safeguard the integrity of the message He entrusted to the Church even when His messengers fail to live up to their moral obligations, and He will do so for the sake of His people whom He came to help. How is this possible? As one ponders this assertion in the light of the testimony of the teachings of Jesus recorded in Scripture, one might ask whether one should abandon faith in the office of the presidency as a democratic institution because of the failures of some of our political leaders like Nixon or Clinton? So should one abandon faith in the teaching office of the Church of Jesus because of the failures of some of its official leaders? This comparison will only seem valid if one clearly understands the attitude that a Christian believer in the Catholic tradition is expected to take toward official Church teaching on moral issues. This issue is both simple and complex, and merits further treatment.

Conscientious Church teachers weigh carefully the moral issues that they adjudicate, and usually they are careful to indicate the level of certitude they would have the hearer attach to their judgments on certain issues. Very few issues are decided with "infallible" declarations.

Nonetheless, each judgment of Church leaders on moral issues—because of the authority they were given by Jesus—deserves a reverent presumption in favor of its truth.[31] For this reason, whenever the reaction of the Church member is one of honest doubt about the judgment of Church leaders on an issue, that person should study the Church's position as carefully and openly as he or she can, and pray for God's guidance of his or her decision. If Christians believe that Jesus can be true to His promise to be with the Church's teachers in their teaching until the end of time (See Matthew 28:19-20), then they must take seriously their own duty to respect the Church's teaching authority as Jesus' voice speaking today and giving moral guidance, even while they recognize that finally they must make their own decisions about what is God's will for them and for the good of the world in which they live.

A very good explanation of this complex issue was given in a pastoral letter that was written by the German bishops on September 22, 1967, and appeared in an article in the monthly journal *Catholic Mind*.[32]

17   [T]here is a difficult problem that needs careful appraisal, since it concerns the faith or the relationship to the magisterium [teaching authority of the Church] of many Catholics today even more than in the past. We refer to the fact that in the exercise of its task the ecclesiastical magisterium can fall into error, and indeed has been known to do so. The Church has always been aware of this possibility, has catered for it in its theology, and has developed rules of procedure for such a situation. *This possibility of error does not arise with those decisions whose promulgation demands the absolute assent of faith—namely those promulgated by the solemn definition of a Pope or General Council or through the ordinary magisterium.* [The *Catholic Mind* editor defines "ordinary magisterium" as "the teaching authority of the universal episcopate when the bishops are not gathered in a General Council but concur in a single viewpoint as one to be definitively held." [33]]

It is historically incorrect to maintain that subsequently the Church has been found to be in error on such dogmas. ...

This process just referred to must not be confused with the obvious fact that beside the unchangeable divine power, there is in the Church a changeable human power too. ...

18   Thus we are concerned with error and the possibility of error in the non-defined teachings of the Church, which in their turn demand very differ-

ent degrees of assent. We must recognize that the business of life in general must proceed according to the best certitude available. We have to make decisions that from the theoretical standpoint cannot be regarded as absolutely sure, and yet which, since they are the best available, must be respected as valid norms for thought and action. Everyone experiences this in his own life; the doctor in his diagnosis is familiar with it, and so is the statesman in his assessment of the political situation, and the decisions that flow therefrom. The Church, too, in its teaching and practice cannot always propose either to give a definitive decision or simply to remain silent and leave everything to the decision of individuals. To protect individuals, and ultimately the substance of faith, the Church must make doctrinal pronouncements which are binding to a limited degree, despite the danger of error in particular matters. Since these are not definitions of faith, they are to some extent provisional and entail the possibility of error. Were it not so, the Church could hardly proclaim the faith as a living reality, nor explain it, nor apply it to new human situations. In this kind of situation, the individual Christian, and indeed the Church as a whole, is like a man who has to follow the decision of an expert who he knows is not infallible.

19   The fact that the faithful are to be instructed on the nature and limited scope of one of the provisional ecclesiastical pronouncements of disputed meaning does not on that account make it part of the preaching and catechesis. However, this has already been dealt with. Whoever believes that he must follow his own opinion having "a better appreciation than the Church," must ask himself soberly before God and his conscience, whether he has the necessary breadth and depth of theological expertise to deviate from the explicit teaching of ecclesiastical authority. Such a situation is conceivable, but subjective conceit and idle arrogance will have to be answered for before God's judgment.

20   The normal pattern of a Catholic's life of faith will entail serious efforts to understand and assimilate even a provisional pronouncement of the Church. Just as in everyday life there is no escaping from far-reaching decisions that have to be made on the basis of fallible insights with only as much reliability as these can yield, so in Church affairs it would be shameful and dishonorable to hesitate in one's attitude to the Church's teaching on the ground that it cannot yet be considered as definite. ... It is possible that the Church's doctrinal development proceeds too slowly in particular instances. But in making such a judgment, one must be prudent and discreet. Doctrinal development takes place in a Church with a human timescale; it cannot advance more rapidly than the safeguarding of the substance of the faith will permit.

21   We [bishops] have no need to fear that we are depriving our contemporaries of the answer to current problems by presenting the mind of the Church in this way. The sincere questions of our time, to which we must respond in faith, frequently oblige us to ponder anew the truths of faith and in this way new emphases may appear. This is not to call faith into question; on the contrary it serves to deepen our grasp of divine revelation and the teachings of the Church. Of this we are convinced, and experience bears it out; we do not wish to be untrue to the Catholic faith nor to a single truth thereof; we understand the faith solely in the Church, and thus do we seek ever more deeply to possess it.

In summary, then, to carry on the values of Jesus and to apply them to the ethical issues of new times, the Church continues to give authoritative guidance and instruction to its members. Some of its pronouncements are quite definitive, some are provisional and given more tentatively but after careful consideration of the issues at hand. Definitive pronouncements—e.g., prohibition against hatred of any other human being—are at the core of our Christian faith, and if we refuse to accept them, we place ourselves outside the community of those who accept Jesus as Lord. In the case of the provisional ethical decisions issued by Church authorities, Catholic Christians are obliged to weigh those with reverence, to try in all intellectual honesty to find wholehearted reasons for obeying them. It is not inconceivable that sometimes a faithful Catholic's conscience will not permit him or her to accept such a Church directive, but he or she ought to behave then with prayerful humility, modesty, and charity.

SECTION HIGHLIGHTS

Like most other forms of education, moral (ethical) education involves the guidance of a community in which elders transmit wisdom and values. This is true of the moral education of Catholic Christians: they learn about the fundamental values taught by Jesus from their elders, and they also benefit from the wisdom those elders have gained as they have sought to apply Jesus' principles to moral questions unheard of in His time.

Though every Christian individual ultimately must follow his conscience, it is foolish to think that each Christian person does not depend on the Christian community for his or her knowledge of Jesus' values or that each Christian in working out his or her responsibilities may with impunity disregard the wisdom that the Christian Church has acquired from its perennial efforts to apply Jesus' values to modern problems.

A number of passages in the Gospels demonstrate that Jesus wanted the leaders of the Christian Church to exercise teaching leadership and to give authoritative moral instruction in His name to the Church community after He ascended from earth.

Though there is evidence in the Gospels that Jesus foresaw that Church leaders might sometimes fail in their duty to provide good example and sound governance, there is also evidence that He nonetheless wanted His followers to listen with a spirit of respect and obedience to their teaching.[34]

In their 1967 letter, the German bishops said that there are two kinds of authentic Church teaching: infallible definitions and authoritative provisional pronouncements of Church teachers.

The "infallible definitions" referred to by the German bishops are those promulgated by solemn definition from the Pope or a General Council, or through the ordinary magisterium.

Infallible moral teaching of "the ordinary magisterium" is any teaching taught outside a General Council by all the bishops of the Catholic Church all the time as a truth which must be held: e.g., the evil of infanticide.

Infallible definitions by the magisterium deserve a Catholic's absolute assent of faith.

In their 1967 letter, the German bishops explained that just as doctors must render their best judgments about the health issues confronting their patients even when they are not absolutely certain of their diagnoses, so Catholic bishops cannot always wait until they reach absolute certitude about a moral issue before they render their best opinion in an authoritative magisterial pronouncement.

In virtue of the theological expertise and authority and grace granted to the bishops by the Holy Spirit, these provisional moral teachings, the German bishops say, should be regarded by Catholics with reverence and with a serious effort to weigh these teachings with a disposition to find in favor of their truth.

The German bishops do not exclude the possibility that in some cases a Church member may in good conscience "deviate from the explicit teaching of ecclesiastical authority," but they warn of the danger of "subjective conceit and idle arrogance" and declare that "the normal pattern of a Catholic's life of faith will entail serious efforts to understand and assimilate even a provisional pronouncement of the Church."

QUESTIONS

Answer the following questions on a separate piece of paper. Write in complete sentences.

1.   Re-present two Gospel passages in which Jesus is seen giving authority to Church leaders to teach His followers in His name after He has ascended from earth.

2.   Re-present one Gospel passage in which Jesus seems to have anticipated the possibility of scandalous behavior by Church leaders, and one Gospel passage

where Jesus indicates that His followers should nonetheless be docile to the teachings of disedifying teachers.

3. Give one example of a moral teaching of "the ordinary magisterium" that is infallible and deserves the wholehearted assent of every Catholic.

4. Give a specific example of a provisional moral teaching of the Church.

5. Explain what attitude the German bishops say Catholics should have toward provisional Church teachings.

6. What did the German bishops say about the situation where a person feels that he or she cannot in good conscience assent to a provisional official teaching of the Church?

PART THREE:

THE ROLE OF NATURAL LAW IN THE FORMATION OF CHRISTIAN CONSCIENCE

A.   WHY THE CATHOLIC CHURCH ADDS NATURAL LAW TO ITS TEACHINGS

What would Jesus have thought about artificial insemination, the procedure in which a couple uses the sperm of a third party to fertilize one of the woman's eggs? Which economic system would Jesus have found to be the most just: capitalism, Marxism, or socialism? What would Jesus have taught about birth control, especially to young married couples who economically are unable to support a child? Would Jesus have condemned the practice of euthanasia, the so-called "mercy killing" of the elderly or terminally ill? How would he have viewed affirmative action, the practice of consciously hiring minorities over other qualified applicants in order to rectify past injustices such as slavery?

The problem with answering the foregoing questions is that neither Jesus nor Scripture *explicitly* addressed any of them. Though the Old and New Testament certainly provide many general moral principles relating to sex, economics, and discrimination, specific questions involving the morality of artificial insemination, capitalism or socialism, and affirmative action were simply not relevant to the Jews or the early Christians. Like all men, the Jews of the Old Testament and the early Christians of the New Testament were people placed in a particular time in history in a particular part of the world. Just as contemporary Americans would be unlikely to engage in a detailed discussion of the ethics of polygamy—a practice that is virtually obsolete in the United States—the Jews and the early Christians would never have had the need to address explicitly the morality of artificial birth control. The emergence of new technology has been accompanied by the emergence of equally new ethical dilemmas, dilemmas that the people who wrote the divinely inspired books of the Bible never faced. And over and above technology, each era of human history has its particular challenges. Needless to say, the authors of the Bible, no matter how divinely inspired they were, could not have foreseen or anticipated *every* difficult moral dilemma humanity would ever face. Life is simply too detailed; there are too many particular circumstances. What, then, is a conscientious Christian supposed to do?

Unlike the fundamentalist or evangelical branches of Christianity, the Catholic faith has always recognized that God has given to people more resources than just Scripture to solve their earthly dilemmas. As noted in Part One of this chapter, the Catholic approach to using Scripture in the realm of ethics is not the *Sola Scriptura* approach. Though it is surely the most important source and should be the starting point for all critical moral reflection, the Bible is not the sole source of ethical knowledge for Catholics. All of humanity is, indeed, corrupted by original sin, but the Catholic Church believes that all people—regardless of their religious conviction and despite their fallen state—have imprinted in them basic and general moral principles that they are able to apply to particular situations through the use of reason. The Church also believes that through rational reflection on human experience, people can learn about their own nature and discover God's plan for the world in the way that He has designed creation. Thus, in addition to the explicit *divine* laws put forward in Scripture or the *human* laws that people make in order to regulate society, the Church believes that there also is a *natural* law written into the hearts and minds of human beings that reveals God's will.[35]

And if the Catholic Church is, indeed, correct in its belief in natural law, there is an additional advantage bestowed upon Catholics. If, in fact, all people—regardless of religious conviction—have access to this divinely inscribed natural law, then Catholics can hope to have fruitful moral dialogues with people of all religions and even the non-religious. Catholics have nothing to fear from honest, rational debate about any ethical issue; they can benefit from such discussions, as well as hope to share what they have learned about the divine plan with all people of good will. Indeed, when the popes have written encyclical letters putting forth a particular position regarding faith or morality, they have traditionally addressed these letters not only to the priests and the faithful but also to "all men of good will." If the only people worth listening to are the ones who believe in or are quoting from Scripture, there will not be much common ground for moral discourse, especially in a multicultural society such as the United States. Natural law, in effect, can be an avenue for bridging the gaps that unfortunately separate Christians and individuals of different faiths from one another.

Hopefully, you have gathered a little understanding of the usefulness of natural law in interfaith and interpersonal discussion of moral issues. Here is what lies ahead of you in the remainder of this chapter: B) a careful analysis of four common misconceptions about the meaning of the term "natural law"; C) a positive exposition of the essence of natural law as it is developed through the writing of St. Paul, St. Thomas, and the authors of this text; D) five specific examples of natural law theory in action—St. Thomas' justification of private property and of the permissibility of stealing in extreme necessity, as well as his natural law case against polygamy; and Pope John Paul II's natural law arguments against capital punishment and euthanasia. Let us look at those topics now.

B.   WHAT NATURAL LAW IS NOT

It may seem odd that an explanation of natural law would begin with an explanation of what natural law *is not*, but the word "natural" has so many meanings that it is necessary at the outset to dispel some possible misconceptions about what the Church could mean by "natural" law. According to one rather modest dictionary, for example, "natural" has 21 different (though occasionally related) definitions, most of which have little or nothing to do with natural law as the Church understands it. Below is a list of some common misconceptions about natural law.

B1. Natural Law and the "Back to Nature" Movement

One of the most natural misunderstandings people have about natural law is that it somehow refers to a rejection of artificial or man-made things in favor of things made by nature. Though this misconception of natural law does resemble aspects of the Church's understanding of this concept, natural law does *not* mean that natural things are to be preferred to man-made ones. Advocates of the legalization of mari-juana often make a "natural law" argument of this sort: "Marijuana comes from na-ture, and all things in nature are good; therefore, marijuana is good." Needless to say, the Church rejects this logic; rocks are natural as well, but dropping them on babies is immoral—in fact, just as immoral as dropping a man-made can of Crisco on a baby. People often incorrectly believe that the Catholic Church condemns artificial in-semination or the use of contraceptives, for example, because they are man-made. The Church's condemnation of these procedures or devices, however, does not focus on the mere fact that they are artificial but, rather, on what they are used for. The Church, for instance, has no moral qualms with automobiles, pacemakers, calcula-tors, thermometers, or food preservatives; they are used for good purposes.

Because they are made in the image of God, people have been given dominion over all creation, including their own actions. People even improve upon nature. Medicine, for example, enables the immune system to rejuvenate the body in ways that it never could if left to its own devices. Thus, "natural" things or states of affairs are not always preferable to man-made things or states of affairs. If scientists could cure muscular dystrophy or Down's Syndrome by altering an embryo's gene code, then the Church would wholly endorse such a measure as in keeping with natural law—even though the child would "naturally" have been born with a disability.

The Church *does* at times declare that certain areas of life or creation cannot be tampered with or manipulated. For example, the *Catechism of the Catholic Church* states that any attempt to influence the genetic code of an embryo or developing life is immoral unless it is directed toward healing the patient.[36] Trying to engineer people with certain traits, such as blond hair or high intelligence, violates human dignity and integrity, according to the Church. In this example, the Church does maintain that what nature or God has planned for each individual *is* clearly preferable to what human beings might try to do to him. But that position is not the same as the position that natural things are always preferable to man-made ones, as the preceding para-graphs make clear.

B2. Natural Law and the Birds and the Bees

"Why doesn't the Catholic Church allow or approve of homosexual unions or masturbation? I thought that they believed in natural law? Just look at the animal kingdom. Aren't there cases of homosexual activity and masturbation in monkeys and other animals?"

Without fail, arguments of this sort are always mentioned whenever the notion of natural law is discussed. Though a moment's reflection is enough to demonstrate that such a view is manifestly ridiculous, there has been a tendency among both supporters and detractors of natural law to argue that people should somehow take wild animals as their model for behavior. Indeed, this popular misconception is most probably the result of arguments that people (maybe even some Catholic religion teachers) have offered in the past. "Homosexuality or masturbation," it may have been argued, "is against God's will. You don't see such things in nature, do you?" Likewise, some theologians, such as St. Thomas Aquinas, *have* used examples of other animals in the midst of discussions surrounding natural law and the immorality of some sexual sins, such as fornication.[37] One critic of the Catholic Church's position on artificial birth control made this mistake twice; first, he essentially argued that the Church was wrongly basing its views of natural law too closely on the behavior of *lower* animals, and then secondly, he advised that the Church should have observed the actions of *higher* animals, such as primates.[38]

Unfortunately, the only time most people have ever heard of natural law—if they ever have heard of it—has been in relation to sexual matters such as artificial birth control, homosexuality, or masturbation. So, when people were taught that these activities were "contrary to natural" or "against natural law," it was only to be expected that some of them would draw parallels between the patterns of sexual behavior of wild animals and the "natural law" of the Catholic Church. But being utterly selfish, stealing from the poor, and lying under oath are equally contrary to natural law, though they have nothing to do with sexuality. Obviously, the Church's rejection of selfishness, theft, and lying did not come from observations of the mating of cheetahs or raccoons!

The truth of the matter is that the Church's understanding of natural law has very little, if anything, to do with the traits people share with birds and bees or any other creature in nature. Whatever "monkey business" does or does not go on in the monkey house at the zoo or in the jungles of central Africa is irrelevant to human morality or natural law. Human beings are indeed animals, and as such, they do share many functions with lower creatures—reproduction, the rearing of young, eating, sleeping, etc. But God's plan for any one species of animal or any combination of animals should not be considered a blueprint for human behavior. Hamsters eat their young; dogs copulate and then immediately abandon their partners; and black widows bite the heads off of their mates. Clearly, no one, except perhaps cannibalistic serial killers or psychopaths, believes human beings should engage in such offensive activities. God's "law" or plan for any one species of animal is already written into the fiber of that creature; this law—one an animal must invariably follow—we call "instinct." But God's plan for man is quite distinct from that for animals.

B3. The "It's Only Natural for a Person To ..." Argument and Natural Law

One of the perfectly legitimate meanings of the word "natural" is something like "not out of the ordinary" or "common." Indeed, it is perfectly "natural," if the word is understood as a synonym for "common," for people to lie, cheat on their spouses, or hoard all of their riches for themselves. Though, admittedly, a misconception of this sort rarely finds its way into any sophisticated discussions of natural law, it does slither in on occasion, especially in attempts to justify immoral behavior. Invariably in the context of a discussion of natural law, someone makes an argument of the following sort: "Clearly, there is nothing unnatural or immoral about masturbation, for the vast majority of all men and a not-insignificant number of women engage in this practice." Or, recently during a much-publicized political scandal involving adultery and lying in public, people who supported this politician repeatedly argued, "Of course, he is going to lie about his marital infidelity. It's only natural for a person to try to conceal his wrongdoings. Who wouldn't do the same in this situation?"

Needless to say, the simple fact that something is a regular occurrence in human affairs does not mean it is in keeping with natural law, as the Church understands that notion. Nothing is more common or natural than hatred, selfishness, greed, lust, deception, and lechery, but none of these emotions or actions are in keeping with natural law. In fact, the saints, who have lived the most extraordinary and "unnatural" lives, have most closely followed natural law or God's plan for them.

B4. "If It's Involuntary, Then It's Natural"

This misconception of natural law is a very subtle one, for not only does it closely parallel the "man-made vs. natural" misconception mentioned above but it also closely relates to several important truths about morality. This misunderstanding of natural law is almost exclusively found in the arguments of Catholics (and non-Catholics) who argue that the Church should sanction homosexual actions. For example, Andrew Sullivan—a noted author and a former editor of the periodical *The New Republic*—put forward the following argument in an interview for the Jesuit magazine *America*:

> It is bizarre that [the Church would maintain that] something can occur naturally and have no natural end [i.e., goal or purpose] ... [Homosexuality] is involuntary. The church has conceded this: Some people seem to be constitutively homosexual ... Yet [according to the Church] the expression of this condition, which is involuntary and therefore sinless—because if it is involuntary, obviously, no sin attaches—is always and everywhere sinful! ... Philosophically, it is incoherent, fundamentally incoherent.[39]

Sullivan's argument is very convincing because it contains at least two statements that are true. First, as we learned in the foregoing sections on sin and the parts of human actions, no one should be blamed for things that are not under his control. If *being* gay is, indeed, an involuntary condition—as it appears to be and the *Catechism* acknowledges—then certainly no one should be blamed for being gay. Second, we commonly do refer to things that are involuntary as "natural." Hence, if some people are born with an inclination toward people of the same sex, then being gay is certainly a "natural" condition.

But without getting into the details of this raging controversy, it is clear that not everything that is a "natural" condition is in keeping with natural law or God's plan for humanity. *Natural inclinations do not necessarily make behavior flowing from them more in keeping with natural law.* Evidence exists that certainly suggests that some forms of alcoholism may be inherited. That is to say, some people may unfortunately have been born with a predisposition for alcoholism; they may have a type of depression that is temporarily relieved by the effects of alcohol or they may experience a more pleasing effect from alcohol than the average Joe experiences. Likewise, there may be evidence to show that pedophiles—i.e., people who are sexually attracted to children—may be suffering from an involuntary or genetic condition. Yet, it is obvious that drinking to excess and molesting children are clearly wrong, whether or not alcoholics or pedophiles are "born that way." Regardless of one's position on the issue of homosexuality, it is clear that the simple fact that a predisposition is involuntary or inborn is not enough reason to argue that acting on this predisposition is healthy or in keeping with natural law.

C.   WHAT NATURAL LAW IS

C1. St. Paul and Natural Law

Ironically, one of the best introductions to natural law—a source of moral knowledge distinct from Scripture—is Scripture itself. As mentioned in Chapter Three,[40] St. Paul recognized that, even apart from Scripture, all human beings have access to God's moral laws through the use of their own reason. Writing to a new community of Christians that had arisen in Rome, Paul explained in some detail how the wicked often try to exonerate themselves of all blame. Apparently, some people, perhaps even some Romans, were trying to absolve or excuse themselves because, they claimed, God had not explicitly revealed His laws to them nor had anyone explicitly taught them about these laws. But Paul responded in the following way:

> [T]he wrath of God is revealed from heaven against all ungodliness and wickedness of men who by their wickedness suppress the truth. For what can be known about God is plain to them, because God has shown it to them. Ever since the creation of the world his invisible nature, namely, his eternal power and deity, has been clearly perceived in the things that have been made. So they are without excuse (Rom. 1:18-20).

Here, Paul is rebuking these men for their wickedness despite the fact that they are claiming ignorance. What is clear from this passage is that Paul believed that God's moral laws for humanity could be known without being explicitly revealed to a person, as the Ten Commandments, for instance, were explicitly revealed to Moses. By honestly and vigilantly attending to "the things that have been made," i.e., to creation, people should be able to ascertain God's plan for humanity. Whether or not the Romans were truly sincere in their pleadings with St. Paul is unclear from the text of his Letter to the Romans, but regardless, Paul is telling them that the "writing was on the wall" all along; all they had to do was read it.

Later in the same letter, Paul is discussing the issue of God's final judgment of human beings. Now, the Romans of course were not Jews, and there must have been many questions in the minds of the Romans whether they were considered to be second-class members in this new branch of Judaism that followed Jesus. But Paul reassured the Romans that "God shows no partiality" and that merely being a Jew is not what is ultimately important. "[God] will render to every man according to his works," Paul states, and then, he puts forward the following observation:

> For it is not the hearers of the law who are righteous before God, but the doers of the law who will be justified. When Gentiles [i.e., non-Jews] who have not the law do by nature what the law requires, they are a law to themselves, even though they do not have the law. They show that what the law requires is written on their hearts, while their conscience also bears witness (Rom. 2:14-15).

In this passage, Paul reveals another vital aspect of the Church's understanding of natural law. Not only is God's law clearly evident in "the things that have been made," i.e., *in the design of creation*, but it is also *"written on [people's] hearts,"* i.e., present in the soul of every human being. By listening to one's conscience and applying reason, a person can use his or her own God-given resources to arrive at moral truths; each person has within himself an imprint of God's eternal plan for humanity.

C2. St. Thomas Aquinas and Natural Law

As Pope John Paul II mentioned in a recent encyclical, the Catholic Church reserves a special place in its intellectual heritage for Thomas Aquinas, a man who devoted his life to reflection on theological and philosophical issues. When we take a more detailed look at natural law "in action," we will see some of St. Thomas' specific applications of natural law to particular moral issues. However, before taking a specific look, it is necessary to take a general look at some of his observations about the meanings of the words "law" and "natural" in order to understand more fully and precisely what is meant by the term "natural law."

According to Thomas, the word "law" can be used either in a broad and general way or in a more specific way. When people ordinarily speak of law, they usually refer to rules that are put into writing and are passed by some form of government for the benefit of a community. For instance, there are (or were) laws forbidding handguns in the District of Columbia, and there are laws that forbid murder, stealing, and perjury in every state in the union. Likewise, there are laws that have originated from God that are similar to the laws passed by governments. For instance, the Ten Command-ments are laws forbidding various actions of the followers of Yahweh (as well as all of humanity) that were given by God for the good of individuals and of the community.

When the Church refers to "natural law," however, she is not really referring to law in this specific sense. Though Aquinas believed that there were certain very gen-eral principles that all people have imprinted in them by God—for example, "Do good and avoid evil"—he obviously did not believe that all of God's divine laws were secretly stored in people's minds, like files in a filing cabinet. The belief in natural law is not the belief that, for example, all people are born with every moral law imprinted in their mind. If people were so born, then no one would ever really have any dis-agreement about morality; morality would be like math, a discipline in which there is virtually absolute certainty and consensus. Though every person has been given some very basic and general natural principles of morality, the specific embodiment of those principles—especially in laws that are tailor-made to fit the needs of a particular situ-ation—require effort and deliberation, not merely instinct.

In a broader sense, however, a "law" for Aquinas is merely *a rule or principle that guides something to its telos or fulfillment.* So, for example, "instinct" in a way would be a "law" for all animals, for instinct guides animals toward their proper course of ac-tion.[41] One could say, for instance, that geese have a natural inclination or instinct to fly south for the winter; hence, one could say that one of the laws of being a goose is the inclination to fly south for the winter. This "law" inside of them guides them toward their telos; it allows them to survive the frigid northern winters and, hence, continue to prosper. Likewise, in a plant or even in an inanimate substance such as water or fire, we could say that each of these things has its own nature or "law" which guides it to its natural end. Indeed, when people speak of the "laws of nature" they mean the word "law" in a sense similar to this sense of law. The laws of nature are the rules or principles that govern the world, that guide everything to its proper fulfill-ment.

Understood in this sense, the true "law" of man is *reason,* for according to Aquinas, when properly exercised, this power will guide humans to their proper fulfillment or at least to the greatest fulfillment of which they are capable in this life. Unlike ani-mals and inanimate things that are wholly and completely guided by their instincts or internal laws and cannot but fulfill God's plan for them in everything they do, hu-mans must struggle and deliberate over what God's law is. And once they do their best to discover what actions will lead to their fulfillment (and to the fulfillment of those around them), they are still free to obey or disobey the guidance that their reason provides.

For Aquinas, then, humans are the most God-like of creatures, for they alone among all of creation are able to take an active part in the governance of the world, as something like a co-creator or director with God. As Aquinas states, "Now among all others, the rational creature is subject to Divine providence in the most excellent way, in so far as it partakes of a share of providence, by being provident both for itself and others."[42] Whereas God alone provides for the fulfillment and regulation of all of

His irrational and inanimate beings, human beings join with God in ruling themselves as well as the world.

Humans are free to obey or disobey the guidance of their reason, but for Aquinas, this fact should not lead one to believe that humans are freely creating moral rules or making it up as they go along. To believe in natural law is to believe that when people are using "right reason," i.e., using their reason properly, they will *discover or uncover the objective and eternal law* that God has laid down for them to follow. To reason well in regard to moral matters is to understand God's plan for humanity.

Of course, as a Christian, Aquinas believed that reason alone was not sufficient to guide human beings to their ultimate telos: supreme happiness in the next life, a life of eternal friendship with God. Humans *do* need divine revelation through Scripture, in addition to natural law, to come to a full understanding of their eternal destiny. And of course, not all people are able to follow the guidance of their reason, for everything from desire and peer pressure to impatience and original sin is constantly clouding the commands of reason. But despite these limitations and impediments, human beings can discover, albeit in an imperfect way, God's moral law.

C3. A Brief Summary of Some of the Main Tenets of Natural Law

Keeping in mind, then, the brief sketch of natural law given above, it will be helpful at this time to outline a number of the essential features or main tenets of Catholic natural law theory.

+ Natural law is a source of moral knowledge independent of the divine laws given through revelation or Scripture, though it is certainly compatible with and incomplete without Scripture and the teachings of Jesus.

+ All rational creatures have within them this natural law, regardless of their religion or culture. The natural law is innate in all people (i.e., present in them independently of choice) and applicable to all people (i.e., no one is exempt from its commands).

+ Knowledge of the teachings of natural law can be ascertained through the use of one's reason and conscience as well as through reflection on the design of creation or "the things that have been made."

+ To believe in the natural law is to believe in an objective moral order that can be grasped by human reason. Right reasoning in regard to moral matters *is* God's eternal or divine law in regard to moral matters.

D.   NATURAL LAW IN ACTION

Up to this point in our inquiry into natural law, there have been very few specifics given about this subject; only its broad and general principles have been provided. Thus, in order to appreciate fully the Church's teaching on natural law, it will be helpful to look at a number of natural law arguments that have been given over the years.

D1. St. Thomas Aquinas

In addition to his more theoretical and abstract work on natural law, St. Thomas Aquinas, using reason and the knowledge available to him at his time in history, put forward natural law arguments about nearly every moral matter at issue in the Middle Ages. Indeed, some of Aquinas' natural law arguments from the 13th century are no longer applicable to the modern world. Time, experience, and an increased understanding of the natural world have rendered some of his arguments obsolete. But for the most part, his arguments continue to hold much authority in the eyes of the Church, and they are an excellent introduction to natural law.

D1a. Why the existence of private property is in keeping with natural law

Though in the United States, the land of the greatest material gifts and materialism in the history of the world, there has not been much serious debate about the morality of owing private property, the same is not the case throughout the world. In fact, some countries like China and North Korea openly advocate "communistic socialism," an economic arrangement envisioned by Karl Marx in which all private ownership of property would eventually cease and everything would be held in common. Likewise in antiquity, from the opposite end of the spectrum, the apostles of Jesus Christ were said to be "of one heart and soul, and no one [of them] said that any of the things which he possessed was his own, but they had everything in common" (Acts 4:32). Likewise, no full-fledged Jesuit owns anything, not even an automobile. Could it be argued on the basis of any one of these models that private ownership of property is evil?

Aquinas addressed this question, using rational observation of the material world and human nature:

> [I]t is legitimate for a man to possess private property; indeed it is necessary for human life for three reasons. First, everyone is more concerned to take care of something that belongs to him than of something that belongs to everyone or to many people, since in the case of common property he avoids efforts by leaving its care to others, as occurs when one has a large number of servants. Secondly, human affairs are more efficiently organized if the proper care of each thing is an individual responsibility. There would only be confusion if everyone took care of everything in a disorganized fashion. Third, peace is better preserved among men if each one is content with his property. So we see that quarrels frequently arise among those who hold a thing in common and undivided.[43]

That Aquinas clearly speaks the truth about the necessity of private property is easily demonstrated through examples. In regard to the first argument, it is obvious to anyone who has ever visited a public restroom that the proper care of material goods requires private ownership; the reason private bathrooms in people's homes are clean and public restrooms are scarier than a Stephen King novel is that individuals or families own private bathrooms. They will be using the bathroom more than anyone else will, so they tend to keep it clean and orderly. Because no one really owns a public bathroom, someone must be paid to clean it, and even though someone is paid to clean a public bathroom, it is clear that, in general, private citizens are more attentive toward their own bathrooms than most employees are toward public ones. Virtually no one would prefer to use a public bathroom to a private one. In regard to the second argument, it is obvious that a division of labor makes for much more efficient work. In an automobile factory, every worker is given a specific task, for it would be chaos if everyone worked on the whole of every car. In this same vein, the institution of private property efficiently divides labor throughout the population; everyone takes care of his or her own items. Thirdly, anyone who has ever given one gift to two small children knows that chaos and screaming is the immediate result. Though close friends or family members are usually able to share possessions without too much acrimony, the same is usually not the case with strangers. Imagine what life would be like if no one in a neighborhood (or town or city) owned a car but, rather, only had access to one common pool of cars. Who would take care of them? How many fights would break out over who was to use the newer, more stylish, or more comfortable cars?

D1b. Is it permissible to "steal" in cases of necessity?

But in endorsing the right to private property, Aquinas was not endorsing Reaganomics or a bloodthirsty, capitalistic competition for material goods. Material goods, such as food, clothing, and shelter, should only be regarded as means to higher, more spiritual goods, such as faith, hope, and love. Additionally, Aquinas would have fully endorsed the practice of religious communities such as the Jesuits who give up their material possessions in order to devote themselves fully to God and to prevent themselves from becoming too closely attached to earthly goods. Though all people need some level of property to sustain themselves or their family, love of private property can be a dangerous thing when people spend *too much* time or effort maintaining, loving, acquiring, or taking pride in their possessions.

Additionally, human beings should be ready and willing to share their goods with others who need them. *Indeed, Aquinas argues that in emergencies or cases of extreme need, in which people cannot legally obtain the material goods—food, shelter, or medicine—they need in order to live, they can take from the abundance of other people without sinning.* As mentioned above, material goods are to be regarded merely as a means of sustaining ourselves so that we may pursue a higher calling. But it is clear to Aquinas that God created the material goods of this world—all the plants and animals as well as inanimate things—for the needs of *all* people.[44] The fruits of the earth do not come to humanity with nametags attached. Though private ownership of these fruits of the earth is certainly necessary for an orderly existence, no man-made law or system of distributing property can undo what the *Catechism* calls "the universal destination of goods."

Of course, Aquinas did not mean that, for instance, because my neighbor has three BMW's and I only own one, I am permitted to take one of his or that I am free to steal a CD player if I cannot afford one. "The universal destination of goods" does not mean that all people must have the same number of goods or that no one is entitled to luxuries. Aquinas clarifies this issue:

> [I]f there is an urgent and clear need, so urgent and clear that it is evident that an immediate response must be made on the basis of what is available, such as when a person is in imminent danger and cannot be helped in any other way—then a person may legitimately supply his need from the property of someone else, whether openly or secretly. Strictly speaking, such a case is not theft or robbery.[45]

Imagine the following scenario. A homeless man finds himself caught in the storm of the century. The snow is piling up as the temperature continues to plummet into the single digits. Nightfall is fast approaching. Because of the drastic conditions, nobody from the state relief services has come by to take people to the shelter, as they usually do in inclement weather. Desperate, the man begins to knock on doors, but no one answers his pleas; people have seen too many news reports to trust a stranger. As he begins to lose feeling in his fingers and toes, the man realizes that he is in danger of losing his extremities to frostbite. Could he die out here? With no other recourse available to him, the man breaks a grocery store window and climbs inside for the night.

Regardless of the judgment the police or courts would pass on this man, Aquinas would maintain that his actions were in keeping with the natural order of things. In fact, this man is not really even stealing, breaking and entering, or trespassing; he is merely, in a sense, reclaiming what was properly destined for him in the first place. As Aquinas puts it, "In cases of necessity everything is common property"; a time-out in the "game" of private ownership of property must be called so that the ultimate destiny of the material goods of this world can be fulfilled. Private property is a secondary or subordinate institution, one that is necessary for the ordinary course of life but is temporarily and automatically put on hold in cases of extreme need or imminent danger.

D1c. The natural law case against polygamy

Now that the Mormons have officially renounced the practice of polygamy, the issue of the morality of having many spouses is virtually unheard of in America (except perhaps on the Internet, where nothing is unheard of). Except when a bizarre tale of a traveling salesman who has lived a double life with two separate families appears in the news, there is almost no discussion of this practice. But monogamy—the practice of having only one spouse—was not always the lifestyle of choice. For instance, the Jews of the Old Testament, such as Abraham and Jacob, had two wives, and in his famous work *The Republic*, Aristotle's teacher Plato recommended that wives be held in common. Additionally, even today the religion of Islam expressly allows polygamy, although in practice monogamy is still the overwhelmingly predominant arrangement.

From the teachings of Jesus and the vision of sexuality and marriage that is put forward in the New Testament, however, it became clear over time to nearly all Christians that monogamy was the social structure sanctioned by God and most in keeping with His plans for humanity. For example, there are no cases of polygamy mentioned in the New Testament, and whenever the rules in regard to marriage are mentioned, it is explicit or implicit that the sacrament is intended to be received by one man and one woman. For instance, in Mark 10:7-9 when Jesus is asked about the propriety of divorce, he repeats the Old Testament teaching that "the two shall become one flesh" in marriage, that man and woman are "no longer two but one flesh," and that "[w]hat therefore God has joined together, let not man put asunder."

However, there is no explicit commandment against polygamy even in the New Testament, and even if there were, why would Muslims, Jews, or pagans who do not believe in the divinity of Christ bother to listen to such a commandment? Here again, we find two of the most important reasons why the Church adds natural law to her teachings: to go beyond what is written in Scripture as well as to communicate with non-Christians in a moral discussion.

For the foregoing reasons, Thomas Aquinas composed his *Summa Contra Gentiles* or, roughly, "Summary Against the Gentiles." Here Aquinas meant the term "Gentiles" to mean "non-Christian," not "non-Jew" as the New Testament authors used it. Aquinas composed this work in order to help 13th century Dominican missionaries in their efforts to convert the Jews and Muslims in Spain and North Africa to Christianity.[46] Though all of the reasons that Aquinas puts forward in his arguments are compatible with the Scriptural vision of marriage and sexuality in the New Testament, they go beyond those books to provide further arguments—ones that non-Christians as well could appreciate—for the position that monogamy is God's sanctioned social arrangement.

Of all animals, Aquinas noted, human beings have the greatest concern for their offspring. Though there are, unfortunately, dead-beat dads and mothers who abandon their children in dumpsters, the overwhelming majority of men and women who have children devote the best parts of their lives to them. Men work long hours at jobs they often abhor to feed, clothe, and educate their children, and mothers are often so caring and protective of their children that they are willing to die for them. Not coincidentally, this desire to care for one's offspring is vital to the achievement of a child's happiness. When they are born, children are defenseless and helpless, and unlike any other creature on the planet, they cannot run forever solely on instinct. Their reason needs to be developed, a task that takes a very long time. Hence, parents need to care for the needs of their children for a significant number of years—in some ways, for a lifetime.

But what, asks Aquinas, would happen to this arrangement if women, for example, were allowed to have many husbands? Suppose that one woman had three or four husbands, and she were to find herself pregnant. Who would be the father of this child? If she were having relations with all of her husbands, none of them could ever be certain that the child is his progeny. According to Aquinas, such a practice by nature stifles the natural desire of a father to know, love, and care for his offspring.[47]

Admittedly, however, the more common arrangement in history has been that one man could marry many wives, and in this situation, the man and the women would know perfectly well whose child belongs to whom. What objection, then, does Aquinas raise in regard to this arrangement? In regard to the well-being of the off-spring, Aquinas observes that it would be nearly impossible for the father to be a *father* to the children of many wives. For instance, if a man were to have four wives, each of whom bore four or five of his offspring, it would be nearly impossible for him to earn enough money to support these children. Modern fathers can hardly support their two to three children, let alone the dozens that would be possible in a polygamous arrangement. Additionally and perhaps more importantly, it would definitely be im-possible for a father to provide the proper amount of attention to each of his children, especially after he has to work to provide for their material needs. Could he even remember all of their names? How much "quality time" could he spend with each of his children? As a matter of fact, most of these children would be virtually fatherless, and as the modern single-parent family has demonstrated, the difficulties a fatherless child faces are often insurmountable.

Furthermore, the polygamous arrangement is not only devastating to the chil-dren; it is disastrous for the spouses, particularly the women. Though child rearing is certainly central to the institution of marriage, it is not the only component. Unless marriage is to degenerate into a mere economic and reproductive agreement, a deep friendship should be at the heart of any marriage. As Aquinas notes:

> [F]riendship consists in an equality. So, if it is not lawful for the wife to have several husbands, since this is contrary to certainty as to offspring, it would not be lawful, on the other hand, for a man to have several wives, for the friendship of wife for husband would not be free, but somewhat servile. And this argument is corroborated by experience, for among hus-bands having plural wives the wives have a status like that of servants.[48]

Though Aquinas does not mention the specific culture(s) that he had observed, reason and modern experience of polygamous cultures confirm his suspicions about this disordered arrangement. Common sense dictates that such a household would necessarily result in the subordination of the wives to the status of servants. Because sexual desire is largely based on physical attraction, the youngest and most beautiful woman would invariably end up being the predominant or exclusive sexual partner in the domestic arrangement; she would be the most physically desirable as well as the most physically able to bear children. However, as experience demonstrates and adults are well aware, the youngest and most beautiful woman is not always the wisest or most fit for conversation. Though the husband may acquire younger wives for the sake of reproduction and sexual pleasure, he is more likely to confide in the wife or wives who are more his age, for they have more shared experiences with him and are wiser because of their years. In short, there will inevitably be a division of labor among the women according to their character and physical characteristics, a division that cannot but result in rivalries and emotional dysfunction among the wives.[49]

Finally, Aquinas notes, "[S]trong friendship is not possible in regard to many people ... Therefore, if a wife has but one husband, but the husband has several wives, the friendship will not be equal on both sides."[50] As anyone who is employed or is a full-time student knows, stable and intimate friendships are not possible with many people. If people are compelled to work eight hours a day and to sleep another eight, they have at most eight hours a day to devote to developing meaningful relationships with others. Indeed, even eight hours is an exaggeration; for most modern people, one to two hours would probably be much more accurate. Additionally, even if a person is exceedingly popular, he or she is likely to have only one or two very mean-ingful relationships. Though there may be people we greet in the hall everyday on the way to class or at the water fountain, and there may be a group of friends with whom we associate at parties, only one or two of our friendships have deep roots. As any college graduate knows, most people only stay in touch with a few friends from their high school days. Time and human nature do not permit any other arrangement. Similarly, a polygamous marriage is doomed to be a lopsided and shallow arrange-ment. Though the wives may be wholly devoted to their husband, "the friendship will not be equal on both sides"; the husband cannot be wholly devoted to any one of his wives in virtue of the relationship itself. He does not have the time nor could he have the emotional or mental reserves to fulfill the needs of each of his wives. The husband and wives in a polygamous relationship cannot possibly forge the types of bonds that a monogamous husband and wife have forged through a singular devotion to one another.

D2. Two Modern Examples: Pope John Paul II on the Death Penalty and on Proper Care of the Terminally Ill

Though St. Thomas Aquinas' foundational work on natural law continues to speak to Christians even in the 21st century, further reflection and reasoning on God's design for humanity is and will always be necessary. Each age faces its particular moral uncertainties, due in large part to technological advancement and cultural upheaval. Consequently, theologians and "all people of good will" must continue to search their hearts and minds, as well as analyze the design of creation, in order to discern God's will.

D2a. Is the death penalty in keeping with natural law?

Continuing the natural law tradition of St. Paul and St. Thomas Aquinas, Pope John Paul II composed an encyclical letter in 1995 entitled *The Gospel of Life*. In this encyclical, the Pope calls upon all people of good will to revere and protect life, and he strongly condemns virtually all assaults on the gift of life, from abortion to euthanasia or "mercy killing."

Of course, murder is one of the oldest sins of mankind; the 21st century did not invent it, and Pope John Paul II was certainly not the first person in the Judeo-Christian tradition to speak on these issues. Indeed, the first book of the Bible, Genesis, declares, "Whoever sheds the blood of man, by man will his blood be shed; for God made man in his own image" (9:6). Furthermore, Catholic theologians for nearly two thousand years have unanimously condemned the direct or intentional taking of innocent life. However, the Pope rightly believed that the traditional Catholic teaching needed to be emphasized and re-evaluated in light of modern Western culture. Though the 21st century did not invent murder, it has certainly glorified and institutionalized it. As the rampant violence in cities and the grisly massacres in high schools throughout the country have amply demonstrated, our society runs the risk of embracing and of modeling what the Pope calls "the culture of death." The infinite value of human life, grounded in the fact that human beings are made in God's image, depreciated substantially in the last few decades of the last century. All times have had vicious men and petty thugs, but the present era seems to have industries and whole social structures devoted to the destruction of human life. From the violence prevalent in the media to the millions of unborn people aborted every year, the West seems to be a factory of death.

Against this dreary background, the modern person is faced with a serious dilemma: What should be the Christian response to capital punishment, the practice of executing criminals?

Unquestionably, the Old Testament does at times endorse the practice of the death penalty. As the passage from Genesis above illustrates, the ancient Jews believed that death was a fitting punishment for certain crimes, and as passages from Exodus through Deuteronomy further illustrate, they prescribed death for everything from murder and kidnapping to witchcraft and disrespect toward one's parents. However, the New Testament is more ambiguous and silent on the subject. Death penalty opponents like to cite the Gospel of John 8:3-11, the story in which Jesus forgives an adulteress who is about to be stoned to death for her sin; they maintain that this passage demonstrates that mercy should prevail over the demands of justice.[51] Death penalty advocates like to cite the Letter of Paul to the Romans 13:15 that states that governors and governments have been given their authority from God, and they are empowered to use their "sword ... to execute [God's] wrath on the wrongdoer."[52]

How are Christians to decide the proper stance on this complex and perplexing issue? Life is, indeed, of infinite value, but what are we to do when an aggressor threatens the safety of a particular person or the security of an entire community? Can we protect ourselves or our loved ones without violating the sanctity of human life? Could one even use lethal force if such force were necessary to protect oneself or his loved ones?

After much discussion of the Biblical view of the inviolability of human life, the Pope employs some natural law reasoning in order to refine the Biblical views on life and the need for defense and punishment. At the heart of the notion of the defense of oneself and others is the idea of self-love. The Pope observes that God has instilled in every person an indissoluble *love for himself or herself*. Indeed, this fact of self-love is explicitly mentioned in the second great commandment: "You shall love your neighbor *as yourself*."[53] Thus, the fact that life is intrinsically valuable and that people naturally love themselves led the Pope to conclude that people have a "true right to self-defense." Additionally, anyone—such as a mother, father, or policeman—entrusted with the lives of other people not only has a *right* to defend those who depend on them for their well-being but also a grave *duty* to do so. Basing his conclusions on the design and natural inclinations of the human person, the Pope has reasoned that the legitimate defense of others and oneself is in keeping with natural law.

But what side is one to take when the legitimate love of oneself requires that *lethal* force be used against an aggressor, i.e., force that could result in the end of a human life? According to Scripture and the traditional teachings of the Catholic Church, God alone has the authority to take life *intentionally*. So, if an aggressor were to break into a home, threatening the lives of one's family members, must the father refrain from using lethal force against this aggressor, even if lethal force would be the only way to stop this man from harming his family? Would the use of such force violate the consistent teaching of the Church that God alone has the power over life and death?

According to the Pope, *one should never use deadly force against an aggressor unless it is absolutely necessary, i.e., unless no other means are deemed possible to render him incapable of doing further harm*. For example, suppose an assailant armed with a knife entered a home through a window, and upon hearing a suspicious noise, the father of this family were to search the house armed with a gun. If, after seeing the gun, the aggressor attempted to flee the house through a window, the father would not need to shoot this man to protect himself and his family; he should immediately notify the police and leave the matter in more competent hands. Indeed, if he *were* to shoot this man, he would be using disproportionate and unnecessary force; though scared and probably angry, the father himself would be guilty of committing a crime and violating God's law. However, if the intruder were lunging for one of the family members in order to harm him or her, then the father would be justified in shooting this armed assailant, if no other effective means of stopping the intruder were available. In this scenario, the death of the intruder—if he were to die—would clearly not be the intention of the father. Such a case would be an instance in which a person's actions would have a double effect; one is intended—saving the life of a family member—and the second is not—killing the attacker. In fact, in this scenario, the Pope would reason that "the fatal outcome [would be] attributable to the aggressor whose action brought it about," not to the father who put an end to the aggression.[54] In a sense, the *criminal's* act was so violent and irreversible that *it* brought about a state of affairs in which the criminal's death was the only way the father could bring about a good end.

However, one may ask, "What exactly does any of this have to do with the death penalty?" According to the Pope, the death penalty should be evaluated in view of the principle formulated above, *one should never use deadly force against an aggressor unless it is absolutely necessary, i.e., unless no other means are deemed possible to render him incapable of doing further harm.* Here, the Pope quotes the *Catechism of the Catholic Church*:

> If bloodless means are sufficient to defend human lives against an aggressor and to protect public order and the safety of persons, public authority must limit itself to such means, because they better correspond to the concrete conditions of the common good and are more in conformity to the dignity of the human person.[55]

After a criminal has been apprehended by the police and placed in prison, society should ask itself the following question, according to the Pope: Can we protect public order and our people—those inside and outside of the prison—without killing this criminal? If we *can* achieve these goals with "bloodless means," we should do so, for more unnecessary killing only adds to a "culture of death." Moreover, if executed, the offender himself would be permanently cut off from rehabilitation and the redemptive love of God.

So, can society protect itself against apprehended criminals using bloodless means? The Pope responds, "Today … as a result of steady improvements in the organization of the penal system, such cases [in which only death would protect the public order and the safety of persons] are very rare, if not practically non-existent."[56] In the days of Thomas Aquinas or perhaps even today in a place like Gilligan's island, it might very well be the case that society could only be protected by executing the criminal. If the technology of a given era or in a given part of the world is so primitive that the probability of the prisoner escaping or injuring/killing another inmate is high, the Pope would probably maintain that the death of a particularly vicious criminal would be warranted. If the crew on Gilligan's island or the Yanomamo of South America encountered a criminal as wily and deadly as Hannibal Lecter or John Dillinger, they would probably be acting wisely if they simply hung him, for their primitive prisons would probably fail to protect their communities. However, this primitive state of affairs does not exist in most parts of the world today. Of course, no system is foolproof; all human endeavors, including the court systems that rule on the guilt or innocence of suspected killers, are liable to fail. But given our current level of prison technology, the Pope concludes, the death penalty should be practically, if not completely, non-existent.

D2b. Is euthanasia permissible according to natural law?

Criminals, however, are not the only undesirable or vulnerable people who are threatened by our culture of death. The Pope also believed it was necessary to address the ethical question of "euthanasia," the question of whether or not it is morally permissible to intentionally take the life of a terminally ill or elderly person. If people *request* that their life be taken in order to relieve their pain or protect their family from the emotional and financial perils of a prolonged death, should doctors be legally or morally permitted to administer a lethal drug "to put them out of their misery"?

Neither terminal illness nor old age is a new subject. It is not as if either has suddenly emerged onto the scene of human history calling out for an ethical evaluation. However, according to the Pope, at least two new developments in our culture warrant a new application of traditional Catholic principles to the experience of dying. First, as the Pope states, medical technology has advanced beyond what anyone, save perhaps a science fiction author, could have imagined a few decades ago:

> By using highly sophisticated systems and equipment, science and medical practice today are able not only to attend to cases formerly considered untreatable and to reduce or eliminate pain, but also to sustain and prolong life even in situations of extreme frailty, to resuscitate artificially patients whose biological functions have undergone sudden collapse, and to use special procedures to make organs available for transplanting.[57]

In many ways, such advances are invaluable; they allow men and women to live fuller and longer lives, with less pain and often much more hope. Virtually every family can reflect on the great gifts that have been bestowed on them by the medical profession. Grandparents are able to live much longer; cancer is no longer necessarily a death sentence; and advanced medications and methods of surgery have given new life to innumerable patients with heart disease. However, this newfound mastery over the human body has, unfortunately, led many in our culture to believe that human beings have become the ultimate *masters of life and death*. Basing their views on Genesis and natural law, Christians, on the contrary, have always argued that man is a steward or caretaker of all creation, having dominion over all the earth, including himself, but ultimately, they maintain that only God can intentionally give or take life; "It is I who bring both death and life," says the Lord in Deuteronomy 32:39. Faced with this new cultural outlook, both doctors and terminally ill patients themselves have become emboldened and blinded by the possibilities technology has provided. Frankenstein's monster has been set loose upon the world.

Second, in addition to the advances in technology, another related aspect of our culture has changed drastically, itself fueled by advances in technology. As the Pope notes, because of the advances in technology—especially in the West—the ability to live a relatively pain-free life with vast material goods has put a new face on the dying process. "When the prevailing tendency is to value life only to the extent that it brings pleasure and well-being, suffering seems like an unbearable setback, something from which one must be freed at all costs," observes the Pope. Not only have technological advances bloated humanity's view of its place in the cosmos, but they have also made pain and death seem absolutely intolerable. Our technologically-fueled economic system and the creature comforts that it has provided have resulted in a culture that places the greatest premium on efficiency and pleasure. Needless to say, the elderly and the terminally ill do not have much of a share in either of these; they are not "productive" members of society, as that term is currently understood, and they suffer, both physically and emotionally. In our culture of death, we seem to have little room for them.

What, then, does right reason and the natural law tell us about God's plan for the dying? Is it ever permissible to intentionally take the life of a terminally ill person, if he or she requests it? If not, is it required that every conceivable measure be taken to prolong life as long as humanly possible?

It should come as no surprise to anyone that the Pope—who calls on all people of good will to cherish all life, even the lives of the most *contemptible and vicious* criminals—would condemn any intentional taking of *innocent* human life. Though euthanasia or "physician-assisted suicide" is often driven by apparently good motives— a desire to be released from physical or mental anguish or to release one's family from the emotional or financial burden of a prolonged death—it is still suicide, a gravely immoral act. Suicide violates the Old Testament teaching that God alone has the power over life and death (Dt. 32:39; 2 Kg 5:7; 1 Sam. 2:6) as well as the New Testament teaching that "your body is a temple of the Holy Spirit within you, which you have from God ... You are not your own; you were bought with a price" (1 Cor. 6:19-20).

Furthermore, according to the Pope, natural law likewise militates against the practice of suicide and euthanasia. As he states, "[Suicide] involves the rejection of love of self and the renunciation of the obligation of justice and charity towards one's neighbor, towards the communities to which one belongs, and towards society as a whole."[58] As mentioned before in regard to self-defense, human beings have a natural self-love by which they seek good things for themselves. Needless to say, suicide is a renunciation of this self-love; instead of trying to preserve oneself in being, the perpetrator of this immoral act rejects his or her natural inclinations and the hope perpetually offered by God. Moreover, suicide is an offense against society. In an age in which "autonomy" or "self-rule" has become the prominent "virtue," it may be difficult to see that human society is an intricately woven fabric of relationships. Pro-choice and pro-euthanasia activists are fond of proclaiming, "Women/dying people have a 'right' to do what they want with their body," but both abortion and suicide are ultimately very destructive of the fabric of society. The loss of any life leaves an immeasurable hole in any family's or community's life, and suicide casts a pall over the loved ones; there is a certain shame and sadness that invade the families of suicide victims. Furthermore, with each suicide, physician-assisted or not, the value of human life slowly decreases; life becomes more expendable and disposable, and society becomes more callous and inhumane.

Arguing for the same position as Pope John Paul II, Fr. Robert Spitzer, SJ, has noted that euthanasia actually does a great disservice to society. Though it may appear that society would be better off if it were rid of its weakest members, "[w]eakness elicits compassion, and compassion civilizes us all."[59] In other words, despite their suffering and lack of productivity, the dying have a vital role to play in society; they bring out the best in nearly all men and women. Though there will always be tyrants and rogues who will victimize the weakest members of society, the vast majority of people learn such virtues as patience, attentiveness, and compassion when they are brought face to face with the most dependent and helpless children of God. For perhaps the first time in many people's lives, they are able to leave their hectic schedules and competitive natures behind and care for the sick. In addition to prematurely stripping the patient of his or her life, physician-assisted suicide strips society of an entire segment of the population who are specially called to civilize and humanize the rest of the race.

In closing, however, it should be noted that the Pope is highly attuned to the needs of the patient and does not rest all of the weight of his natural law argument on one's duty to society. Pain is often redemptive, and it often brings a person face to face with her limitations and own mortality. Pain cuts through the banality of existence and helps the victim clarify her relationship with God; the patient becomes aware of her ultimate dependence on God. Keeping these observations in mind, however, the Pope is not averse to the practice of administering any of the latest pain medications to a patient, as long as they are not given in order to shorten life or to deprive the patient of consciousness unnecessarily. Indeed, it is even in keeping with natural law for a dying patient to refuse extraordinary treatments whose risks are disproportionate to any of their expected benefits. For example, a ninety-year old woman who is suffering from inoperable brain cancer is not called upon to subject herself to a new, experimental chemotherapy drug, especially one that might immediately kill her or produce horrific side-effects.

The issues of euthanasia and capital punishment deserve further analysis and debate, and may be the subject of deeper study later in the year when you study specific moral issues. The point of mentioning these issues at this juncture in our course is to provide specific examples that will enable you to understand how reasoning and natural law are utilized in the Catholic moral tradition.

This section concludes the examination of the components at work in the formation of a Catholic's conscience. The final chapter, which follows immediately, will familiarize the reader with some very practical tools that can help people who are trying to live a good Christian life. These will constitute the last part of An Introduction to Catholic Ethics.

SECTION HIGHLIGHTS

The Catholic Church holds that although humanity is, indeed, corrupted by original sin, every human person—regardless of his or her religious convictions and in spite of his or her fallen state—has imprinted within, basic and general moral principles that he or she is able to apply in particular situations through the use of reason.

If, in fact, all men and women have access to this divinely inscribed natural law, then Catholics and other Christians can hope to have fruitful moral dialogue with people of all religions and even with non-religious people.

There are misconceptions about the concept of natural law:

> *Natural law theory does not hold that natural things are ipso facto to be preferred to man-made ones.*

> *Natural law theory does not hold that animal behavior should be the moral standard for human behavior.*

> *Natural law theory does not hold that because certain human misbehaviors are commonplace—e.g., lying or marital infidelity—they are morally right, or that uncommon choices, such as vowed celibacy, are wrong because they are "unnatural."*

> *Natural law theory does not hold that what is involuntary—e.g., the disposition to alcoholism or a homosexual orientation—should be acted upon because it is "natural."*

St. Paul, in his Letter to the Romans, maintained that non-Christians who denied God's existence and practiced selfish sexual excesses should have known better because of "the natural law" that is "written on their hearts"(Romans 2:14-15).

Thomas Aquinas maintained that, unlike lower forms of creation that comply with nature's plan for them simply by following their instincts, humans comply with God's plan for them (His "Law") by using their reasoning power rightly and by doing what their right reason tells them to do. Thus, humans join with God in ruling themselves as well as the world and have a dignity higher than that given to other animals.

Review and master the four bullet items in section C3.

The following are examples of natural law theory in action:

> *According to Aquinas, since experience shows that property given to a certain person is better cared for than property not given to anyone's care at all and since property parceled out to specific persons rather than left 'up for grabs' is less likely to cause strife, the existence of private ownership of property is in accord with the natural law.*

> *Aquinas also maintains that because God made material goods for the sake of ALL of his children, a person in dire straits—in danger of dying from want—may take the property of a person who has an abundance of goods in order to save his or her life or the lives of his or her family. In other words, the practice of private property can be temporarily suspended if the original purpose for material goods is not being met.*

> *Aquinas maintains that reason shows that polygamy is an unhealthy human arrangement: it causes friction and jealousy among multiple spouses, leaves certain children feeling neglected and slighted by the single dominant spouse, and militates*

against the formation of a partnership of healthy friendship and equality between husband and wife.

John Paul II maintains that Scripture and reason (natural law) teach us that the Creator and not humans are masters of human life and therefore humans do not have the right to take the life of another human unless it is necessary to do so to prevent that person from taking one's own life. Since, in the modern era, killers can be effectively imprisoned for life, there is no need to execute a killer. For imprisonment alone will protect society, and this form of punishment shows a greater respect for the sanctity of human life.

John Paul II also maintains that since humans are stewards, not masters, of life, which is sacred, and since human weakness and sickness evoke humanizing compassion and humbling patience—both Christ-like virtues—euthanasia is not right.

QUESTIONS

Answer the following questions in writing on a separate sheet of paper. Use complete sentences.

1. In your own words, explain what is meant by the theory of natural law.

2. In the opening of this section on natural law, what do you learn about why using the theory of natural law is important for the Christian who wants to help to develop a world that is more moral and more just?

3. Show why the following understandings of natural law are wrong:

    a. "Natural law theory holds natural things are to be preferred to man-made things."

    b. "If animals do it, it is natural (and right) for humans to do it as well."

    c. "What is commonplace—i.e., done by the majority of human persons—is natural, and what is natural is right."

    d. "If people are born with an unwanted (involuntary) tendency, they are not to blame if they act on it; it is natural to do so."

4. T-F — St. Paul believed in natural law. (Support your answer with evidence from Scripture.)

5. Give one example of natural law in action. Explain clearly why it is natural law, not another moral theory, at work in your example.

CHAPTER SIX:
TOOLS FOR DISCERNING GOD'S WILL

J udging the morality of human actions is sometimes most difficult. Some guidelines have been developed over time that can help a person to make good decisions. These guidelines do not replace the important use of Scripture and of the Church's teachings, but they complement them. They have been developed by Christian theologians and by a Christian saint, St. Ignatius Loyola. This section contains three sets of such guidelines, together with a daily exercise useful for keeping focused on God and good.

A.   GUIDELINES FOR DIFFICULT SITUATIONS[1]

Sometimes in life one has to choose between what appear to be two negatives, a choice popularly described as "choosing the lesser of two evils." The believer maintains that, in actuality, finding and choosing the right alternative—the one that God wants—opens that desperate situation to the transforming and redeeming action of God so that what appears as a dead end is really not! Nonetheless, the situation will appear to our eyes to be a dire one, in which both alternatives seem wholly negative, rendering the entire situation hopeless. For example, the situation of an elderly parent who has Alzheimer's and can no longer be easily cared for at home, or a woman diagnosed with terminal cancer and told that she can either receive chemotherapy, which will cause discomfort but may delay death, or prepare for almost certain death in a given time. In such cases, the choices do not look good, but they are choices.

Listed immediately below are eight cases that involve such choices and note what choices were made. Write down your evaluation of each choice ("right" or "wrong") and explain the reasons for your evaluation. After you finish, we will look at your evaluations and then see how the Catholic Church has traditionally approached such cases.

1.   A person shoots an armed man who broke into his house and was charging him with the weapon.

2.   A person shoots and kills a person who was in the process of stealing his car.

3.   A surgeon operates on a pregnant woman with a cancerous uterus to remove the uterus. A by-product of the removal of the uterus is that the enclosed fetus dies. Without the removal of the cancerous uterus, both the mother and the fetus would certainly die.

4.   A surgeon amputates a person's gangrenous leg to save a patient's life. This was the only available choice other than allowing the patient to die from gangrene.

5.   By injecting serum into a person, a surgeon could have saved a person's leg and life. Instead, she chose to amputate the leg.

6.   A person smokes cigarettes for relaxation and enjoyment despite the fact that this practice has been shown to be a serious long-term risk to his health and life.

7.   A woman uses donor insemination to have a child since her husband is infertile. She realizes that there is a serious risk that such a procedure might cause tension and instability in her marriage.

8.   A person ordered to do so by a totalitarian regime kills an innocent "enemy of the people" as a condition to win the release of his own family who are held hostage and threatened with death by that government.

To judge the morality of complex human actions such as these, the Catholic Church argues that one must break them down into their essential components, viz., their objects, intentions, and circumstances. As we learned in Part Four of Chapter Four, the object is *what* the person has chosen to do—it is the concrete, physical action a person has taken; the intention of an action is *why* a person has chosen the object in question; and the circumstances are the *secondary factors* surrounding either the moral agent himself or the content of the action itself. And as we also learned in that section, both the object and the intention of an action must be good in order for an action as a whole to be morally praiseworthy. Additionally, the specific circumstances of each case must be taken into consideration, for on occasion, they too can be deciding factors as to whether or not an action as a whole is morally praiseworthy.

Keeping these basic concepts and guidelines in mind, we can come to some conclusions about the cases above. First, we can ask, "Do any of the cases above involve objects that are inherently bad?" If so, these actions are not to be condoned. In light of this question, it is clear that cases 7 and 8 cannot be approved, however much sympathy we may feel for the parties involved. According to the Catholic Church, donor insemination or any other practice, such as *in vitro* fertilization, that severs or dissociates the sexual act from the procreative act is always to be condemned; no good intention or unique set of circumstances can make acts of this sort good. Likewise, the intentional taking of innocent life is always to be condemned, regardless of the good consequences that one believes would be secured by doing so. In both cases, as compassionate Christians, we should emphasize that the parties found themselves in truly difficult circumstances, and this fact should be taken into consideration when evaluating their level of guilt. Nonetheless, their actions as a whole are not to be condoned.

Second, we can ask, "Do any of the cases above involve evil intentions?" or, more precisely, "Do the people involved desire the evil effects that would be produced by their decision or are they, as it were, merely unwanted by-products of their decisions?" If the people involved do intend the evil effects, then their actions are not to be condoned. Cases 2 and 5 might arouse our suspicion in this regard. Why, we may ask, is the person in case 2 so eager to use deadly force to stop a car thief? Does he know this criminal and is merely using the occasion of the attempted theft to exact revenge on him for a prior wrong? And why would the surgeon in case 5 opt to remove a leg that she can save with a serum? Does she secretly intend to cripple this patient because of some prior wrongdoing? Or is the surgeon performing unnecessary surgery because she is greedy and will make more money by doing so? From the descriptions given above, however, one cannot definitely determine the intentions of these people. But let us assume that all of the cases involve people with good intentions; e.g., the policemen want to protect the public, the surgeon wants to save the patient's life, etc. How, then, are we to evaluate these actions?

The problem with evaluating cases 1 through 6 is that all of them, at least apparently, involve good intentions and none of them involve objects that are clearly defined as inherently evil by the Catholic Church. Medical procedures and acts of self-defense are unquestionably essential to human life, and it is hard to determine whether inhaling cigarette smoke is inherently bad—for not everything that is potentially physically harmful is necessarily bad, as any proud mother who endured the trauma of birth knows. What makes the evaluation of these cases problematic is that each involves two effects, a good one and a bad one, and the question is "How is one to evaluate actions that have both good and bad effects?"

In order to evaluate actions that do not have evil objects or evil intentions but do have good and bad effects, the Catholic Church has offered the following guideline as an aid: Ask "Is the good end intended by this act proportionate to the bad effect?"[2] Now, in order to apply this guideline to the cases above, we obviously must come to some understanding of what "proportionate" means, and this is no easy undertaking. Over the centuries, theologians and philosophers have disagreed over how to interpret this concept, but in general, at least three inter-related ways of understanding the concept have come to the surface.

First, to say that a good end or effect is "proportionate" to a bad effect is to say that the good effect has been achieved in a way that minimizes the bad effect as much as possible. Given this understanding of "proportionate," one would have to conclude that the surgeon's action in case 4 was properly proportionate; given our current level of medical knowledge, amputation was the one way to save the patient from dying of gangrene. For this same reason, we would have to conclude that the surgeon's action in case 5 was not properly proportionate, for suffering the pain of a needle is not nearly as evil as suffering the loss of a limb. And again, the person in case 6 who decided to smoke for relaxation did not act for a proportionate reason; there are other, less dangerous ways to relax and enjoy oneself than smoking.

Second, to say that a good end or effect is "proportionate" to an evil one is to say that the good end is of sufficient value to tolerate the evil effect.[3] Putting the matter in the form of a question, one could ask, "Is the good achieved by this act good enough to warrant the evil that will be produced as a by-product?" Given this understanding of "proportionate," one would have to conclude that the person's action in case 2 was not proportionate, for the value of a car, no matter how expensive or beloved, could never be compared to the value of a human life. Likewise, the person's decision to smoke in case 6 can be condemned as being disproportionate, for temporary relaxation and enjoyment do not warrant the permanent damaging of one's health and the shortening of one's life. But cases 1, 3, and 4 are all proportionate in this sense, for all of these cases aim at preserving one of the highest goods, human life. Though the removal of the fetus in case 3 would result in its death, the woman *and* the fetus would have died if the cancer had been allowed to spread unchecked. Had the woman risked the life of her unborn baby for the sake of cosmetic surgery or some similarly trivial reason, then her action would not have been proportionate to the good end, viz., a more beautiful or youthful appearance. But she did not act for such a trivial end; she acted to preserve her life.

Third, to say that a good end or effect is "proportionate" to an evil one is to say that the evil effect does not undermine the value that is aimed at in the action as a whole. Given this understanding of "proportionate," one would have to conclude that the person's action in case 8, for example, was not proportionate, for someone who killed an innocent person to win the release of another innocent person would be undermining the principle on which his action was based. Killing innocent human beings to preserve the lives of other innocent human beings is contradictory and unprincipled. Likewise in regard to case 2, it could be argued that the person who shot and killed a car thief actually undermined the very value he believed he was defending. The person shot and killed the thief in order to protect his rights, safeguard his property, or preserve public order, but the use of lethal force against someone who is merely stealing property actually undercuts these goals; this type of vigilante activity actually threatens the public order by creating an environment in which private property is valued more than human life. In other words, in regard to actions that have a good and a bad effect, we must ask ourselves why we are performing them and then judge whether, as a whole, they really promote the type of goals we are trying to achieve.

B.   GUIDELINES FOR READING ONE'S FEELINGS

Guidelines, such as the ones mentioned above, are often helpful tools for discerning God's will in difficult situations. But the type of cases mentioned above are relatively rare in human life. The moral quandary of a pregnant woman who is stricken with uterine cancer certainly makes for lively debate in an ethics class, and though we may encounter problems such as these at some point in our lives, the day-to-day struggle to be a virtuous and holy human being is usually quite different in nature from the struggles of the people mentioned above. In particular, most people who have made a commitment to becoming better human beings must struggle with their emotions and conscience on an everyday basis. "Am I being too lax in my behavior?" a person may wonder, or again, "Is this voice inside me—telling me that my desires for the opposite sex are unhealthy and need to be reigned in—one that I should listen to or one I should ignore?"

St. Ignatius Loyola laid out a set of guidelines for reading and analyzing these often-conflicting and confusing feelings. Ignatius, a genius in psychology and spirituality, was a careful student of human emotions in general, and through reflection and observation, he was able to set forth a number of helpful suggestions for reading these feelings.

He spoke first about the feelings one has when one has not been a very good person, i.e., when one has been acting out of selfishness or out of very evil motives. In this context, he also spoke about what happens when a person in that situation begins a reform of his or her life.

Before such a person opts to reform, the person can feel troubled about his or her lifestyle: e.g., "I am messing up everyone's life, including my own, by my drinking." He or she can also have another feeling: "Forget it. Lighten up. Be happy. Forget it!" Or "How can you expect to live if you try to change? It is impossible." Ignatius, who had had such an experience himself, noted: "In this situation, the first inspiration—*turmoil*, together with the sense that change is necessary—is *from God*. The second inspiration—*denial*, together with the sense that change is impossible—is *from the Evil Spirit*."[4]

In the case of the person who has opted to begin to reform but then experiences turmoil together with a voice that says, "You can't keep this up," and overall, a sense of temporary depression, Ignatius noted: "This movement comes from the Evil Spirit, and not from God." Whereas, *when a person who is reforming his life feels delight, joy, and peace, it is God who is coming* to encourage the person to put his or her life together.

In the case of those people who have begun to reform their lives but are experiencing temptation to despair and depression, Ignatius urges them not only to hang in there but even to try to fight against those feelings of discouragement by praying more or making a stronger effort to be good to others. God will see the person through, he counseled, and give the person new peace and encouragement. One who is on the path of reform should never make a change of direction when he or she is feeling tempted and depressed. Instead, according to Ignatius, he or she should stick with the original resolution made when he or she felt inspired to be good.

For the person who has lived a good life for a long time and is trying to lead an even better one, Ignatius counseled that usually the person should have feelings of basic peace and that the inspirations that come from God will usually come gently like a drop of water on sponge. By contrast, an inspiration from the evil spirit will hit such a person the way a waterfall hits a stone ledge below; it will cause a big splash of confusion and turmoil and cause him or her to be discontent with the peace he or she had been feeling.

Ignatius advises such a good person to be humble when he feels especially "good" and especially "inspired," and to remember humbly how weak he has felt when attacked by temptation. Says Ignatius, one can be grateful for such "holy feelings," but one should also remember that those feelings are gifts from God.

If a holy feeling of God's presence and God's encouragement to be good comes to a person without any apparent previous cause, then Ignatius says, that movement can be trusted; it comes from God.

A final bit of wisdom Ignatius offered was that if this person who generally strives to be good falls, he or she should go back over his or her life and find out how the Evil Spirit misled him or her: "How did the Evil Spirit deceive me? What weakness in me did the Evil Spirit capitalize on?" Ignatius' philosophy here is: "Take the time to learn from your mistakes."

This line of reflection may seem to be a bit too pious. But people might be more open to try to absorb some of his guidelines if they recall that Ignatius lived a worldly life until he was wounded in battle, and then did a lot of intense introspection while confined to bed, recovering from his wounds, before deciding to reform his life. Indeed, even after his choice to reform, he experienced temptation to commit suicide! His *Spiritual Exercises* has been praised by non-believing psychologists as the work of a person who was a genius in his knowledge of the operations of the psyche.

What has been presented here is the bulk of his guidelines, but not all of them.

C.   GUIDELINES FOR CHOOSING BETWEEN TWO GOODS[5]

In life, we sometimes have to decide not only between "two evils" but also between "two goods"—between getting married or choosing to be single as a religious or priest, between pursuing one's post-college job immediately or choosing instead to spend a year in service of the poor as young people do who join volunteer corps like the Jesuit or Mercy Volunteer Corps, between keeping one's fortune for the security of oneself or one's family or giving away some of this fortune as some philanthropists have done.

Ignatius offered these guidelines for making decisions of this sort. He noted that there are three different situations in which one can confront such decisions.

The first is when one gets a thunderbolt from heaven like St. Paul, who was knocked off his horse and heard a voice calling him to a change of religion, or like Fr. Pedro Arrupe, SJ, the recently deceased leader of the Jesuit order, who, before beginning his graduate studies in medical school, saw a miraculous cure of a paralyzed polio victim at Lourdes and was led by that experience to recognize a call to serve Jesus by joining the Jesuits. In such experiences, there is hardly any room for doubt. This kind of experience is rather uncommon.

The second is when one feels somewhat pulled in two different directions. For example, upon finishing college, one feels drawn both to give a year of one's life to living among the poor in service but also to go on with a career she has been preparing for with the idea of helping others by being a good doctor, lawyer, or whatever occupation she has chosen. As one asks God's help with these options, one seems to get constant consolation from God for one of the options—i.e., she consistently feels God's presence and encouragement telling her to go with one of these options rather than another. This is a second type of situation. In this situation, Ignatius would recommend that one take some serious time to pray carefully for divine guidance about such serious choices, and he would urge a person who feels constantly consoled to believe that God is speaking to her about what is best, to trust her feeling and confidently to give herself to follow that choice.

The third situation Ignatius speaks of is a situation like the second, except that prayer yields no constant clear feeling of consolation, i.e., of God's presence saying: "Make this choice rather than that." In such a situation, Ignatius suggests that after a person has asked God's guidance and recalled the reason for human existence—viz., to do God's will and serve God with all her strength and her talent—the person should carefully write down all the pros and cons for the two options, and see which choice fits because it seems more reasonable. Then, she asks God to bless that choice. He also suggests two other tactics that might help the person get the desired clarity: imagining what advice one would give to a friend who asked about such a choice, or imagining how one will feel with either of these choices as they appear before God on judgment day. Ignatius concludes that after a person reaches some clarity through this method, the person should still beg God to accept and to *confirm* the choice she is making and to make it clear to the person that this is indeed what God wishes by *surrounding the choice with much consolation.*

These are Ignatius' techniques for making a good choice when one is looking at decision between two goods.

D.   A DAILY GUIDE FOR STAYING FOCUSED ON GOD AND THE GOOD

Ignatius suggests a very simple exercise of prayer that you could use to stay focused on God and on leading a good life. Each day, begin your day by offering your actions to God and Jesus. Then at the end of the day, reflect upon the many choices you made and the feelings you experienced throughout the day. Ignatius recommended to people he directed in the spiritual life the following method of prayer to be used especially at the end of the day. He recommends an "examination of consciousness" that goes as follows:

✢   First, recall with gratitude the personal gift you have received from God.

✢   Second, ask for God's help to see how the day went and whether you have continued on the path of generous service of God according to the inspiration you have received for contributing to a better world, the inspiration that shapes your vision of what you could do this day.

✢   Third, review the day to see if you have stayed on course; ask, "What characterized my activity today?"

✢   Fourth, where you moved off course, ask God's forgiveness.

✢   Fifth, resolve to amend your life and make plans to live in closer union with Jesus tomorrow. How will you struggle to make the world better tomorrow? You could conclude this exercise with the Our Father: "Thy Kingdom come, Thy will be done on earth as it is in heaven."

This exercise in the evening, together with some personalized offering of one's day to God in the early morning, make two bookends for the practice of solid Christian living.

QUESTIONS

Rather than provide highlights for this chapter, the questions below will exercise your grasp of the aids given above. Using complete sentences, write your answers to the following questions on a separate piece of paper.

1. Do the written exercise prescribed on page 209. State what choice should be made in each case, and why.

2. Change case 7 on page 210 so that both parents are in total agreement about donor insemination. Would this course of action be morally correct? If not, why?

3. If your life has been fairly "cruddy" up to now, does Ignatius think that the Evil Spirit will bother your conscience? Explain.

4. If you are leading a very good life and begin to be troubled with discouraging worries and difficulties, from which Spirit—Good or Evil—does Ignatius think your difficulties and worries are coming? Explain.

5. You have violated your principles and to your shame have done wrong, but now you intend to get back on track. What would Ignatius encourage you to do as soon as you have a little time to yourself?

6. If you have been leading a fairly good life but now feel tempted to discouragement, what two strategies would Ignatius suggest to you?

7. Do you think that Ignatius' guidelines for choosing between two "goods" will help you to make choices about your career or vocation some day? Why or why not?

8. What are the three different kinds of situations Ignatius says people find themselves in as they ponder a serious life-choice between two good possibilities?

9. Explain how Ignatius suggests that someone arrives at a choice between two good possibilities when he or she does not experience constant divine consolation or inspiration favoring one possibility over another.

10. Christians should offer each of their days to God with the promise that they will try to make a difference for good in the world. Write a brief morning prayer offering God your day.

11. What does the examination of conscience aim to do for a person trying to live a serious Christian life?

NOTES

CHAPTER ONE:
INTRODUCTION, TEST CASES, AND RELATIVISM

1   Aristotle, *Nicomachean Ethics* in *Introduction to Aristotle*, ed. Richard McKeon (Chicago: University of Chicago, 1973), 348.

2   The relation of circumstances to the other parts of a human action—the object and the intention(s)—will be discussed in detail in chapter 4.

3   For a fuller treatment of this issue see the appendix of C.S. Lewis' *The Abolition of Man* (New York: Collier Books, 1947), 93-121.

4   Ibid., 96.

CHAPTER TWO:
SECULAR ETHICAL SYSTEMS

1   Mortimer Adler, "A Sound Moral Philosophy" in *Reforming Education: The Opening of the American Mind* (New York: Collier Books, 1977), 254.

2   Aristotle, 561.

3   Ibid., 567.

4   Ibid., 369.

5   Ibid., 541.

6   Ibid., 378.

7   Ibid., 378-9.

8   *Catechism of the Catholic Church* (Mahwah: Paulist Press, 1994), §1806.

9   St. Augustine, *Confessions*, trans. John K. Ryan (New York: Doubleday, 1960), 248.

10 St. Thomas Aquinas, *Summa Theologica*, trans. Fathers of the English Dominican Province (Allen: Thomas More Publishing, 1948), I-II, q. 3, a. 8.

11 St. Ignatius Loyola, *Spiritual Exercises: A Literal Translation and a Contemporary Reading*, trans. David Fleming, SJ (St. Louis: Institute of Jesuit Sources, 1978), #23.

12 *Catechism*, §1804.

13   Ibid., §2559.

14 For this reason, Kant's moral philosophy is often described as being "deontological"

in character. In Greek, the word "deon" means "necessary" or "obligatory." A moral theory is "deontological" if it emphasizes that certain acts *must* or *must not* be done, regardless of their consequences; the worth of an act resides in the act itself, not what follows from it. Aristotle's ethics, it will be remembered, was "teleological" in nature; it emphasized that human choices were directed toward the *goal* of human fulfillment. And in the next part of this chapter, we will address a "consequentialist" ethic or one that is based on the results of one's actions.

15   Immanuel Kant, *Grounding for the Metaphysics of Morals with On a Supposed Right to Lie because of Philanthropic Concerns*, trans. James W. Ellington (Indianapolis: Hackett Publishing Company, Inc., 1993), 7.

16   There is a tension in Aristotle's thought about the value of courage or a couragous act. At times, Aristotle does seem to value courage because it is necessary for human happiness, but at other times, he praises certain actions as being "noble," or worthy of praise regardless of their consequences. For example, giving one's life in a battle for a just cause would be noble for Aristotle, but given his beliefs about God and immortality, it would be hard for him to make the case that this action would lead to happiness. Being dead is not really conducive to being happy, for Aristotle did not believe in personal immortality. He could not justify the giving of one's life for a noble cause the way a Christian would, viz., by arguing that such an action would lead to or somehow contribute to one's happiness in the next life.

17   Kant, 7.

18   This example is an elaboration of one given by James W. Ellington in his notes to Kant's *Grounding for the Metaphysics of Morals*, 10-1.

19   Ibid., 19.

20   Ibid.

21   Ibid., 30.

22   Ibid., 31.

23   Ibid., 32.

24   Ibid., 36.

25   Onora O'Neill, "The Moral Perplexities of Famine and World Hunger," in *Matters of Life and Death: New Introductory Essays in Moral Philosophy* (New York: Random House, 1980), 322.

26   Immanuel Kant, *Lectures on Ethics* (Indianapolis: Hackett Publishing Co., 1963), 239.

27 John Stuart Mill, *Utilitarianism* (Indianapolis: Hackett Publishing Co., 1979), 7.

28 Ibid., 8.

29 Ibid., 10.

30 Ibid., 16

31 Ibid., 17.

32 Cynthia Rostankowski and Manuel Vasquez, *Ethics: Theory and Practice* (Upper Sadle River: Prentice Hall Professional Technical Reference, 1984), 104-5.

33 See, e.g, §§1755, 1756, and 2271.

34 John Harris, "The Survival Lottery," in *Contemporary Moral Problems*, ed. James E. White (Belmont: Wadsworth Publishing Company, 2000), 226.

35 Aquinas, II-II, q. 66, a.7. The translation of this passage has been slightly altered from that of the English Dominican Province translation.

36 Ronald Dworkin, *Taking Rights Seriously* (Cambridge: Harvard University Press, 1985), 188.

37 In fairness to Dworkin, it should be noted that, in the quote above, he only states that this definition holds "in most cases."

38 John Locke, *Second Treatise of Government* (Indianapolis: Hackett Publishing Co., 1980), 9.

39 It is interesting to note that the first paragraph of the Declaration of Independence also uses the phrase "law of nature" in this Lockean way.

40 According to Locke, though, children are naturally subject to their parents' authority until they reach adulthood.

41 Locke, 19.

42 Ibid., 25.

43 Tom Regan, "The Case for Animal Rights" in *In Defense of Animals*, ed. Peter Singer (Oxford: Blackwell, 1985), 22.

44 Ibid., 21.

45 Ibid., 13.

46 John Rawls, *A Theory of Justice* (Cambridge: Harvard University Press, 1971), 12.

47 Ibid., 302.

48 This line of reasoning about rights conflicts has been used by philosopher Judith Jarvis Thomson in her article "A Defense of Abortion" [in *Moral Problems*, ed.

James Rachels (New York: Harper and Row Publishers, 1979)]. Thomson writes, "I am arguing only that having a right to life does not guarantee having either a right to be given the use of or a right to be allowed continued use of another person's body—even if one needs it for life itself" (140). If, Thomson argues, you were to wake up one morning and find that a group of fanatical music lovers had surgically attached you to a famous unconscious violinist so that he can use your kidneys to stay alive, you would not be obligated to let him use your body. Just because the violinist has a right to life and needs your body—because of your blood type—does not mean he is therefore entitled to the use of your body. And in a similar fashion, the mere fact that an unborn baby has a right to life does not entitle him or her to the free use of the mother's body. So, in some cases, there is actually no conflict between a baby's right to life and the mother's right to do as she pleases with her body.

49   *Catechism*, §1930.

50   Ibid., §2273.

51   John XXIII, *Peace on Earth*, §11 in *Seven Great Encyclicals* (Glen Rock: Paulist Press, 1963).

52   Cited in Mary Ann Glendon, *Rights Talk: The Impoverishment of Political Discourse* (New York: The Free Press, 1991), 79.

53   Ibid., 108.

CHAPTER THREE:
TRANSITION TO CATHOLIC ETHICS

1   For an excellent treatment of this very subject, one to which certain sections of this chapter refer, see chapter four of Peter Kreeft's *Making Choices: Practical Wisdom for Everyday Moral Decisions* (Ann Arbor: Servant Books, 1990), 39-50.

2   *Catechism*, §1804. Italics have been added for emphasis.

3   Ibid., §1954.

4   This passage is also used by Peter Kreeft in his discussion of the relationship between God and morality. See Kreeft, 42.

5   The "natural" or human virtues include both moral virtues, such as temperance and fortitude, as well as intellectual virtues, such as mastering mathematics or physics. Throughout this section, only moral virtues will be referred to, for obvious reasons.

6   Aristotle maintained that there is a part of the human being, reason, that survived death, but his understanding of immortality is nothing like the Catholic belief in immortality, which involves a resurrection of both the body and soul of

a human being. Aristotle's god was much too busy contemplating his own perfect nature to have any concern for measly human beings. Hence, no such loving relationship was possible between his god and human beings.

7   Aquinas, *Summa Theologica*, I-II, q. 62, a.1.

8   Mother Teresa, *A Simple Path* (New York: Ballantine Books, 1995), 73-4.

9   *Catechism*, §1822.

10   Ibid., §1827.

11   Ibid., §1822.

12   Mother Teresa, 80.

13   Ibid., 55.

14   *Catechism*, §1814.

15   Ibid., §1817.

16   Ibid., §1822.

17   *A Pilgrim's Journey, The Autobiography of Ignatius of Loyola*, trans. Joseph Tylenda, SJ (Wilmington: Michael Glazier, Inc., 1985), #1, p. 7.

18   St. Ignatius Loyola, *Spiritual Exercises*, #23.

19   Ibid.

20   This quote by David O'Brien is cited in the introduction to Dorothy Day's *Selected Writings: By Little and By Little*, ed. Robert Ellsberg (Maryknoll: Orbis Books, 1992), xvii.

21   Dorothy Day, *The Long Loneliness* (San Francisco: Harper Collins Publishers, 1952), 42.

22   Ibid., 24.

23   Ibid.

24   Ibid., 29.

25   Ibid., 43.

26   Dorothy Day, "Peter Maurin: A Poor Man" in *Selected Writings: By Little and By Little*, ed. Robert Ellsberg (Maryknoll: Orbis Books, 1992), 126.

27   Dorothy Day, "Room for Christ" in *Selected Writings: By Little and By Little*, ed. Robert Ellsberg (Maryknoll: Orbis Books, 1992), 96.

28   See Dorothy Day, "The Scandal of the Works of Mercy" in *Selected Writings: By Little and By Little*, ed. Robert Ellsberg (Maryknoll: Orbis Books, 1992), 99.

29 Cited in the introduction to *Selected Writings: By Little and By Little*, xxxix.

30 Dorothy Day, "Here and Now" in *Selected Writings: By Little and By Little*, ed. Robert Ellsberg (Maryknoll: Orbis Books, 1992), 102.

31 Lawrence S. Cunningham, *The Meaning of Saints* (New York: Harper & Row Publishers, Inc., 1980), 65.

32 See King's sermon "The Drum Major Instinct" in *I Have a Dream: Writings and Speeches that Changed the World*, ed. James M. Washington (San Francisco: Harper Collins Publishers Inc., 1986), 180-92.

33 Martin Luther King, Jr., "Pilgrimage to Nonviolence" in *I Have a Dream: Writings and Speeches that Changed the World*, ed. James M. Washington (San Francisco: Harper Collins Publishers Inc., 1986), 58.

34 Ibid.

35 Ibid., 59.

36 Martin Luther King, Jr., "An Experiment in Love" in *A Testament of Hope: The Essential Writings and Speeches of Martin Luther King, Jr.*, ed. James M. Washington (San Francisco: Harper Collins Publishers, 1986), 19.

37 Quoted in Martin Luther King, Jr., "Our Struggle" in *I Have a Dream: Writings and Speeches that Changed the World*, ed. James M. Washington (San Francisco: Harper Collins Publishers Inc., 1986), 5.

38 Martin Luther King, Jr., "Facing the Challenge of a New Age" in *I Have a Dream: Writings and Speeches that Changed the World*, ed. James M. Washington (San Francisco: Harper Collins Publishers Inc., 1986), 23.

39 Martin Luther King, Jr., "I See the Promised Land" in *I Have a Dream: Writings and Speeches that Changed the World*, ed. James M. Washington (San Francisco: Harper Collins Publishers Inc., 1986), 203.

40 David J. Garrow, *Bearing the Cross* (New York: William Morrow and Company, Inc., 1986), 625.

41 Ibid., 587.

42 Much of this biographical sketch of Thomas More is drawn from *The Encyclopedia Britannica* (Chicago: Encyclopedia Britannica Inc., 1987) vol. 8, 312-5 and the *New Catholic Encyclopedia* (Washington, D.C: The Catholic University of America) vol. IX, 1136-9.

43 *Encyclopedia Britannica*, vol. 8, 314.

44 *New Catholic Encyclopedia*, vol. IX, 1139.

45 *Encyclopedia Britannica*, vol. 8, 315.

46 Much of the information about the life of Pedro Arrupe, SJ, is taken from *Pedro Arrupe, SJ* by George Bishop, published in India but available from Loyola University Press in Chicago.

47 Ibid., 37.

48 Ibid., 40.

49 Ibid., 41.

50 Ibid., 343.

CHAPTER FOUR:
KEY CONCEPTS FOR UNDERSTANDING CHRISTIAN ETHICS

1 Cited in *Catechism*, §1730.

2 Sir Isaac Newton, *Principia Mathematica, Vol. II: The System of the World* (Berkeley: University of California Press, 1969), 544.

3 Bertrand Russell, "Has Religion Made Useful Contributions to Society?" in *Why I am not a Christian* (New York: Simon & Schuster Inc., 1957), 40.

4 *Catechism*, §1735.

5 Aristotle, 370.

6 *Catechism*, §1730.

7 Cited in ibid., §1848.

8 Cited in ibid., §385.

9 Ibid., §404.

10 "[A]s one man's trespass led to condemnation for all men, so one man's act of righteousness leads to acquittal and life for all men," says St. Paul in his Letter to the Romans (5:18).

11 See, for example, the sermon "You are Accepted" in *The Shaking of the Foundations* (New York: Charles Scribner's Sons, 1976).

12 This section is fundamentally an exposition of parts of §1853 of the *Catechism*.

13 The Catholic Church has traditionally recognized two types of ignorance in regard to sin, "vincible" and "invincible" ignorance. Succinctly put, a person who suffers from "vincible" ignorance might not know that what he is doing is wrong, but he *should* have known what he was doing was wrong; his ignorance in regard to a particular act might lessen his culpability, but he is still blameworthy for *not knowing* the proper course of action. However, a person who suffers

from "invincible" ignorance not only does not know that what he did was wrong, but he could not have been expected to know given his circumstances. A person who is invincibly ignorant is not to be blamed for his action, even if the object of the action is disordered.

14   In general, if a person's free will or knowledge is *completely absent or obstructed*—i.e., not merely lessened—then he is not guilty of any kind of sin, either mortal or venial.

15   Cited in the *Catechism*, §1863. The parenthetical remark has been added for the sake of clarity.

16   Richard M. Gula, SS, *Reason Informed by Faith: Foundations of Christian Morality* (New York: Paulist Press, 1989), 124. The last sentence has been italicized for emphasis.

17   Ibid., 136.

18   Ibid., 137-8.

19   Ibid., 139.

20   Ibid., 147.

21   Ibid., 148-50.

22   For the most part, the section to follow is an exposition of Article 4 of Section One of Part Three of the *Catechism of the Catholic Church*. Examples and some commentary have been added for the sake of clarification, but the substance of this section is the same as that section of the *Catechism*.

23   This example is used by Peter Kreeft in *Making Choices: Practical Wisdom for Everyday Moral Decisions*, 31.

CHAPTER FIVE:
SCRIPTURE AND TRADITION: SOURCES FOR
THE FORMATION OF CONSCIENCE

1   See, for example, Senis Bayly and Royal W. Rhodes, *The Faith of Christians* (Philadelphia: Fortress Press, 1984), 21.

2   *Catechism*, §101.

3   This story is related in Betrand Russell's, *Religion and Science* (Oxford: Oxford University Press, 1961), 51-2.

4   See, for example, Donald G. Bloesch, *Essentials of Evangelical Theology, Volume 1: God, Authority, and Salvation* (San Francisco: Harper & Row Publishers, Inc., 1978), 66.

5   *Catechism*, §107.

6   Bloesch, 69. Italics added for emphasis.

7   It is true that there is much that appears to be history in the Bible, and some of these writings are, indeed, intended to be historical accounts. Historians have verified some of these historical events, such as the crucifixion of Christ, but other events, such as the capture of Jericho in the book of Joshua, have not been verified. As Christians we do believe that many parts of the Bible—especially the Gospels that describe the life, words, and deeds of Jesus and his followers— *do* in fact reveal a great detail of factual, historical information. But even the history *as history* is not always the point.

8   Understood in the scientific or historical sense of the word, "accuracy" is often not the central concern of either the Bible itself or the person who is reading it. Christians of all denominations regularly turn to the Bible for instruction, encouragement, consolation in times of grief, or even the simple pleasure of hearing an edifying story. Because of the great debates in this century over whether "creationism" or "evolution" should be taught in schools and the scholarly interest in "the search for the historical Jesus"—i.e., the effort to distinguish myth and historical additions from the actual words, deed, and events of Jesus' life— there has been an inordinate amount of energy spent on the science and history present in Scripture. Hopefully, the foregoing comments will illustrate to what extent these debates have misunderstood the Christian understanding of the "infallibility" of Sacred Scripture.

9   St. Augustine, *Confessions*, 320.

10   See *Catechism*, §76.

11   Ibid., §119.

12   St. Augustine, 320.

13   This quote, from Vatican II, is cited by Richard M. Gula, SS in his *Reason Informed by Faith*, 165 [#16 of the Document on Priestly Formation.]

14   See Gula, 166.

15   These three passages are cited by G.E.M. Anscombe in her article "War and Murder" in *Moral Problems* (New York: Harper & Row Publishers, Inc., 1979), 401, in an effort to demonstrate the way that pacifism misinterprets and denigrates the Old Testament.

16   *Catechism*, §107.

17   The five tasks explained in this section are based on the tasks described by Kenneth R. Himes, OFM, in "Scripture and Ethics: A Review Essay," *Biblical Theology Bulletin* 15 (April 1985): 65-73. Additionally, Richard Gula, SS,

building upon Himes' work, has also explained these tasks in his *Reason Informed by Faith*, 167-72. The section to follow is largely based on the work of these two theologians. However, the examples provided in the present text are quite different, and the "methodological task" has been abbreviated. Additionally, the "Christocentric Principle" is not one of Hime's or Gula's tasks, though it is perfectly compatible with the four they do discuss.

18   Gula, 167

19   Joseph A. Fitzmyer, *The Gospel According to Luke* (X-XXIV) (New York: Doubleday & Co. Inc., 1986), 1063.

20   Ibid.

21   Pheme Perkins, *Reading the New Testament, An Introduction* (New York: Paulist Press, 1978), 142.

22   The following description of a Matlock episode is taken from memory. None of the quoted phrases are direct quotes from the television show; they are paraphrases.

23   Several complex questions on this topic could be answered in a more detailed treatment of the specific issue of God's prescriptions concerning marriage and divorce – the "Pauline privilege," the "Petrine privilege," and the meaning of Matthew 19:9. But the indicated contrast between Jesus' teaching about this topic and the teaching of Moses is accurate and serves to illustrate the Christocentric task.

24   *Catechism*, §107.

25   Ibid., §§80-5.

26   Ibid., §§85-7.

27   In his "Galileo" (*New Catholic Encyclopedia*, Vol. VI, 254), J.J. Langford states, "Galileo was made to kneel and abjure the Copernican opinion, sentenced to imprisonment, and given a 'salutary penance' to recite. The prison sentence was never imposed, though Galileo remained under house arrest in Florence for the rest of his life. The condemnation was the act of a Roman congregation and in no way involved infallible teaching authority. But the theologians' treatment of Galileo was an unfortunate error; and, however it might be explained, it can not be defended."

28   For a clear explanation of how the Church arrived at its conclusion about inauthentic gospels, see Luke Timothy Johnson, *The Real Jesus* (New York: HarperCollins, 1996), 148-66.

29   The Roman Catholic Church Council at Trent rejected the idea that this passage from John's Gospel could be used to show that the power to forgive sins had

been given to each of Christ's faithful and declared that the passage should be understood to speak of the power exercised by the priest in the sacrament of reconciliation. On pages 1041-5 of his Anchor *Commentary on John's Gospel,* Raymond Brown treats the complex issue of how modern biblical scholarship would view this passage.

30   See, for example, St. Ignatius Loyola's "Rules for Thinking with the Church" in his *Spiritual Exercises,* #352-70.

31   *Catechism,* §892.

32   Cited in Karl Rahner, SJ, "Non-infallible Pronouncements," *Catholic Mind* 69 (December 1971): 20-2.

33   Ibid., 28. Cf. Vatican Council II, *Lumen Gentium,* #25.

34   Cf. The Anchor Bible, *The Gospel according to Luke* (X-XXIV), Joseph Fitzmyer, SJ (New York: Doubleday & Co. Inc., 1986), 989. Fitzmyer writes in commentary on Jesus' teaching in Luke 12: "Well, who is the faithful and prudent manager whom the master puts over his staff to distribute to them a food allowance at the proper time? The implication is that the 'manager' represents someone placed in authority over others, not just over material possessions, but those who are under the *kyrios.* The evangelist could be referring to community officials."

35   It should be noted that a belief in natural law also helps to explain how most cultures have had the same basic moral principles, as was documented to some extent on pages 16-18 above.

36   See *Catechism,* §2275.

37   For instance, in Book III, Chapter 122 of his *Summa Contra Gentiles* [trans. Vernon J. Bourke (Notre Dame: University of Notre Dame Press, 1975)], Aquinas makes a comparison between the fact that birds require two parents to rear offspring and the fact that humans likewise require two parents to raise their offspring properly. Though Aquinas was not saying human parents should stay together to raise their young because birds do the same, it is easy to see how this type of misunderstanding could have been generated.

38   See Robert Heaney, "Sex, Natural Law and Bread Crumbs" in *America* (February 26, 1994).

39   "'I'm Here': An Interview with Andrew Sullivan," interview by Thomas H. Stahel, SJ, *America* (May 8, 1993), 113.

40   See B1 in Chapter Three.

41   Note the similarity here between the specific sense of law and the more general one. Civil and divine laws are also rules in this more general sense. A man-made law against speeding or the divine law against adultery is a "rule or principle that guides something to its telos or fulfillment." Speeding laws are intended to preserve order and lives on the highway so that people can go about their business and live happily. Likewise, God prohibits adultery so that families and the social order will be preserved. Faithful husbands and wives provide models of love for their offspring, and ultimately, fidelity to one person fosters individual responsibility, patience, and temperance, virtues that fulfill husbands and wives themselves.

42   Aquinas, *Summa Theologica*, I-II, q. 91, a. 2.

43   Ibid., II-II, q. 66, a. 2.

44   Notice here that Aquinas' reflections on this matter are perfectly in line with the Biblical view of creation given in Genesis 1:26-29:

Then God said, "Let us make man in our image, after our likeness; and let them have dominion over the fish of the sea, and over the birds of the air, and over the cattle, and over the earth, and over every creeping thing that creeps upon the earth." So, God created man in his own image, in the image of God he created him; male and female he created them. And God blessed them, and God said to them, "Be fruitful and multiply, and fill the earth and subdue it; and have dominion over the fish of the sea and over the birds of the air and over every living thing that moves upon the earth." And God said, "Behold, I have given you every plant yielding seed which is upon the face of all the earth, and every tree with seed in its fruit; you shall have them for food."

45   Aquinas, *Summa Theologica*, I-II, q. 66, a. 7.

46   For more on this issue, see the introduction to *St. Thomas Aquinas on Politics and Ethics*, edited by Paul E. Sigmund (New York: W. W. Norton & Company, 1988), xv.

47   Of course, this argument arose in a time before the development of DNA paternity testing. However, the availability of this test does not do away with the power of this argument. In addition to the fact that DNA testing is still unavailable to the vast majority of the world's population, the *need* for this test in polygamous relationships proves that these relationships are themselves disordered. For example, it may be the case that liposuction, a modern technique for removing fat, can do away with much, if not all, of the harms of overeating, but that fact in no way indicates that overeating is not wrong or harmful. Overeating creates a condition in which liposuction or some kind of remedy is necessary; similarly, polygamy creates a condition in which DNA testing or some kind of remedy is needed. Clearly, both overeating and polygamy are undesirable practices.

48   Aquinas, *Summa Contra Gentiles*, Bk. III, chap. 124, §4.

49   The story of Abram, who took on another wife because his first wife Sarai did not bear him a son, in Genesis 16, shows both this division of labor within the marriage as well as the rivalries that result from this division.

50   Aquinas, *Summa Contra Gentiles*, Bk. III, chap. 124, §5.

51   "The scribes and the Pharisees brought a woman who had been caught in adultery, and placing her in the midst, they said to him, 'Teacher, this woman has been caught in the act of adultery. Now in the law Moses commanded us to stone such. What do you say about her?' This they said to test him, that they might have some charge to bring against him. Jesus bent down and wrote with his finger on the ground. And as they continued to ask him, he stood up and said to them, 'Let him who is without sin among you be the first to throw a stone at her.' And once more he bent down and wrote with his finger on the ground. But when they heard it, they went away, one by one, beginning with the eldest, and Jesus was left alone with the woman standing before him. Jesus looked up and said to her, 'Woman, where are they? Has no one condemned you?' She said, 'No one, Lord.' And Jesus said, 'Neither do I condemn you; go, and do not sin again.'"

52   "Let every person be subject to the governing authorities. For there is no authority except from God, and those that exist have been instituted by God. Therefore he who resists the authorities resists what God has appointed, and those who resist will incur judgment. For rulers are not a terror to good conduct, but to bad. Would you have no fear of him who is in authority? Then do what is good, and you will receive his approval, for he is God's servant for your good. But if you do wrong, be afraid, for he does not bear the sword in vain; he is the servant of God to execute his wrath on the wrongdoer."

53   See Pope John Paul II, *The Gospel of Life* (Boston: Pauline Books & Media), no. 55. Having a healthy love of oneself should not be confused with being "selfish." All people should and do naturally desire their own happiness. To desire happiness for oneself is to will something good for oneself, and to will something good for oneself is to love oneself. Thus, good people actually love themselves more than "selfish" ones, for they find true happiness by loving God and their neighbors. Selfish people mistakenly think that happiness is to be found by directing everything toward themselves and hoarding good things, and they end up miserable.

54   Ibid.

55   Ibid., no. 56.

56   Ibid.

57   Ibid., no. 64.

58   Ibid., no. 66. Note that *Catechism* §2282 and §2283 emphasize that many take their own lives out of desperation, which diminishes responsibility, and that we should pray for those who have done so.

59   Robert Spitzer, SJ, "The Case Against Active Euthanasia" in *University Faculty for Life, Life and Learning IV: Proceedings of the Fourth University for Life Conference*, ed. Joseph W. Koterski, SJ (Washington: University Faculty for Life, 1995), 94.

CHAPTER SIX:
TOOLS FOR DISCERNING GOD'S WILL

1   This section of chapter six is largely an exposition of elements of "the principle of double effect," a set of rules or guidelines for judging the morality of actions that have two effects, one good effect that is intended and another bad one that is not intended.

2   The notion of "proportionate reason" can be traced back to St. Thomas Aquinas, in particular his arguments for the legitimacy of self-defense. *Summa Theologica* II-II, q. 64, a. 7 is the *locus classicus* of this notion, as well as the principle of double effect in general.

3   This way of understanding "proportionate" has run into disfavor in some theological circles, for in their estimation, it sounds too much like "consequentialism" or "utilitarianism." See, e.g., Richard Gula, SS, *Reason Informed by Faith: Foundations of Catholic Morality*, 272ff.

4   This quotation is a paraphrase of #313 of *The Spiritual Exercises* of St. Ignatius. The quotations which follow below in section B are paraphrases of the "Guidelines for the Discernment of Spirits," ##313-336 of *The Spiritual Exercises of St. Ignatius.* See *The Spiritual Exercises of St. Ignatius, A Literal Translation and Contemporary Reading*, 204-19.

5   This section will largely be an explanation of ##175–188 of St. Ignatius' *Spiritual Exercises*. See ibid., 107-13.

SELECT BIBLIOGRAPHY

Adler, Mortimer. "A Sound Moral Philosophy." In *Reforming Education: The Opening of the American Mind*. New York: Collier Books, 1977.

Anscombe, G.E.M. "War and Murder." In *Moral Problems*, ed. James Rachels. New York: Harper & Row Publishers, Inc., 1979.

Aristotle. *Nicomachean Ethics*. In *Introduction to Aristotle*, ed. Richard McKeon. Chicago: The University of Chicago Press, 1947.

Aquinas, Thomas. *St. Thomas Aquinas on Politics and Ethics*. Ed. and with an introduction by Paul E. Sigmund. New York: W.W. Norton & Company, 1988.

_____. *Summa Contra Gentiles: Book Three: Providence Part II*. Trans. Vernon J.Bourke. Notre Dame: University of Notre Dame Press, 1975.

_____. *Summa Theologica*. Trans. Fathers of the English Dominican Province. Allen: Thomas More Publishing, 1948.

Augustine. *Confessions*. Trans. John K. Ryan. New York: Doubleday, 1960.

Bayly, Senis and Royal W. Rhodes. *The Faith of Christians*. Philadelphia: Fortress Press, 1984.

Bloesch, Donald G. *Essentials of Evangelical Theology, Volume I: God, Authority, and Salvation*. San Francisco: Harper & Row Publishers, Inc., 1978.

Branch, Taylor. *Parting the Waters*. New York: Simon and Schuster, Inc., 1988.

Brown, Raymond. *Commentary on Luke's Gospel*. In *The Anchor Bible*. New York: Doubleday & Company Inc., 1986.

Day, Dorothy. *Selected Writings: By Little and By Little*, ed. Robert Ellsberg. Maryknoll: Orbis Books, 1992.

Dworkin, Ronald. *Taking Rights Seriously*. Cambridge: Harvard University Press, 1958.

Fitzmyer, Joseph A., SJ. *The Gospel According to Luke (X-XXIV)*. In *The Anchor Bible*. New York: Doubleday & Company Inc., 1986.

Garrow, David J. *Bearing the Cross*. New York: William Morrow and Company, Inc., 1986.

Glendon, Mary Ann. *Rights Talk: The Impoverishment of Political Discourse*. New York: The Free Press, 1991.

Gula, Richard, SS. *Reason Informed by Faith: Foundations of Christian Morality*. New York: Paulist Press, 1989.

Harris, John. "The Survival Lottery." In *Contemporary Moral Problems*, ed. James E. White. Belmont: Wadsworth Publishing Company, 2000.

Heaney, Robert. "Sex, Natural Law and Bread Crumbs." In *America* (February 26, 1994).

Himes, Kenneth R. "Scripture and Ethics: A Review Essay." *Biblical Theology Bulletin* 15 (April 1985): 65-73.

Johnson, Luke Timothy. *The Real Jesus*. New York: Harper Collins, 1996.

Kant, Immanuel. *Grounding for the Metaphysics of Morals with On a Supposed Right to Lie because of Philanthropic Concerns*. Trans. James W. Ellington. Indianapolis: Hackett Publishing Company, Inc., 1993.

_____. *Lectures on Ethics*. Trans. Louis Infield. Indianapolis: Hackett Publishing Company, Inc., 1963.

King, Martin Luther, Jr. *I Have a Dream: Writings and Speeches that Changed the World*. Ed. James M. Washington. San Francisco: Harper Collins Publishers Inc., 1986.

King, Martin Luther, Jr. *A Testament of Hope: The Essential Writings and Speeches of Martin Luther King, Jr.* Ed. James M. Washington. San Francisco: Harper Collins Publishers Inc., 1986.

Kreeft, Peter. *Making Choices: Practical Wisdom for Everyday Moral Decisions*. Ann Arbor: Servant Books, 1990.

Lewis, C.S. *The Abolition of Man*. New York: Collier Books, 1947.

Locke, John. *Second Treatise of Government*. Indianapolis: Hackett Publishing Company, Inc., 1980.

Loyola, Ignatius. *Spiritual Exercises: A Literal Translation and a Contemporary Reading*. Trans. David Fleming, SJ. St. Louis: Institute of Jesuit Sources, 1978.

_____. *A Pilgrims' Journey, The Autobiography of St. Ignatius of Loyola*. Trans. Joseph Tylenda, SJ. Wilmington: Michael Glazier, Inc., 1985.

Mill, John Stuart. *Utilitarianism*. Indianapolis: Hackett Publishing Company, Inc., 1979.

Mother Teresa. *A Simple Path*. New York: Ballantine Books, 1995.

Newton, Isaac. *Principa Mathematica, Vol. II: The System of the World*. Berkeley: University of California Press, 1969.

O'Neill, Onora. "The Moral Perplexities of Famine and World Hunger." In *Matters of Life and Death: New Introductory Essays in Moral Philosophy*, ed. Tom Regan. New York: Random House, 1980.

Perkins, Pheme. *Reading the New Testament, An Introduction*. New York: Paulist Press, 1978.

Pope John XXIII. *Peace on Earth*. In *Seven Great Encyclicals*. Glen Rock: Paulist Press, 1963.

Pope John Paul II. *The Gospel of Life*. Boston: Pauline Books & Media, 1995.

Rahner, Karl, SJ. "Non-infallible Pronouncements." *Catholic Mind* 69 (December 1971): 20-2.

Rawls, John. *A Theory of Justice*. Cambridge: Harvard University Press, 1971.

Regan, Tom. "The Case for Animal Rights." In *In Defense of Animals*, ed. Peter Singer. Oxford: Basil Blackwell, Inc., 1985.

Rostankowski, Cynthia and Manuel Vasquez. *Ethics: Theory and Practice*. Upper Sadle River: Prentice Hall Professional Technical Reference, 1984.

Russell, Bertrand. "Has Religion Made Useful Contributions to Society?" In *Why I am not a Christian*. New York: Simon & Schuster Inc., 1957.

_____. *Religion and Science*. Oxford: Oxford University Press, 1961.

Spitzer, Robert J., SJ. "The Case Against Active Euthanasia." In *University Faculty for Life, Life and Learning IV: Proceedings of the Fourth University Faculty for Life*, ed. Joseph A. Koterski, SJ. Georgetown: University Faculty for Life, 1995.

Sullivan, Andrew. "'I'm Here': An Interview with Andrew Sullivan," interview by Thomas H. Stahel, SJ. In *America* (May 8, 1993).

Thomson, Judith Jarvis. "A Defense of Abortion." In *Moral Problems*, ed. James Rachels. New York: Harper & Row Publishers, Inc., 1979.

Tillich, Paul. "You are Accepted." In *The Shaking of the Foundations*. New York: Charles Scribner's Sons, 1976.

EPILOGUE

Y ou have completed *An Introduction to Catholic Ethics*. Whether you accept all of its principles or not, you will now be in a better position to understand the perspectives taken in Catholic tradition on a number of specific ethical issues. Perhaps, in your school, your instructor will now supply you with a Catholic Ethics Reader that, with the instructor's help, will enable you to grasp the "what" and the "why" of the Catholic positions on a number of specific issues related to human life, sexuality, culture, substance abuse, and personal integrity. Below is an annotated bibliography that catalogs scripture-passages, segments of the *Catechism of the Catholic Church*, and articles that pertain to those issues. Included in the bibliography for a number of those topics are articles at odds with the Catholic position. Your instructor will help you to weigh those articles critically and fairly, and tell you the grounds on which the Catholic tradition rejects their arguments. This collection of specific ethical issues focuses on personal ethical issues more than issues of social justice.

[Note #1: Permission to re-print cited below articles often—not always—involves payment of a fee.]

[Note #2: The bibliography below is of mixed value for practice in applying principles of Catholic ethics to disputed issues touching on personal ethical decisions. Some of the sites provide articles *pro* and *con*; others do not. All the sites touch on issues of personal ethics.]

A.   HUMAN LIFE ISSUES

1.   Abortion:

    a.   Biblical texts:

        The Bible does not explicitly treat this topic. It is probably much better to ask if abortion is in keeping with *the spirit of reverence for human life, regard for the authority of God over life and death, and subordination to God's will* found throughout the Bible than to attempt an argument based on a single text. Texts sometimes referred to in debate about this issue are the following: (pro-life citations) Jeremiah 1:5; Psalm 139: 13, 14-16; Isaiah 49:1; Luke 1:41-44; (pro-choice citations) Exodus 21: 22-25; Genesis 2:7; Ezekiel 37: 8-10.

    b.   *Catechism of the Catholic Church*: §§2270-2275.

    c.   Articles *against abortion*:

        Andrew C. Varga, "Abortion" in *The Main Issues in Bioethics* (Mahwah, N.J.: Paulist Press, 1984), 57-73. This article presents a very good overview of the history and the main issues touching abortion. [Rights and Permissions, Paulist Press, FAX: 201-825-8345.]

        Francis J. Beckwith, "Shifting the Focus of the Abortion Debate,"

University Faculty for Life, Life and Learning V: Proceedings of the Fifth University for Life Conference (1995), 331-49. This article is an important thoughtful response to the arguments of Judith Jarvis Thomson's article "A Defense of Abortion." [Permission to use this article and the article against active euthanasia by Robert Spitzer, SJ, listed below may be obtained by writing to Rev. Joseph Koterski, SJ, Department of Philosophy, Fordham University, Bronx, N.Y. 10458-5148.]

d.   Article *in defense of abortion*:

Judith Jarvis Thomson, "A Defense of Abortion," *Philosophy and Public Affairs, vol. 1, no.1* (Princeton University Press, 1971), 45–64. This article is the "summa" for "pro-choice" advocates. [Princeton University Press' Copyright Division, FAX: 978-750-4470.]

e.   Note: It is appropriate to inform discussants about the methods used in abortions.

2.   Capital Punishment:

a.   Biblical texts:

Capital punishment advocates cite Old Testament passages like Exodus: 12, 15-17, Leviticus 20:10-13, which declare a person should be killed for certain acts. They also cite passages like Genesis 7:6, 19:24 and 38:10 or 2 Samuel 11:1-12:13, where God kills or threatens death to a wrongdoer. Two New Testament texts cited are Romans 13:1-5 and Acts of the Apostles 5:1-11.

Capital punishment opponents cite New Testament texts like John 8:3-11, Romans 12:17-21, Deuteronomy 32:35, and the spirit of Jesus' teachings about love of one's enemy and about the Christian's duty to forgive.

b.   *Catechism of the Catholic Church*: §§2263-2267.

c.   Articles *in favor of the death penalty*:

Michael Pakaluk, "Till Death Do Us Part," *Crisis*, Sept., 1989. [Article available at *Crisis*, P.O. Box 1006, Notre Dame, IN 46556; permission available at FAX: 202-861-7790, at 1814 N Street, N.W., Washington, D.C. 20036.]

d.   Articles *against the death penalty*:

Richard L. Nygaard, "'Vengeance is Mine,' Says the Lord," *America*, vol. 171, no. 10, Oct. 8, 1994, 6-8. [*America*, 106 West 58th Street, New York, N.Y. 10019.]

Robert F. Drinan, SJ, "Catholics and the Death Penalty," *America*, vol. 171, June 18, 1974, 13-5.

3.   **Euthanasia:**

   a.   Biblical passages:

   Perhaps, Romans 14:7-9.

   b.   *Catechism of the Catholic Church:* §§2276-2279

   c.   Article/video *for euthanasia:*

   60 Minutes has an interview-video of Dr. Jack Kirvorkian in which he makes his case for active euthanasia. [Cf. *60 Minutes*, 524 West 57th St., New York, N.Y. 10019, Phone: 212-975-3247, 1-800-848-3256.]

   Peter Singer, *Practical Ethics* (Cambridge: Cambridge University Press, 1993), 176-8, 193-200.

   d.   Article *against euthanasia:*

   Robert Spitzer, SJ, "The Case Against Active Euthanasia" in *University Faculty for Life, Life and Learning IV: Proceedings of the Fourth University for Life Conference* (1975), 80-97. [Cf. A1c above for address where this article may be obtained.]

B.   SEXUALITY ISSUES

1.   Heterosexual Norms Before and After Marriage:

   a.   Biblical Passages:

   Mark 7:21; 10:2-12, 19; Matthew 5:27-28; 19:1-8; 1 Corinthians 6:13-20; 7:12-6; Ephesians 5:5-6; Hebrews 13:4; 1 Timothy 1:8-11.

   b.   *Catechism of the Catholic Church:* §§2348-2372; §§1646-1653.

   c.   Articles on *chastity:*

   Mary Patricia Barth Fourqurean, "Chastity as Shared Strength: An Open Letter to Students," *America*, November 6, 1993,10-4.

   Mitch Finley, "Cohabitation: A Perplexing Pastoral Problem," *America*, July, 1993,16-7.

   d.   Articles on *use of artificial contraception within marriage:*

   [i] *for:*

   Robert Heaney, "Sex, Natural Law, and Bread Crumbs," *America*, February 26, 1994, 12-6.

   [ii] *against:*

   Janet E. Smith, "Barnyard Morality," *America*, August 13, 1994,12-4.

   Janet E. Smith, "*Humanae Vitae* Made Some Bold Prophecies: Two Decades Ago. Did They Come To Pass?" In *Why Humanae Vitae was Right: A Reader* (San Francisco: Ignatius Press, 1993), 519-31. [Ignatius

Press, Post Office Box 1339, Ft. Collins, CO 80522-1339, Phone: 1-800-651-1531, FAX: 1-800-278-3566.]

2. Homosexuality:

a.   Biblical Passages:

The Bible says nothing about homosexual orientation. Homosexual actions are spoken of in the following passages: Genesis 19:1-11; Leviticus 18:22; 20:13; Romans 1:18-27; 1 Corinthians 6:9-10.

b.   *Catechism of the Catholic Church*: §§2357-2359.

c.   Articles about *marriage of homosexuals*:

[i] *for*:

Andrew Sullivan, "Let Gays Marry," *Newsweek*, June 3, 1996, 26-7.

"'I'm Here': An Interview with Andrew Sullivan," *America*, May 8, 1993, 5-9.

[ii] *against*:

William Bennett, "Leave Marriage Alone," *Newsweek*, June 3, 1996, 27.

John F. Harvey, OSFS, "Arguments from Revelation and Reason in Favor of the Official Teaching of the Church" in *The Homosexual Person: New Thinking in Pastoral Care* (San Francisco: Ignatius Press, 1987), 309-19. [Cf. above, for addresses for permissions for Ignatius Press, under "Heterosexual Norms," last entry.]

3. Cultural Issues, Free Speech, and Pornography:

a.   Biblical passages:

Matthew 5:27-30; Philippians 4:8-9; Romans 13:11-14; Galatians 5:16-26.

b.   *Catechism of the Catholic Church*: §§2284-2287, §2351, §2354, §§2523-2525.

c.   Articles on *media*:

Michael Medved, "Denial Behavior" in *Hollywood vs. America* (New York: HarperCollins Publishers, 1992), 239-52. HarperCollins Publishers Inc., Permissions Dept., General Books Group, Phone: 212-207-7534 or *www.harpercollins.com/permissions/*]

Joe McNamara, "Television Is Corrupting American Society" in *Opposing Viewpoints: Mass Media* (Farmington Hills, MI: Greenhaven Press, 2002), 1-9. [cf. 27500 Drake Rd., Farmington Hills, MI 48331-35-35, Phone: 248-699-8006 or *permissions@galegroup.com*.]

American Medical Association, "Media Violence Should Be Treated as a

Public Health Problem" in *Opposing Viewpoints: Media Violence* (cf. loc. cit. supra), 1-6.

Elizabeth Thoman, "Media Literacy Education Can Address the Problem of Media Violence" in *Opposing Viewpoints: Media Violence* (cf. loc. cit. supra), 1-6.

d.   Article on *U.S. culture*:

William J. Bennett, "America Faces a Moral Crisis" in *Opposing Viewpoints: American Values* (cf. loc. cit. supra), 1-8.

e.   Article on *pornography*:

Victor B. Cline, "Pornography Use Results in Abnormal Sexual Behavior" in *Opposing Viewpoints: Human Sexuality* (cf. loc. cit. supra.), 1-7.

f.   Article on *censorship*:

Robert H. Bork, "The Case for Censorship" in *Slouching Toward Gomorrah* (New York: HarperCollins Publishers Inc., 1997), 140-53. [Cf. address given above in "c" of this section for instruction on how to obtain permission to publish HarperCollins material.]

Dorothy Allison, "The Porn Problem," (originally, appearing as "Obscenity Laws Threaten Free Speech") Glamour, January 1995.

4.   Drug and Alcohol Abuse:

a.   Biblical passages:

Luke 21:34-36; Romans 13:11-14; Galatians 5:16-24; 1 Corinthians 6:9-11.

b.   *Catechism of the Catholic Church*: §§2290-2291.

c.   Articles on *alcoholism*:

Rita Rubin, "The Debate: What Makes an Alcoholic?" *Miami Herald*, Jan. 20, 1987, B1.

Larry Thompson, "Alcoholism Leaves Its Mark," *Anchorage Daily News*, March 13, 1988, G1.

d.   Article on *marijuana*:

National Institute of Drug Abuse, "A Fact Sheet on Marijuana." [Seven pages of facts available on line from the Web-site for the National Institute of Drug Abuse: *http://www.nida.nih.gov/MarijBroch/ Marijteenstxt.htmj*.

John P. Walters, "The Myth of 'Harmless' Marijuana," *The Washington Post*, May 1, 2002, A25.

5.   Integrity:

a.   Biblical Passages:

Genesis 1:26-29; Exodus 20:15-16; Deuteronomy 5:19-20; 24:14-15; 25:13-16; Amos 8:4-6; Proverbs 18:5; 19:9; Sirach 21: 28; Matthew 5:33; 5:37;19:18; Luke 19:18; John 1:14; 8:12; 8:32; 8:44; 12:46; 16:13; Romans 3:4; 2 Corinthians 8:9; Ephesians 4:24-25; 1 Peter 2:1; James 5:4.

b. *Catechism of the Catholic Church*: §§2401-2412; §§2450-2454; §§2464-2470; §§2475-2485.

c. Articles:

Articles on cheating, lying, stealing are available in reference to recent corporate scandals, and in connection with cheating scandals at universities and military academies. None is supplied here.

ABOUT THE AUTHORS

Rev. Lucien F. Longtin, SJ, is a Jesuit priest currently teaching seniors at Gonzaga College High School in downtown Washington, D.C. Fr. Longtin is a graduate of St. Joseph's Prep in Philadelphia, Pa. He holds an A.B. in classics and an M.A. in education from Fordham University, pontifical licentiates in philosophy and in sacred theology from Sacred Heart College in Woodstock, Md., and an M.A. in religious education from The Catholic University of America in Washington, D.C. Ordained a Jesuit priest in 1965, he has spent all of his years of priestly ministry in secondary education, teaching religion and helping in the administration of Jesuit high schools.

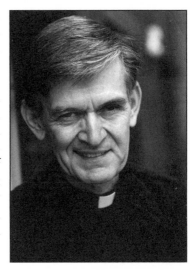

Andrew Peach teaches philosophy and theology at Boston College. Dr. Peach holds a B.A. in theology from Georgetown University in Washington, D.C., and an M.A. and Ph.D. in philosophy from The Catholic University of America in Washington, D.C. Prior to his current position, he taught philosophy at King's College in Wilkes-Barre, Pa., and theology and philosophy at Gonzaga College High School in Washington, D.C. Dr. Peach currently resides in Watertown, Ma., with his wife, Kathryn, and their children, Lucien and Bridget.